Poetry makes things happen

Poems, essays, texts, afterwords, blurbs, notes...

jim leftwich

LBP

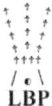

LUNA BISONTE PRODS
2021

Poetry makes things happen
Poems, essays, texts, afterwords, blurbs, notes…

Publication credits

Angry Old Man magazine
Arteidolia
Brave New Word magazine
Eileen Verbs Books
experiential-experimental magazine
Galatea Resurrects
Luna Bisonte Prods
mOnocle-Lash Anti-Press
Otoliths

Book design: C. Mehrl Bennett

ISBN 9781938521690

lulu.com/spotlight/lunabisonteprods

LUNA BISONTE PRODS
137 Leland Ave.
Columbus, OH 43214 USA

Page# **Table of Contents**

Poetry makes things happen
afterword to *Dropped In The Dark Box* by John M. Bennett

Open your book to page 6 and read "*towel in the furnace*". Would there be any time if we didn't say anything? I say the answer is yes, but it would be a different kind of time. Imagine enduring or enjoying a Thanksgiving dinner with your extended family, four or five generations of your extended family. The clock says dinner lasted fifty-three minutes. Your family members have twenty other opinions. The clock is a fact. Our experiences are alternative facts. If we didn't say anything our world would be only the clock. We speak rusted time disbound if soaked in tongue wet and dusty. Only a clock could prefer the fact of the clock to the poems of human experience.

Open your book to page 12 and read "*found the fistula,*" which might be thought of as a kind of mini *ars poetica.* Agglutination is the clumping of particles. The particles in question here are the l e t t e r s of the alphabet. These particular particles, when clumped, are called words. Their deglutination in a poem is fakery, also known as artifice or poetic device. The fistula in the title is an abnormal or surgically made passage. The energy of the-poem-in-the-poet passes through this artificial opening, across the gap of an imaginary mindspace, shared by all (via the anarchic telepathy of the poem), all the way over to, the reader. Okay.

Now, open your book to page 31 and read "*grave gravel.*" From one perspective, possibly that of the poet, there is no poem entitled "*grave gravel.*" Do not let that discourage you from reading it. Read it in all directions. It is many poems at once. Maybe get together with some of your friends and read it in many directions at once. Or go hear the Be Blank Consort perform. Some of what you hear from them will sound like the shoe cheese cheese shoe of "*grave gravel.*"

Open your book to page 57 and gaze for more than a moment at "*Transduction of a Caligramme by Guillaume Appolinaire.*" Stare at it. Attempt to decipher its inherently polysemic calligraphy. Turn to page 58 and read the transliteration of the transduction. Then return to page 57 where you will find the reading process, while still much slower than for example the pace employed for reading the front page of your local newspaper, less frequently frustrated by futile attempts to determine which of Bennett's several languages has given us the word "*choctiton.*" Poems by definition thwart any attempt at an easy and simple reading. Perhaps all poems are at least partially about reading. All visual poems are always primarily about reading, about the construction of meanings, about the collaborative process of constructing meanings by a reader and an author. The inherently polysemic nature of Bennett's calligraphic visual poems foregrounds the slow process of collaboratively constructing a range of meanings as a reading.

Open your book to page 94 and read the poem entitled "*the stroke mastication.*" Near the center of the poem is an exceptionally large capital *'F'.* We recall, upon encountering this '*F*', that line two ends with the letter '*f*', allowing us to read both "*lag*" and "*flag*" as distinct words across the line-break.

suction open f
lag yr chest a

When we arrive at the central 'F' we will have just passed the word "ogstorm", a truncated neologism. Appearing on the next line, just below "ogstorm," the large 'F' completes the coinage "fogstorm". Perhaps the (temporary) absence of the initial 'f' is intended to increase the fogginess of the word. In the line following the capital 'F' we find the partial words "aceless" and "aze," both of which are meaningfully completed by the addition of the floating 'F'. That complete line

aceless aze con

followed by the line

amintion o it's

forces the brain to watch itself as it actively invents possible meanings, selecting and discarding among them.
con animation. no.
confirmation not even close confamintion no.
con T amination no.
ammunition badminton no & no etc & etc until the mind gives up...
It is an interesting swarming search to watch as it unfolds. Especially since it is happening in one's own mind.

Open your book to page 122 and read "*the lunch X.*" At the end of line two into the beginning of line three we have ten letters, an em space, and a line break strategically combined / aligned / sequenced to do the work of two words comprised of twelve letters (and an em space)

wat ch
owder

watch chowder

Concoct meanings as you wish, sort and sift them at your pleasure, discard them in the end and simply (which in context means complexly) enjoy the machinery of the poem at work. This is the what and the why of many a Bennett poem. It takes some effort to get to it, but it is always worth the work. Poems make things happen. Little things, yes, but worlds are made of little things, lives are made of little things. A poem should mean and be and do, simultaneously and sequentially.

The second poem on page 122 is entitled 'X'. It builds the word "*div orce*", taken from line one of "*the lunch X,*" beginning with the letter '*d*' and continuing, one letter at a time, to "*divorc.*" Following "*divorc*" is a blank line, and then "*divorcaTexe e.*" Cf. *divert*, from *di-* 'aside' + *vertere* 'to turn'. See also the origins of verse, Old English *fers*, from Latin *versus* 'a turn of the plow, a furrow, a line of writing', from *vertere* 'to turn'; reinforced in Middle English by Old French *vers,* from Latin *versus* .

Consider Isidore Isou, *from Introduction à une Nouvelle Poésie et une Nouvelle Musique.* Paris: Gallimard, 1947:
Still IX Words are family garments.
        Poets enlarge words every year.
        Words already have been mended so much they are in stitches.
Pathetic X   People think it is impossible to break words.
Still X   Unique feelings are so unique that they can not be
        popularized. Feelings without words in the dictionary
                disappear.
Pathetic XI   Every year thousands of feelings disappear for lack
                of a concrete form.
Still XI   Feelings demand living space.

If we have mixed feelings/thoughts about Isou, perhaps it is because we have mixed thoughts/feelings about poetry, as we should, as the poem -- any poem, every poem -- demands of us, and as each component of each poem uniquely requires of us... letters, spaces, line breaks,
words, phrases, lines, sentences, stanzas.

Read a poem once and you know that it exists. Read it twice and you might think you know some of what it means. Read it three times and you suspect it of nonexistence. The poem will not sit still for your inspection. It will not stand for scrutiny. While reading it the fourth time you suspect you have some sort of slithering, slippery, shape-shifting chimera before your eyes. It is made of signs and sings and sounds and sooouuunds, slimy shifting symbols and sticky surfaces.

d
di
div
divo
divor
divorc
divorcaTexe e

Poetry makes things happen, makes us happy, makes us happy by making things happen.

February 2019

ALPHABET NOIR by Nico Vassilakis
(c_L Books, Portland, OR, 2016)

Alphabet Noir 1

i like the size of Alphabet Noir. if i place my wrist on the lower left corner and spread my fingers my hand is almost exactly the size of your book. i know some of what i will find inside this book, so i begin by looking and touching and measuring. soon i'll start reading. first i read the blurbs. Blonk is on it: writing in general leads to more writing; poems in particular lead to more poems. having finished with the back cover i begin reading by flipping through from back to front, pausing a few times when something -- page layout and design, typographical contrasts -- catches my eye. I notice on page 59 your reference to Solt's new poet-reader. 50 years later we still feel the need.

A New Poet-Reader
jim leftwich
04.19.2017

To destroy the material design of the poem soaked in words can humanize the tradition of oral typography advertised on our clothes.

Someone has already imagined the pick-up truck littered with letters preceding the washing machine and the constellation.

The worlds of contours floundering in coincidence are flooded with visual poems.

The world as a visual poem is the cosmic material itself.

Spirituality wishes to form in writing the peculiar contemporary fish suddenly historical.

Facts are lost in the silent environment.

Poets are fragments of an impossible poem.

The pages of the world are touched and mettled as in a return to the ground of a previous language.

Neither goat nor peyote, the perception of an exploration lies in the design of its making.

The present is not the only hymn of the real.

Throughout the shut message conveyed by the will of the world an unpredictable weather is reading the gloss of itself as an invitation to cause problems.

Semantic freedom tarnished by a penetrating framework.

Letters occupy the common carom of an arrow in style.

Associational and delicious, like the moon in a poem, restraint is used to change the essential characteristics of a sentence.

Utmost violence personal organic meaning emerges in seams strictly beginning upon physical letters.

Organic tooth-magic arrangement also paragraphs and parentheses, tracking its own golden elephant through the sparkle of an ageless crystal, words staring intently into their econometric hourglass, perfect balloons neutral shining warnings, simple decorative meanings hiding in the trash adapt to expensive garbage, so yields the turtle, do not hesitate before these beautiful spells, horizontal and ultimate in your semantic space.

Imagine the poems as a playhouse created by reversals in silence.

Tempted by the sun, the sounds of emphatic clarity are unnecessary.

Ideology is born in the nascent morals of method and structure.

Form foams; firm fires; farms famish; ferns feet; fur furls.

Their identity is wide and bold, like the flexible velocity of the poem.

"Curse yet goat" becomes in practice the ghost of a hybrid given.

The soul of the word in the street is the light of the word on the feet.

Remove the sun: more words!

Managed aesthetic patterns are poetry.

Paper is a visual poem about linguistic content.

Elsewhere!

Suitable!

Typeface!

Carnival!

Lower-case!

Interpretations!

Seen!

Text!

There!

To!

Required!

Styles!

Relationships!

Alphabet Noir 2

page 49
"Maurice Lemaitre says, for the first time with poetic Lettrism and hypergraphic Lettrism, PAINTER and POET are one and the same (because the genre has become the same).

The question is really how far one can go in reducing and limiting the elements of a genre and still be considered part of that genre." (Vassilakis)

hypergraphy = post-writing = textimagepoems (when the person approaching the coniunctionis of text and image is moving from text, as a writer, toward image -- to join the writing, which they have already been making, with the image, in order to expand and/or enhance the writing)

the situation is somewhat different when the person approaching the mysterium of textimage work is moving from image, as a visual artist, toward the text -- to join their visual art, which they have already been making, with text, in order to expound and/or enchant the image

"The important thing Lemaitre points out is the vulnerability of syntax, more than semantics, to such manipulation." --Johanna Drucker, Hypergraphy: A Note on Maurice Lemaitre's 'Roman hypergraphique'

Ed Corbett: "I intend my work as poetry." (1952)
Black Mountain Review #7, front cover by Ed Corbett (1957)

In recent years some folks working under the rubric of "asemic writing" seem to have reversed Ed Corbett's intention, by asserting in varying degrees of explicitness that they intend their writing as visual art.

Alphabet Noir 3

AINT BASEBALL GREAT.
A
A
A
.

That's how the letters begin to plan their escape from the word. Once the long A's have escaped -- a word is a submarine, rhyme opens the hatch, the long 'A's pop out onto the deck (it's a movie about World War II), link hands and dance in circles under the midday sun (they look like yellow m & m's, in contrast to the infinitely deep blue sea) (our cartoons are designed to make us feel better about our wars) -- the words are no longer intact.

INT BSEBALL GRET. (or GRT).
The syllogism in air.

A word is a balloon.
These balloons are losing air.
Vowels are air.

Reading a poem is like swimming or dancing, said Robert Creeley. Writing a poem, too, is like swimming or dancing.

A poem exists so we can be with it. So I can be with it. So you can be with it.

"Vassilakis," writes Crag Hill in his introduction to Alphabet Noir, "wants the notion/s of letters living life outside the constraint of a word scrum to be available to all."
There is a video of Creeley talking. He says a poem isn't there to take you to its meaning any more than swimming is there to take you to the other side of the lake, any more than dancing is there to take you to the other side of the room.
The first line of Creeley's book Pieces is: "as real as thinking."
Vassilakis: "I think vispo is a kinetic mirror."
Creeley: "no thing less than one thing"
Vassilakis: "I am very interested in drawn letters. I am not though so interested in written letters."
Creeley:
"There is no trick to reality—

a mind

makes it, any
mind."
Vassilakis: "Visual language is dependent on the virus that infects it. The constant task of the field is to suppress and acquire information in order to assure its lock on power."

If the rhymed vowels can escape, then other related letters also can escape. The two T's can go, leaving us with
IN BSEBALL GRE. (or GR).
The two B's can follow:
IN SEALL GRE. (or GR).
Then the two E's (assuming there are two E's):
IN SALL GR.
The two L's:
IN SA GR.

On the table behind the book or beneath the screen we find the liberated letters dancing to a poem by Robert Creeley, or swimming in Lake Eden at Black Mountain College:

AAATTBBEELL
ATABAETLBEB
LLEEBBTTAAA
LALAEAEBTBT

More disheveled than the previous one, say is more plagiarism than asemic to hair everywhere.

"That distance or measurement where content is vulnerable to corruption." --Nico Vassilakis
Yvonne Rainer: "I'm interested in how things don't work, putting things together that don't fit." (2012)

"To confound the dictionary by eroding cohesion between the letters that form words." --Nico Vassilakis
Kitasono Katue: "I always felt a distance from ideology. Ideology is a blank sheet of paper. What is important is method." (1975)

"Then there are aspects of an erupted B dangling off a row of commas." --Nico Vassilakis
John Clarke: "The subjective as objective requires correct processing." (1965)

"The parts of letters you regard as useless are busy, very busy." --Nico Vassilakis

Toni Morrison: "Definitions belong to the definers—not the defined." (1987)

"When no one's looking letters quietly arrange themselves." --Nico Vassilakis
Kitasono Katue: "What I have been thinking about most is that within words there are many words and in each country they are different. What a bother it all is. My meaning is: 'Let's stop using words!'" (1975)

"Letters give way to other letters, to inner letters, tangential letters, ones that wait in the back. You can try to animate these misfits in your mouth. Bring them to life. But here, a letter is eager to be nothing but free of word and able to explore its visual substance." -- Nico Vassilakis

The baseball season finished.
Shit/Enters into it only as an image
It is not for the ears. (p.42)

April 2017
published by Eileen Tabios at Galatea Resurrects

blurb for Frozen Heatwave, by steve dalachinsky & Yuko Otomo

If we begin at the beginning we begin with chapter 35, in which the physiology of the central nervous system is illustrated by an image of a placard, with the word "America" typed on it, stuffed into a toilet bowl, and we think to ourselves "ok, so that's why it's called frozen heatwave." But we are easily misled and clearly mistaken. "If you see something / say worker" it says on page four and I say "workers, plural" -- one who wrote the non-italic lines, another who wrote the lines in italic, another two who edited and published the book, and a reader. There are five of us here, now six, since you have joined us. Thank yous all around. The first collage (page 11) repeats the phrase "the physiology of the central nervous system," adds a cut-away view of a Rubik's cube floating in interstellar slash neural space, where the inside meets the outside, the infinitely small meets the infinitely large, the rubber meets the road, and the cut fish climbs a graphic lattice to rejoin the cut worm, who over two hundred years ago had already forgiven the plow. A severed head meditates sleepily in the lower right-hand corner. The disembodied brain levitates beyond the first false frame. If you were in New York City between March 21 and July 23, 2017, you could have seen the Lygia Pape: A Multitude of Forms exhibit at The Met. Steve and Yuko were there. What is she saying? asks the poem. In the video at The Met website she doesn't say a word. "in the book of creation / an echo simply becomes / a spider-shaped balloon / to textualize the mystic narrative / of our birth." As a single balloon must stand for a lifetime of thinking about balloons, so each citizen expressed, in the attitude we chose, a complex of attitudes. Collage #2, page 25: the heads of Steve and Yuko floating in a neural roadmap. Now we are beginning to understand. The Frozen Heatwave is a training manual: How To Teach Your Brain To Fish. White wave-patterns on a black background. Wheat planted in a cylinder grows up into a kneeling brain. A muscle promptly and entirely pentagonists. The ghost of 'lectricity howls in the bones of our face. "You write what you want / I write what I want." Making Space: Women Artists and Postwar Abstraction. April 15 - August 13, 2017. MOMA. Collage #3, page 41: A constellated spiderweb-map of the third eye. A brain is a folded serpent. Peripheral vision dripping letteral snakespittle: sa / ons / in. / of / [seasoning] / of / on, / [ironing] / ng / w, / ed [winged] / [wedding] / or- / al [oral]. "non-objective / doesn't mean / formless." "& then [page 47] waiting an hour / in order to arrive in AMERICA / to get into the golden toilet." Collage #4: physiology of central nervous system again. Quasi-calligraphic space-glyphs writing the visual cortex.

August 2017

Arthur, Dying
(a slightly longer than a longish blurb on Arthur Dies: First Chronicle, Vol. 3, by Olchar Lindsann)

Do not think of mass murder inhabiting your memory when the Modern State is being born and is no longer if it ever was static nor simply stratified, these layers in lyrical epic (containing multitudes and more -- contradiction is a kind of clarity) of 2018 redacted unto the next thousand years are less likely than any subversive enthusiasm -- from French enthousiasme, or via late Latin from Greek enthousiasmos, from enthous 'possessed by a god, inspired' (based on theos 'god') -- imploding outwards from an overprinted lyric, upon the past and its pasts, as any capability negative or othersidewayswise towards the letteral accuracy of a proposed recombinative facticity -- it is saying you more than I am saying it and none of that so much as your imagined reading self, underwritten as undermin'd, rageous through flowering countercultures to thanatic dealtcult torture manuals (beneath which we glimpse in palimpsest early drafts of the Monroe Doctrine) -- to this, a sort of last word from one of us who never had any interest much less faith in the validity of anything even similar to the concept of "having the last word" -- in addition to a last and lasting appendix:

Anabasis (Tom Taylor), from Horndog, published by anabasis press, oysterville, wa 2002. Chapter 5, unpaginated: "You think you know the end of this already. It just stops. That's why it's lifelike, it starts and then it stops, all with no apparent reason. Inside that there is love and the rest, and as the rest rests, love goes on. And on. And sometimes off, off course, off base, off and on. On top and off top. Inside out, depends on your point of view. Cola non rafa, don't fuck with Joe Meat, don't tread on me."

...as a sense of Death, individual and ongoing, in every mythic past, but perhaps especially in the multitudinous tales of Arthur, as invading and occupying an inevitable historical future (we see these Times collapse into a swarming current consciousness) (subjectivity is always plural, and always in collaborative process), there are as many entrances as we are willing to muster for ourselves, the text having preemptively welcomed all of us, with all of our potentials, into its actual diction and design, but there is, as Anabasis/Taylor intimates, only one way out, which is of course the entrance into another text.

How should we consider those fragments, juxtaposed, presented in weathered columns, shored as, not against, our ruins? And the cut quotations? Cut-off, not cut-up. Whatever we may think of our own capabilities as readers, as collaborative writers of meanings within the r(e)adically destabilized text, we will without question find ourselves thwarted line-by-line-by phrase-by word-by syllable and phoneme, letter-by-letter in any attempt at becoming comfortable with or within this. How it is broken is where you are interrupted. Why it is fragmented is when you are forced to stop. Against your will. To stop and return and re-read. To reconstruct, reimagine, reinvent your subjectively fictional facts -- the fictions are necessary for the navigation, the actual motion of perceptions and proposals, one following another -- within the ruins of the text. Your mind is being colonized or else you are awakening.

I find myself among these shifting pronouns, looking at you in the mirror.

A training manual, then, out of an ancient poetry as self-help psychology, and into an existential agon -- at us, at everywhere we find our selves. How To... Donald Trump is President. No serious person would have believed you a few short years ago. How To Fry An Egg. How To Wear A Shirt. Supposedly serious journalists are writing about "alternative facts" and our "post-truth" society. The American military has occupied Afghanistan for the last 17 years. How Things Work. Who benefits? Where do they find these people? The question is always, where do we begin? Arthur is a good place to begin. Let's say we want to think about Empire. The trajectory from Empire to Failed State. A pre-history of Arthur begins, begins again, re-begins. We find in fragments as if of the monomyth in daily newspapers and weekly magazines, cut and posited into the poem (it is less difficult than we often think to get the news from poems), lists culled from enhanced interrogation instruction books and evasive quotes from presidents concerning extrajudicial executions. We may still feel as if the tops of our heads have been taken off. We may ask ourselves: how to get in motion, and stay in motion. How to choose, anything, say a single letter of the alphabet, when choosing one means if only for a moment rejecting all the others. Poems, even epic poems, are made one decision at a time. We take our time, and read them that way too. Page 18: "each triumbled overorther fizzzing full". Page 29: "w'ere he swayed and mumbled flashlike syllables". Page 47: "bedeck in plunderfancy ,glancenveloppant". Page 76: "mais all y'our love pour Ablion / is w'armish to my swittersome pensivity". (Also: "b,ubbling". And: "renascendant".) Page 123: "the brythons heard / & briefboldbelde proclamations twitterd travers the real,m".

Having followed the path of a Lucas sequence in search of samples as examples, of a diction in a discourse, we arrive at an expressionistic punctuation, a flamboyant and celebratory excess of generative and generous neologization (among recombinative routes through and around related roots), letteral subtractions and additions, comminglings of French and English, backwards (spells and) spellings. Page 123: "It's true your language – though adjudged taboo – awakens in me small and deep misgivings." This is only a beginning of what and where and how Lindsann's language awakens us in his Arthur. The surfaces open in all directions to the poem as historiography -- the writing out of a history through our current events into a future unfolding towards us as what will have been our historical con-text.

07.06.2018

long blurb for TRANSCENDENT TOPOLOGIES: STRUCTURALISM AND VISUAL WRITING, by Tom Hibbard

Rethinking a system in the reality of language -- language undoubtedly approximate -- discernible in antithetical agency, does not constitute the strict bleakness of an asemic transcendence. As I write this, it is a fine spring afternoon in southwest Virginia. This morning I saw two very small ants walking across a crumpled paper towel. We are sad to see John Bolton return. We are happy to see Paul Ryan depart. Themselves oceans, alphabets access an origin of the earth, the origin of an earth. Ambiguous permanence in the idea of a human architecture. Parenthetical reflections utter handwritten roads. For you, as a reader of visual poetry, the political is often tinted with an indeterminate expressivity. In VISUAL WRITING: CONSCIOUSNESS AND EXISTENCE: LANGUAGE AND THE METAPHOR OF MATTER, Tom Hibbard writes: Mankind's consciousness -- language, art, history, science -- exists above and outside of everything else and judges everything else, not precisely because of a prearranged natural order nor because of certain characteristic "human patterns of behavior" but because the image of reason is capable of completely separating from the presumptive ebb-and-flow of instinctive behavior. Mankind defies infinity. Consciousness precedes matter. In practical terms what this means is that we as human beings have a structural imperative to examine closely and consider with care objects that are apart from us. This applies also to our actions. For you, as a reader of essays about visual writing, war is always state-sponsored mass murder, capitalism hates your worthless guts. Lies about Syria are eerily similar to lies about Venezuela. The tangible meaning of a micro-press poetry publication hovers over our house of dreams. In this way, spontaneous multiplicity articulates the imbricate continuum. I, too, want to read the transcripts of Michael Cohen's threatening telephone conversations. I want MSDNC to be replaced by the Noam Chomsky channel, the Pepe Escobar channel, the Michel Chossudovsky channel. What does this have to do with visual poetry? Precisely this: visual poetry is even more explicitly erotic than collage. Perhaps, too, sexual or erotic childhood civilizations. Visual/sexual impulses in my opinion could be considered writing. Sex is an expression of text, followed by memories of earlier sex. For you, as a reader of blurbs about essays about visual writing, what is theory but the assertion of being in a complex room? Sumerian, the middle of snow, a new world of romantic environments. Authority is appearance. What if Trump refuses a grand jury subpoena? Who do we the people send to arrest him? What if his secret service agents surround him, guns drawn? Are we then beyond the idea of a constitutional crisis and fully into an era of military dictatorship? Tom Hibbard's book, TRANSCENDENT TOPOLOGIES: STRUCTURALISM AND VISUAL WRITING, is as political as you are. It has no other choice. Read it and take notes (handwritten notes, like James Comey and his associates). Track down the books he writes about. Teach yourself how to do what the authors of those books do. Write essays about their work, about your work, about Tom Hibbard's work, about James Comey's work, Michael Cohen's work. Visual writing is trying to teach us one thing, over and over, in a thousand different ways: we live in a shifting constellation; we must read it and write it that way.

April 13, 2018

IN COMPANY: AN ANTHOLOGY OF NEW MEXICO POETS AFTER 1960

After a few practice sessions of nomadic reading I have decided upon a strategy for writing about this hoard and horde of poetical facets, faceted facades, crenelated lineations iterated as crimes against Plato's Republic, with each other through the through-stems, to each other in flight and fight. I read an earlier review and marked it on my mind's map as a territory to be studiously avoided. Thus, having given up on the elephants, which rhyme with the sea, I have decided to begin on page 107, with Larry Goodell's poem entitled "Human Non-Sequitur".

Since the line-break device (that exact sequence of decisions) insists that we focus if only for a moment on the last word of each line, I will extract those words from "Human Non-Sequitur" and use them as a guide to a reading as a writing of IN COMPANY: AN ANTHOLOGY OF NEW MEXICO POETS AFTER 1960, edited by Lee Bartlett, V. B. Price and Dianne Edenfield Edwards (University of New Mexico Press, 2004).

"Human Non-Sequitur" is a sonnet in form, but most of its verse lines are longer than a single printed line. In this particular lexeography I will be using all of the words at the ends of lines on the printed page, even when a single verse line extends to more than one printed line. My choice of how to use the printed page gives me 24 words to work with, rather than 14. This isn't arbitrary. It's simply a way of giving myself permission to include more than 14 poets in this irreview.

Line one of "Human Non-Sequitur" ends with the word "other". I turn to the table of contents, begin with the last page in that table, and read upwards until I find a poet whose name begins with the letter 'o'.

Deanna Ortiz, page 510.
From "Ladders"
"One October night the clear green eyes came to me."

From "Again"
"But wild or wrong arrived in the shotglass everytime,
your green eyes alive as the sea,
a body, and seven hundred miles of waste."

Line two of "Human Non-Sequitur" ends with the word "the". I turn to the table of contents, begin with the last page in that table, and read upwards until I find a poet whose name begins with the letter 't'.

Jennifer Timoner, page 498.
From "The Eye Occupation"
"Can you name ten corpses that begin with the letter O"

From the Abstract for Romanticizing Bataille: Subject-Object Relations and the "Extreme Limit" of Knowledge in Blake, Coleridge, and Shelley, by Jennifer Alla Timoner Dissertation, The University of New Mexico (2001)\

This work begins with the premise that the English romantic poets believed in and valued the subject's unsatisfiable desire to know the objective world, rather than a static knowledge of the object. I show further that the work of Georges Bataille provides a valuable perspective from which to analyze romantic epistemology. Looking at texts that have a long history of epistemological criticism---William Blake's Book of Thel and Visions of the Daughters of Albion, Samuel Taylor Coleridge's The Rime of the Ancient Mariner, and Percy Bysshe Shelley's Alastor---I propose radically different interpretations of the poems based on Bataille's ideas concerning the violent annihilation of subject and object, as well as the sacrifice of meaning represented by poetic language. In part, then, this study contributes to an understanding of romantic poetry as the heterogeneous communication of the anguished, isolate subject.

Line three of "Human Non-Sequitur" ends with the word "stems". I turn to the table of contents, begin with the last page in that table, and read upwards until I find a poet whose name begins with the letter 's'.

James (Jim) Stewart, page 480.
From "On Speed, Or How We Murdered Nostalgia"
"crystal meth is a machine, a tool"
[...]
"I could hear Cassady's voice, and understood how little
his motor-spell-chant-talk really had to do with some magic door"

Line four of "Human Non-Sequitur" ends with the word "&". I turn to the table of contents, begin with the last page in that table, and read upwards until I find a poet whose name begins with the letter 'a'.

Elizabeth Abbott, page 305.
From "Awakening"
"There were no magic words.
'Love is built,' they told her.

Line five of "Human Non-Sequitur" ends with the word "discharge". I turn to the table of contents, begin with the last page in that table, and read upwards until I find a poet whose name begins with the letter 'd'.

Mary Dougherty, page 312
From "Only Death"
"I am pushed to sea
the boat is in flames."

From "Spring In Placitas"
"I'm electric tonight, everything
I touch begins to spark."

From "The Burning of Margaret Moone"
"Flowers of fire grow in my legs.
I lean to the faggots
and flame redeems me."

Line six of "Human Non-Sequitur" ends with the word "fight". I turn to the table of contents, begin with the last page in that table, and read upwards until I find a poet whose name begins with the letter 'f'.

Phillip Foss, page 453.
From "Anascesis and Wreckage"
"these divisions are only for the purpose of knowing: they have no meaning"
[...]
"the chosen poverty rekneading the body into another dirt * perhaps
mircaceous or igneous * fog
you must pass out of these
structures
into a kind of sound in which you cannot recognize your self"
[...]
"what light does sound make?"

Reading, nomadically again, among the results of a google search on the word "anascesis", I come upon The Literary Essays of Thomas Merton, directed specifically to his paper on Pasternak, in which I find the following:

It is therefore instructive to study the scattered allusions in these letters which, added together, provide us with a strikingly coherent formula, a kind of ascesis for survival under totalism. In this, Pasternak falls into a long traditional line of sapiential thought which goes all the way back to the court literature of ancient Egypt, is reflected in such books of the Old Testament as Proverbs and Ecclesiastes, and echoes other wisdoms in India and China.

It is an ascesis of honesty, of work, of loyalty to one's friends, to one's task, and to oneself. It is above all an ascesis of fidelity to life itself and to the human measure. Therefore an ascesis not of rigor and restraint but of openness and response: not of solipsism but of self-forgetfulness, celebration, and love.

Line seven of "Human Non-Sequitur" ends with the word "take". I turn to the table of contents, begin with the last page in that table, and read upwards until I find the second poet whose name begins with the letter 't'.

John Tritica, page 448.
From "Approaching The Equinox"
"To warrant semantic excess
but to define or extend
beyond the bleachers."
[...]
"If you want a poem
find a blank page."
[...]
"To read poetry is to write the world."

coreopsis, noun: a plant of the daisy family, cultivated for its rayed, typically yellow, flowers.
Origin
modern Latin, from Greek koris 'bug' + opsis 'appearance' (because of the shape of the seed).

penstemon, noun, another term for beardtongue.
Origin
modern Latin, formed irregularly from penta- 'five' + Greek stēmōn 'warp,' used to mean 'stamen.'

beardtongue, noun, a North American plant of the figwort family with showy, five-lobed flowers. Each blossom has a tuft of hair on one of its stamens.

Line eight of "Human Non-Sequitur" ends with the word "initiative". I turn to the table of contents, begin with the last page in that table, and read upwards until I find a poet whose name begins with the 'i'.

Mark Ivey, page 513.
From "Golden, New Mexico"
"Gravestones, cut from soft rock, tilt,
their letters become dark mumbles."

Line nine of "Human Non-Sequitur" ends with the word "of". I turn to the table of contents, begin with the last page in that table, and read upwards until I find the second poet whose name begins with the letter 'o'.

Simon Ortiz, page 113.
From "My Mother and My Sisters"

"My oldest sister wears thick glasses
because she can't see very well.
She makes beautifully formed pottery.
That's the thing about making dhyuuni;
it has more to do with a sense of touching
than with seeing because fingers
have to know the texture of clay
and how the pottery is formed from lines
of shale strata and earth movements.
The pottery she makes is thinwalled
and has a fragile but definite balance.
In other words, her pottery has a true ring
when it is tapped with a finger knuckle.

Here, you try it;
you'll know what I mean."

From "The State's claim that it seeks in no way to deprive Indians of their rightful share of water, but only to define that share, falls on deaf ears."

The cosmos is measured by American-made satellites, the land is being razed by Kennecott Copper and Anaconda Corporation monstrosities, and our land has been defined by the RIGHT OF WAY secured by American RAILROADS, ELECTRIC LINES, GAS LINES, HIGHWAYS, PHONE COMPANIES, CABLE TV.

Line ten of "Human Non-Sequitur" ends with the word "communicate". I turn to the table of contents, begin with the last page in that table, and read upwards until I find a poet whose name begins with the letter 'c'.

Denise Clegg, page 508.
From "Five Senses"
"between
cotton and skin
I am young and old
and wholly present"

Line eleven of "Human Non-Sequitur" ends with the word "to". I turn to the table of contents, begin with the last page in that table, and read upwards until I find the third poet whose name begins with the letter 't'.
Victoria Tester, page 422.
From "First Horses, 1519"
"They breathed into our nostrils until our spirits mingled,
and we gave them our speed and flesh
in exchange for their language
of wind."

From "Broken Glass"
"I wonder of she went to California, on
one of those wagonloads of the insane."

Line twelve of "Human Non-Sequitur" ends with the word "other". I turn to the table of contents, begin with the last page in that table, and read upwards until I find the third poet whose name begins with the letter 'o'. I find that there is no third poet whose name begins with the letter 'o', so I move on to the next line in Larry Goodell's poem.

Line thirteen of "Human Non-Sequitur" ends with the word "they're". I turn to the table of contents, begin with the last page in that table, and read upwards until I find the fourth poet whose name begins with the letter 't'.

Toadhouse, page 298.
Allan Graham [aka Toadhouse] in Conversation with John Yau
Brooklyn Rail December 14, 2007

"Well, when we finished this studio, this house, and were moving back in, it had been almost three years since I had done anything. Before that, I had done the collage pieces as well as monochrome shaped-pieces at the same time. So there were works with words and works that were purely visual, and they would be in the studio at the same time—I'd be working on both, and somehow it made sense to me. But when I started back in here and I walked into this brand-new studio in the mountains, I thought, "You know, what I want to deal with is the Toadhouse thing," which was a joke I shared with a poet friend. Toadhouse was the name I gave an underground kiva because Spadefoot toads used to jump in it, and that's where I started writing these notes to myself. The room was twelve feet across and ten feet underground. And I liked that state of mind; there was some kind of a connection with simple words that seemed to take on greater meaning than I could ever imagine. But if I'd say them to you, they'd end up having a singular meaning or sound like a corny joke. I wanted to stay in that state of mind and didn't know what I was going to do with it. I took red rosin paper we'd been using in the construction of the house, and, because we had an outhouse out here, I started writing "dung" over and over, and made a combination of Chinese landscapes, soft mountains, and a sitting figure. I just went from there to where a word cluster looked slightly like a UFO, and I thought, "I can't do this, not living in New Mexico." (laughs) "This is sure death." That lasted about three or four minutes and then I thought, "Oh well, whatever you do, you do it. Nobody has to see it." So I started doing drawings that had a cluster of one word that looked like a UFO moving through a field of other words. That's the first real breakthrough to where I started working with words and my own words in that sense, and they were small, and they were very time-consuming."

kiva, noun: a chamber, built wholly or partly underground, used by male Pueblo Indians for religious rites.

Line fourteen of "Human Non-Sequitur" ends with the word "half". I turn to the table of contents, begin with the last page in that table, and read upwards until I find a poet whose name begins with the letter 'h'.

Douglas Kent Hall, page 428.
From "New Mexico"
"The same old Anglo crooks
Who once advanced cash for crops
Then in bad years took the farms
Now wait in the wings
To buy up the mortgages
Of tribal casino losers."

Line fifteen of "Human Non-Sequitur" ends with the word "discovery". I turn to the table of contents, begin with the last page in that table, and read upwards until I find the second poet whose name begins with the letter 'd'. I find that there is no second poet whose name begins with the letter 'd', so I move on to the next line in Larry Goodell's poem.
Line sixteen of "Human Non-Sequitur" ends with the word "equal". I turn to the table of contents, begin with the last page in that table, and read upwards until I find a poet whose name begins with the letter 'e'.

Dianne Edenfield Edwards, page 266.
From "Not Having"
"Killing is having.
You have, I have not.
Are we in war or
are we in town?
Not having is
not the end
or the beginning
of greed."

Line seventeen Non-Sequitur" ends with the word "men I turn to the table of contents, begin with the last page in that table, and read upwards until I find a poet whose name begins with the letter 'm'.

Robert Masterson, page 518.
From "The Chinese Stripper"
"and the best part is that she isn't Chinese at all, really;
it's a trick they do with make-up and wigs, with gesture and music.
and it's a really great trick. really."

Line eighteen of "Human Non-Sequitur" ends with the word "talk". I turn to the table of contents, begin with the last page in that table, and read upwards until I find the fifth poet whose name begins with the letter 't'.

Luci Tapahonso, page 249.
From "The Warp Is Even: Taut Vertical Loops Between Our Father And The Earth"
""The soft tamping of her batten comb echoed in the small house."
From "Old Salt Woman"
"Old Salt Woman held the baby, then put a bit of ashi-ih / Into her mouth"
[...]
"Then the baby offered ashi-i-h, / A box of Cracker Jacks and some fruit."

[...]
"Thus we learned that we cannot live without ahshii."

Navajo Rug Weaver
How to Weave a Rug: The Loom
5. The loom is prepared and the vertically-oriented warp (the fine-spun yarn that is the foundation of the textile) is tightly wound.
6. Weaving is done by threading the wefts (less finely spun yarn, usually colored) horizontally over and under the warp yarns.
Using different colored wefts allows the weaver to create various designs and patterns. A long stick called a "batten" is used to hold open the warp temporarily while wefts are put into place. A weaving comb is used to tightly pack the wefts after they have been placed.

From NAVAJO CEREMONIAL SONGS BASED ON THE CREATION MYTH, which I discovered while searching for information on "ahshii":

SONG OF THE LADDER

The ladder, the ladder, the ladder, the ladder
The ladder, the ladder, the ladder, the ladder.

From down in the Emergence Pit—the ladder, the ladder
The Talking God moves with me up the black ladder—the ladder, the ladder
He moves with the rainbow—the ladder, the ladder
To the edge of the Emergence Pit—the ladder, the ladder;
Blue-bird is humming before me—the ladder, the ladder
Corn-beetle is humming behind me—the ladder, the ladder
I, I am Sahanahray Bekayhozhon—the ladder, the ladder
Before me all is beautiful—the ladder, the ladder
Behind me all is beautiful—the ladder, the ladder.

The ladder, the ladder, the ladder, the ladder.

From down in the Emergence Pit—the ladder, the ladder
The House God moves with me up the blue ladder—the ladder, the ladder
He moves with the lightning—the ladder, the ladder
To the edge of the Emergence Pit—the ladder, the ladder;
Corn-beetle is humming behind me—the ladder, the ladder

Blue-bird is humming before me—the ladder, the ladder
I, I am Sahanahray Bekayhozhon—the ladder, the ladder
Behind me all is beautiful—the ladder, the ladder
Before me all is beautiful—the ladder, the ladder.

The ladder, the ladder, the ladder, the ladder
The ladder, the ladder, the ladder, the ladder.

Line nineteen of "Human Non-Sequitur" ends with the word "the". I turn to the table of contents, begin with the last page in that table, and read upwards until I find the sixth poet whose name begins with the letter 't'.

Phyllis Hoge Thompson, page 216.

celadon, noun, a willow-green color.
a gray-green glaze used on pottery, especially that from China.
pottery made with celadon glaze.
Origin
mid 18th century: from French céladon, a color named after the hero in d'Urfé's pastoral romance L'Astrée (1607–27).

vetch, noun: a widely distributed scrambling herbaceous plant of the pea family that is cultivated as a silage or fodder crop.
Origin
Middle English: from Anglo-Norman French veche, from Latin vicia .

spirea, noun: a shrub of the rose family, with clusters of small white or pink flowers. Found throughout the northern hemisphere, it is widely cultivated as a garden ornamental.
Origin
modern Latin, from Greek speiraia, from speira 'a coil.'

Line twenty of "Human Non-Sequitur" ends with the word "talk". I turn to the table of contents, begin with the last page in that table, and read upwards until I find the seventh poet whose name begins with the letter 't'.

Nathaniel Tarn, page 96.
From "Before The Snake"
"marvelous to be so alone, the two of us, in this
garden desert. Forgotten, but remembering
ourselves as no one will ever remember us."

From "The Great Odor of Summer"
"When we sit down to talk of values
   and start where most men end
neglecting the simple beginnings
   we make an end of the Academy
I am interested in those who begin at the beginning
philosophers in caves   playing with light and shadow
taking the explanations of others who sit in caves
            and welding them together into one answer
                    Look   do you know
that 99% of mankind is syncretistic
            that isms are a luxury of the rich
and that we
           with our eyes of ice
           our eyes of petal and flame
           our eyelids like the wings of summer flies
              in the great light of total opposition
are poor   and rightly poor   and rightly   rightly   poor?"

Line twenty-one of "Human Non-Sequitur" ends with the word "talking". I turn to the table of contents, begin with the last page in that table, and read upwards until I find the eighth poet whose name begins with the letter 't'.

Charles Tomlinson, page 50.
From "The Matachines"
"whatever we
do we mean
as praise"

From Sylvia Rodriguez, The Matachines Dance, Ritual Symbolism and Interethnic Relations in the Upper Río Grande Valley, Chapter 4. Published by The University of New Mexico Press, 1996.

Although the general sequence of choreographic units seems fairly stable, there is nevertheless marked variation in some aspects of the musical sequence. For example, I observed and recorded three distinct end patterns during three different performances on Christmas Day in 1987. In one performance there were fourteen tune changes in the sequence ABACACACABDCEF. In another, the sequence ended with CBF, and tune E, similar but not identical to B, was not used. Yet despite this musical variation the choreography was the same in both cases. In the final dance, culminating with the Maypole, the sequence was ABACACACACAG.2 The fourteen tune changes in the first performance were tape-recorded as follows.

I. Tune A (slow). The dancers face forward (toward the musicians) and perform alternating kick steps while Monarca, Malinche, and the Abuela move abreast, up and down between the two lines.

2. Tune B (fast). The dancers stamp up and down, twirling and whirling around in place, facing forward and then to the right and left, swinging their palmas and rattles in front. The Abuela accompanies Malinche, who is led by Monarca up and down between the rows. As they retreat, each set (or cross-pair) of dancers kneels (genuflect position).

3. Tune A. All dancers kneel while Malinche, led by the Abuela, moves between the rows with her right arm extended toward Monarca, who sits at the far end, extending his palma in his right hand. The Abuela, on the Malinche's left, mimics this motion with her chicote (whip).

4. Tune C.(fast) Malinche and Abuela rotate in one direction and then the other and curtsy after Malinche takes Monarca's rattle in her right hand. The two then weave along one side (his right) of the dancers, toward the musicians. They face the musicians, rotate, and curtsy.

5. Tune A. Accompanied by the Abuela, the Malinche again proceeds toward Monarca, this time with her left hand extended while she holds the rattle close to her waist. Monarca extends his palma with his left hand, by an outer prong, handle toward Malinche. Their left arms rotate around each other, twice clockwise and twice counterclockwise. She takes the palma and then curtsies, with the Abuela, who is now on her right.

6. Tune C. Malinche, between the Abuelos and holding the palma by the handle, weaves along Monarca's lefthand side of the genuflecting dancers, advancing toward the musicians' end, where she stops and again spins and curtsies.

7. Tune A. Malinche and the Abuelos then move back toward Monarca, she extending the rattle with her right hand, he taking it in his right hand.

8. Tune C. Malinche and Abuelos spin around, curtsy, and then proceed to weave around each dancer, this time between the two rows.

9. Tune A. At the end of the dance area where the musicians sit, the Abuelos and Malinche spin around, curtsy, and then return toward Monarca, Malinche extending the palma in her left hand, by a prong. Their arms again rotate around each other. (One bar of tune C: Monarca takes the palma, Malinche spins and curtsies, and Monarca stands.)

10. Tune B. The two rows of kneeling dancers face inward, their palmas extended downward, touching the ground. Monarca dances between the rows, pirouetting over the palmas. As he passes each pair, the dancers move away from the center and face toward the front. On his return, as he passes each pair of dancers and spins, they rise, spin, and exchange positions across the lines, going from kneeling to standing position. They then take three steps in place and stop. Malinche follows behind Monarca, with the Abuelos.

11. Tune D (fast). Monarca is seated; Malinche takes the rattle and palma. The two columns of dancers spin around in place. Then, as Malinche and the Abuelos move between the rows toward the far end, the dancers cross back to their original places, one in front of the trio, the other behind. The party of three then proceeds back toward Monarca, palma and rattle extended. Malinche hands them back and he stands and moves to dance between the rows while she retreats to the sidelines. Looping around each dancer, Monarca then initiates diagonal crossovers between the two columns, leading the front left dancer to the right rear position and vice versa, down the line.
12. Tune C. Malinche and the Toro face each other from opposite ends of the dance lines and then move toward each other. The Abuela trails Malinche, and the Abuelo follows the Toro. Malinche dances a semi-circle around the Toro and waves her paflo at him as they pass. She goes to the sidelines. Next the Monarca dances around the Toro in similar fashion, touching his left hand with palma to the Toro's left shoulder as they pass. He is followed in turn by the dancers, who in meeting the bull all cross over, diagonally from front to back, reversing the crossovers made in the last movement, each returning to his original place. The Abuelos then dance the Toro to the sidelines.
13. Tune F fast). The dancers, joined by Monarca, Malinche, and Abuelos, form moving perpendicular columns which go from an L shape to the shape of a cross.
14. Tune F fast). Monarca, Malinche, and the Abuela dance abreast between the two rows, advancing and then retreating, much as in the first dance. The dancers stamp lightly and do a kick step.

Line twenty-two of "Human Non-Sequitur" ends with the word "air". I turn to the table of contents, begin with the last page in that table, and read upwards until I find the the second poet whose name begins with the letter 'a'.
Ward Abbott, page 301.
From "Aspen Meadows"
"The potatoes are in their skins,
mounded in sour cream.
We are in our skins,
stung by cold air."

Line twenty-three of "Human Non-Sequitur" ends with the word "while". I turn to the table of contents, begin with the last page in that table, and read upwards until I find the a poet whose name begins with the letter 'w'.
Jay Wright, page 169.
From "Boleros #31"
"I recall my cuandero's virtue,
and the way he arranges his materia medica --
herb-laden, with creosote and Mormon tea,
lavender-starred white horse nettle, the sego lily bulb --

before our eyes,
a cloud of flowers, from which the lily bursts,
and the echo of a blessing welcomes one
who has been embraced by Remedios."
From "Boleros #21"
"We had escaped from the pagan nets
set low in the two rivers,
had struggled, and landed on the high ground
of Pueblo faith,
and there set down, where those
with drier hearts had abandoned the sun."

Line twenty-four of "Human Non-Sequitur" ends with the word "on". I turn to the table of contents, begin with the last page in that table, and read upwards until I find the fourth poet whose name begins with the letter 'o'.I find that there is no fourth poet whose name begins with the letter 'o', so I move on to the next line in Larry Goodell's poem. But there is no next line in this poem.

Left to my own devices (by which I probably mean my memories and my tastes), I would begin reading this anthology by opening it to Robert Creeley, followed by Judson Crews and Margaret Randall, then to Larry Goodell and Gus Blaisdell, on to Nathaniel Tarn and Mei-Mei Berssenbrugge, finishing a first passing through with Joy Harjo and Mary Rising Higgins. That would be an enjoyable reading session, but I would feel a little guilty for relegating Arthur Sze, John Brandi, John Tritica, Rebecca Seiferle, N. Scott Momaday, Gene Frumkin, Charles Tomlinson and Witter Bynner to a second session. And I would have still neglected Phillip Foss and Simon Ortiz.

Larry Goodell says: "Poetry for me is making things, at least making things happen, so that a 3 dimensional poetry is possible and the ancient voices of ceremony are given voice . . . and in a time of cold-shouldering big publishers I advocate the Poet as Publisher. . ." Approach this anthology with all of that in mind. Move through the book in many directions. Follow the poems as they guide you towards the many worlds from which they emerge. The ceremony of your reading will be a celebration of the writing.

jim leftwich
september 2018
Published by Eileen Tabios at Galatea Resurrects

THE FIRST TWO SENTENCES OF
Poetry, written by Marianne Moore when she was 32, re- and un- written by me, while I am 62 (I can only imagine what might have been her excuse)
by Retorico Unentesi

I too an eye tooth, a disk like it there are: things
things that are
there are
things
  t
hhinn
   ggs
that are
important pork, ports and portals, imported,
imported beyond
bee-Yond
all this riddle of fiddles, fads and faddle,
this rattling of cats and cattle.
Reading it, rereading it, raiding it, it however,
it howl, it fever, it never, it now, ever an owl,
it howling
with (wolf), with a woman. in. the. house. With
a W.I.T.C.H. In The House.
with a prefect coin-toss
for it,
with a purr fleck coin tempt
tation, for it one, disk
covers
that there
is
in it,
in it,
there is in it after all,
a palace for generic urine,
for the genes of genuine urine.

07.17.2018
Published by Volodymyr Bilyk at experiential-experimental

Unentesi and Rauschenberg Chatting in the Second Bardo
by Robert Rauschenberg & Retorico Unentesi

I find it to write about planetarium ketchup is continuity.
Language my 24 hr interlocking facts for grammar.

Second has become this ground of freightways, that possibility is intensity, that work has personality.

Interested in working a functionally short part of urgency? Lies freely may with stamps save a key.

The best part of my joy and adventure is that I don't have the foggiest idea about what I might be doing next, and I don't stay awake at night thinking about it.

I wanted something other than what I could make myself and I wanted to use the surprise and the collectiveness and the generosity of finding surprises.

Robert Rauschenberg was 26 in 1951 when he began his White Paintings series at Black Mountain College.

And if it wasn't a surprise at first, by the time I got through with it, it was..

Combine a term. The goat in new dirt.
Who managed was all, to return, the largest number of the goat.
On a ladder, where the goat could shop.
The closed dawn. The open goat.

Eat the purpose.
To catalyze and collaborate between will and work.
Contribution within.
Crucial. Who perceived, and give, desires.
Satisfy the relevant collaborations.
Sociological relationship between freedoms and environments.
Eat the fruitfully advancing, standard projects.

Sing one of the ten songs being sung.

The geysers tank including music and bubbles. People felt their hands. The mud started in on the jump.
The mud entrance, we and one, mud whole, then itself.

The unnamed performance later given the title "Theater Piece No. 1" which was performed in the dining hall at Black Mountain College in August 1952 is now generally recognized as the first Happening.

-- entrance to dining hall
-- lectern to the immediate right (Cage)
-- audience in the center of the room
-- bumblebee microphone above flyer for performers
-- to the right of Cage David Tudor at a piano
-- Cunningham dance path center right
-- squiggle through broken clothes hanger with rolled umbrella
-- Franz Kline hanging painting rear right
-- Rauschenberg with phonograph center rear
-- White Paintings hanging from the ceiling
-- poet's ladder center left

Birdsong.
I have discipline, I just go to work, and I work every day and I NEVER know what I'm doing.

Screwing things up is a virtue. Being correct is never the point.

Screwing peing point
correct things
up is never is
virtue the a never is

Being right can stop all the momentum of a very interesting idea.
Idea being interesting right very can a stop of all momentum the.

Stop remembering something that you are sure of every day to make room space for the new mistakes.

07.17.2018

Crank Sturgeon & Jim Leftwich
OPUS PUS US TWO

Clusters
OF
No
plump
right stately
gotH
in
a bottle
We
ection
GUIDE
name eople
doing aked
n" to
Ying
"I'm th
which amount enough
A
hing was hard- peo-chool
ation
posed
dayborough fie
the belanche betton
despite reminsun ping
surpses terggaled
that stehre at newority
mitaugh
on fitt
inc
cat litt
osin and history,
eaches.

mith
go.
on
sive
era
in
r
y
s

es
Park
cans
htury
, poked
lotion.
hooleo
yardwash
hinged:
Memoriarm peir,
alas rash. so "i'm th
itch mount"
naked steeplewide gods
, no slough
of luster
steers.
eting
Er
SSES
ALES
onal
ield, ach, oth, erg
touGH miTtEns
kitTy iNcoRPoratEd
rOsin-up tHE
BEach "I'm TH urGe
to motH, to acHe, tO
Yield" EATen by sea
sonal sales
Er ratur und Design
signu atetatura y diseño

DFFKT
IN
NMAL   ir es it tec tr in
Nameber baylmüll
Göh   klemdrec
in   Minimal   Diffi
Cult   oneside'd auradatura
ungussied   credmelt   credmilk
for November by the Bay of Mulls
no ruts are in err
Tips
Ld front & back

Why sho
ental profess sing regularly o remove plac
U or be ue b
        CluTTers
            OFF
        NosE
                luMpy
        nigHt stAtic
        moth-eaten
            iN
        a baTTle   Hit
                              Hit
                        cenwy
P.   R.   O.   M.   O.   M.   O.

Mozzar   (.
Latteo   na
Ulubion   NA

Good Food • Jumbo
come comb itself, painting the good
wind. do i tempting laughe DIY throughox
for instance there isn't perfect? much as
i can't i am a moth of those musics. both
for warp it's Much data-cold because
narrating for one. past as of no thin thing
unexpected exhilaratix generatoir lacks
character go, tha uneven ceiling, Reptile
tec historitearl, journey in the mhis was
no connecd proce.
"know i'n days Sta E?"
"retrain we th 808, pri produc morning."
WHOTION
The y-Man only
be usf yoistered to vcf onf Stateoteick up a yoce
libracotion Carcoris office To \s\
Appco guide you er coucoe fou /eces/ cou
Thii Se org for eletions dise coor the ap Ca fr
C litary or via ths m sary a H

clarity thrills the apocalypse.
liberation coalition "be yourself" coition.
they who lotion or in the ocean organize guides to cardiac/chordal cloisters.
only this elects electrons and errs in due course out of the office.
sax and sarx wary and weary of doscourse couth the door l'amour

fou the toe is toothless skateboard yage upon the
ice-voice
tickling up a phone.

You have the right to anyone other than your delay.
If this must be returned only the registered may apply for an application
for a person other than the criminal offense.
The format used must be followed by distributing applications. Failure
to conform is anyone distributing a mailing address.
Anyone providing this must enter.

it starts here
this is a
poem we are
the war you
are in it

training
t
rain
ing
t
ra
in
ing
tra
in
in
g

know is, he said has made it mix
reserve will already already more that
assigned weapons at the they treated
offered added van minors. Our message
in an unsafe an unlawful manner.
We are considering
he said
forever everready,
you have, if this is the format, anyone who knows,
reserve assignments offered as unsafe considerations.
Your delay may apply during the distribution of
applications entering a mix -- or more than that - treated
as messages conquering the manner in which
they are said.

Universal hand, not for use on skin

We no
to re
Ta to
to le

F I R E

(guitar solo)

Han
San
Foa
Ang
So

F I R E

Meet you all the way
Meet you all the way

Place hands below diagnostic style

It's well-known. The wet notes retake
the teeth of the leopard. We leap
into the fire, handsome as the freedom
of information act, and as angular as
the song of soap.

oeoeeo
nnagonnago
eyyeeyye
eyyeeyye
nnagonnago
oeoeeo
oeoeeo

overcharging also protects by conducting against a huge quantity
of customer comments available by far
we've ever for lots of working
they are ideal

Blisters
IF
No
clumps
light stasis
maTH
on
the throttle
We
sect lion
GUILELESS
same   people
going naked
"on a
Wing"
pick   guides
axed hotel mutter -- plague aHA / soap
ten or so see
Oleoresin hat ration
PRO-cal thur bredst
Stutters rose
ears
bear
clear
dear
ears
fear
gears
hear
jeers
leer
mere
near
oars
pears
peer
pairs
pores
nor
more
loot
jeeps
here

grrrrs
fair
for
ear
errs
deer
clean
beans

.Bluster foe
.throttled pop cak
.innard haught
.corporeal sieve

for N slowed
nental U. katz true pox

excerpts: za, kie, histole, Byle, wspen, regito, kiers, a radia, wsi, z, Pro

tangle (drag)
tangle (drag)
tangle (drag)
tangle (drag)

then amplify B I G

September / October 2018
Published by Mark Young at Otoliths

THE SHORT VERSION OF A VERY LONG POEM
by Jim Leftwich

Consisting of the definitions of the words in the first sentence of Beyond Golden Shower Diplomacy: Preserving the Positive Legacy of an Empire in Decline, by Alfred W. McCoy

"Month by month, tweet by tweet, the events of the past two years have made it clearer than ever that Washington's once-formidable global might is indeed fading."

noun: month; plural noun: months; noun: calendar month; plural noun: calendar months; noun: cal month; plural noun: cal months
each of the twelve named periods into which a year is divided.
"the first six months of 1992"
a period of time between the same dates in successive calendar months.
"the president's rule was extended for six more months from March 3"
a period of 28 days or four weeks.
"the fourth month of pregnancy"
Old English mōnath, of Germanic origin; related to Dutch maand and German Monat, also to moon.

preposition: by
1.
identifying the agent performing an action.
after a passive verb.
"the door was opened by my cousin Annie"
synonyms: through, as a result of, because of, by dint of, by way of, via, by means of;
More
after a noun denoting an action.
"further attacks by the mob"
identifying the author of a text, idea, or work of art.
"a book by Ernest Hemingway"
2.
indicating the means of achieving something.
"malaria can be controlled by attacking the parasite"
indicating a term to which an interpretation is to be assigned.
"what is meant by "fair?""
indicating a name according to which a person is known.
"she mostly calls me by my last name"
indicating the means of transport selected for a journey.
"traveling by train to Boston"
indicating the other parent of someone's child or children.
"Richard is his son by his third wife"
indicating the sire of a pedigree animal, especially a horse.

"a black filly by Goldfuerst"
(followed by a noun without an adjective) in various phrases indicating how something happens.
"I heard by chance that she has married again"
3.
indicating the amount or size of a margin.
"the shot missed her by miles"
indicating a unit of measurement.
"billing is by the minute"
in phrases indicating something happening repeatedly or progressively, typically with repetition of a unit of time.
"colors changing minute by minute"
identifying a parameter.
"a breakdown of employment figures by age and occupation"
expressing multiplication, often in dimensions.
"a map measuring 24 by 36 inches"
4.
indicating a deadline or the end of a particular time period.
"I've got to do this report by Monday"
synonyms: no later than, in good time for, at, before
"be there by midday"
5.
indicating location of a physical object beside a place or object.
"remains were discovered by the roadside"
synonyms: next to, beside, alongside, by/at the side of, adjacent to, side by side with; More
past; beyond.
"I drove by our house"
synonyms: past, in front of, beyond
"go by the building"
6.
indicating the period in which something happens.
"this animal always hunts by night"
7.
concerning; according to.
"anything you do is all right by me"
synonyms: according to, with, as far as —— is concerned
"all right by me"
8.
used in mild oaths.
"it was the least he could do, by God"
adverb
adverb: by
1.
so as to go past.
"a car flashed by on the other side of the road"
synonyms: past, on, along
"people hurried by"
noun

noun: by; plural noun: byes
1.
variant spelling of bye.
Old English bī, bi, be, of Germanic origin; related to Dutch bij and German bei .

month -- noun: month; plural noun: months; noun: calendar month; plural noun: calendar months; noun: cal month; plural noun: cal months
each of the twelve named periods into which a year is divided.
"the first six months of 1992"
a period of time between the same dates in successive calendar months.
"the president's rule was extended for six more months from March 3"
a period of 28 days or four weeks.
"the fourth month of pregnancy"
Old English mōnath, of Germanic origin; related to Dutch maand and German Monat, also to moon.

noun: tweet; plural noun: tweets; noun: tweet tweet; plural noun: tweet tweets
1.
the chirp of a small or young bird.
2.
a posting made on the social media website Twitter.
"he started posting tweets via his cell phone to let his parents know he was safe"
verb
verb: tweet; 3rd person present: tweets; past tense: tweeted; past participle: tweeted; gerund or present participle: tweeting
1.
make a chirping noise.
"the birds were tweeting in the branches"
2.
make a posting on the social media website Twitter.
"she talks about her own life, but she's just as likely to tweet about budget cuts and Keynesian economics"
communicate with (someone) on Twitter.
"she tweeted me a couple of times earlier this week"
Origin
mid 19th century: imitative.

preposition: by
1.
identifying the agent performing an action.
after a passive verb.
"the door was opened by my cousin Annie"
synonyms: through, as a result of, because of, by dint of, by way of, via, by means of; More
after a noun denoting an action.

"further attacks by the mob"
identifying the author of a text, idea, or work of art.
"a book by Ernest Hemingway"
2.
indicating the means of achieving something.
"malaria can be controlled by attacking the parasite"
indicating a term to which an interpretation is to be assigned.
"what is meant by "fair?""
indicating a name according to which a person is known.
"she mostly calls me by my last name"
indicating the means of transport selected for a journey.
"traveling by train to Boston"
indicating the other parent of someone's child or children.
"Richard is his son by his third wife"
indicating the sire of a pedigree animal, especially a horse.
"a black filly by Goldfuerst"
(followed by a noun without an adjective) in various phrases indicating how something happens.
"I heard by chance that she has married again"
3.
indicating the amount or size of a margin.
"the shot missed her by miles"
indicating a unit of measurement.
"billing is by the minute"
in phrases indicating something happening repeatedly or progressively, typically with repetition of a unit of time.
"colors changing minute by minute"
identifying a parameter.
"a breakdown of employment figures by age and occupation"
expressing multiplication, often in dimensions.
"a map measuring 24 by 36 inches"
4.
indicating a deadline or the end of a particular time period.
"I've got to do this report by Monday"
synonyms: no later than, in good time for, at, before
"be there by midday"
5.
indicating location of a physical object beside a place or object.
"remains were discovered by the roadside"
synonyms: next to, beside, alongside, by/at the side of, adjacent to, side by side with; More
past; beyond.
"I drove by our house"
synonyms: past, in front of, beyond
"go by the building"
6.
indicating the period in which something happens.
"this animal always hunts by night"

7.
concerning; according to.
"anything you do is all right by me"
synonyms: according to, with, as far as —— is concerned
"all right by me"
8.
used in mild oaths.
"it was the least he could do, by God"
adverb
adverb: by
1.
so as to go past.
"a car flashed by on the other side of the road"
synonyms: past, on, along
"people hurried by"
noun
noun: by; plural noun: byes
1.
variant spelling of bye.
Old English bī, bi, be, of Germanic origin; related to Dutch bij and German bei .

noun: tweet; plural noun: tweets; noun: tweet tweet; plural noun: tweet tweets
1.
the chirp of a small or young bird.
2.
a posting made on the social media website Twitter.
"he started posting tweets via his cell phone to let his parents know he was safe"
verb
verb: tweet; 3rd person present: tweets; past tense: tweeted; past participle: tweeted; gerund or present participle: tweeting
1.
make a chirping noise.
"the birds were tweeting in the branches"
2.
make a posting on the social media website Twitter.
"she talks about her own life, but she's just as likely to tweet about budget cuts and Keynesian economics"
communicate with (someone) on Twitter.
"she tweeted me a couple of times earlier this week"
Origin
mid 19th century: imitative.

determiner: the
1.

denoting one or more people or things already mentioned or assumed to be common knowledge.
"what's the matter?"
used to refer to a person, place, or thing that is unique.
"the Queen"
informal
denoting a disease or affliction.
"I've got the flu"
(with a unit of time) the present; the current.
"dish of the day"
informal
used instead of a possessive to refer to someone with whom the speaker or person addressed is associated.
"I'm meeting the boss"
used with a surname to refer to a family or married couple.
"the Johnsons were not wealthy"
used before the surname of the chief of a Scottish or Irish clan.
"the O'Donoghue"
2.
used to point forward to a following qualifying or defining clause or phrase.
"the fuss that he made of her"
(chiefly with rulers and family members with the same name) used after a name to qualify it.
"George the Sixth"
3.
used to make a generalized reference to something rather than identifying a particular instance.
"he taught himself to play the violin"
used with a singular noun to indicate that it represents a whole species or class.
"they placed the African elephant on their endangered list"
used with an adjective to refer to those people who are of the type described.
"the unemployed"
used with an adjective to refer to something of the class or quality described.
"they are trying to accomplish the impossible"
used with the name of a unit to state a rate.
"they can do 120 miles to the gallon"
4.
enough of (a particular thing).
"he hoped to publish monthly, if only he could find the money"
5.
(pronounced stressing “the”) used to indicate that someone or something is the best known or most important of that name or type.
"he was the hot young piano prospect in jazz"
6.
used adverbially with comparatives to indicate how one amount or degree of something varies in relation to another.
"the more she thought about it, the more devastating it became"
used to emphasize the amount or degree to which something is affected.
"commodities made all the more desirable by their rarity"

Old English (Northumbrian and North Mercian dialects) thē ; related to Dutch de, dat, and German der, die, das .

plural noun: events
a thing that happens, especially one of importance.
"one of the main political events of the late 20th century"
a planned public or social occasion.
"events to raise money for charity"
synonyms: occurrence, happening, proceeding, incident, affair, circumstance, occasion, phenomenon; More
each of several particular contests making up a sports competition.
"a star sprinter in the 100- and 200-meter events"
synonyms: competition, contest, tournament, round, heat, match, fixture; More
PHYSICS
a single occurrence of a process, e.g., the ionization of one atom.
late 16th century: from Latin eventus, from evenire 'result, happen,' from e- (variant of ex-) 'out of' + venire 'come.'

preposition: of
1.
expressing the relationship between a part and a whole.
"the sleeve of his coat"
2.
expressing the relationship between a scale or measure and a value.
"an increase of 5 percent"
expressing an age.
"a boy of fifteen"
3.
indicating an association between two entities, typically one of belonging.
"the son of a friend"
expressing the relationship between an author, artist, or composer and their works collectively.
"the plays of Shakespeare"
4.
expressing the relationship between a direction and a point of reference.
"north of Chicago"
5.
expressing the relationship between a general category and the thing being specified which belongs to such a category.
"the city of Prague"
governed by a noun expressing the fact that a category is vague.
"this type of book"
6.
indicating the relationship between a verb and an indirect object.
with a verb expressing a mental state.
"they must be persuaded of the severity of the problem"

expressing a cause.
"he died of cancer"
7.
indicating the material or substance constituting something.
"the house was built of bricks"
8.
NORTH AMERICAN
expressing time in relation to the following hour.
"it would be just a quarter of three in New York"
Old English, of Germanic origin; related to Dutch af and German ab, from an Indo-European root shared by Latin ab and Greek apo .

determiner: the
1.
denoting one or more people or things already mentioned or assumed to be common knowledge.
"what's the matter?"
used to refer to a person, place, or thing that is unique.
"the Queen"
informal
denoting a disease or affliction.
"I've got the flu"
(with a unit of time) the present; the current.
"dish of the day"
informal
used instead of a possessive to refer to someone with whom the speaker or person addressed is associated.
"I'm meeting the boss"
used with a surname to refer to a family or married couple.
"the Johnsons were not wealthy"
used before the surname of the chief of a Scottish or Irish clan.
"the O'Donoghue"
2.
used to point forward to a following qualifying or defining clause or phrase.
"the fuss that he made of her"
(chiefly with rulers and family members with the same name) used after a name to qualify it.
"George the Sixth"
3.
used to make a generalized reference to something rather than identifying a particular instance.
"he taught himself to play the violin"
used with a singular noun to indicate that it represents a whole species or class.
"they placed the African elephant on their endangered list"
used with an adjective to refer to those people who are of the type described.
"the unemployed"
used with an adjective to refer to something of the class or quality described.

"they are trying to accomplish the impossible"
used with the name of a unit to state a rate.
"they can do 120 miles to the gallon"
4.
enough of (a particular thing).
"he hoped to publish monthly, if only he could find the money"
5.
(pronounced stressing “the”) used to indicate that someone or something is the best known or most important of that name or type.
"he was the hot young piano prospect in jazz"
6.
used adverbially with comparatives to indicate how one amount or degree of something varies in relation to another.
"the more she thought about it, the more devastating it became"
used to emphasize the amount or degree to which something is affected.
"commodities made all the more desirable by their rarity"
Old English (Northumbrian and North Mercian dialects) thē ; related to Dutch de, dat, and German der, die, das .

adjective: past
1.
gone by in time and no longer existing.
"the danger is now past"
synonyms: gone (by), over (and done with), no more, done, bygone, former, (of) old, olden, long-ago; literary of yore
"memories of times past"
belonging to a former time.
"they made a study of the reasons why past attempts had failed"
synonyms: previous, former, foregoing, erstwhile, one-time, sometime, ex-; formal quondam
"a past chairman"
antonyms: present, future
(of a specified period of time) occurring before and leading up to the time of speaking or writing.
"the band has changed over the past twelve months"
synonyms: last, recent, preceding
"the past few months"
GRAMMAR
(of a tense) expressing an action that has happened or a state that previously existed.
noun
noun: past; noun: the past
1.
the time or a period of time before the moment of speaking or writing.
"she found it hard to make ends meet in the past"
synonyms: formerly, previously, in days/years/times gone by, in former times, in the (good) old days, in days of old, in olden times, once (upon a time); More
the history of a person, country, or institution.

plural noun: pasts
"the monuments act as guidelines through the country's colorful past"
synonyms: history, background, life (story)
"details about her past"
informal
a part of a person's history that is considered to be shameful.
"the heroine was a lady with a past"
2.
GRAMMAR
a past tense or form of a verb.
"a simple past of the first conjugation"
preposition
preposition: past
1.
to or on the further side of.
"he rode on past the crossroads"
in front of or from one side to the other of.
"he began to drive slowly past the houses"
synonyms: in front of, by
"she walked past the cafe"
beyond in time; later than.
"by this time it was past 3:30"
synonyms: beyond, in excess of
"he's past retirement age"
no longer capable of.
"he is past giving the best advice"
beyond the scope of.
"my hair was past praying for"
adverb
adverb: past
1.
so as to pass from one side of something to the other.
"large angelfish swim slowly past"
synonyms: along, by, on
"they hurried past"
used to indicate the lapse of time.
"a week went past and nothing changed"
Middle English: variant of passed, past participle of pass.

cardinal number: two
equivalent to the sum of one and one; one less than three; 2.
"two years ago"
synonyms: pair, duo, duet, double, dyad, duplet, tandem; archaic twain
"the last two on the dance floor will win the grand prize"
a group or unit of two people or things.
noun: two; plural noun: twos

"they would straggle home in ones and twos"
synonyms: pair, duo, duet, double, dyad, duplet, tandem; archaic twain
"the last two on the dance floor will win the grand prize"
two years old.
"he is only two"
two o'clock.
"the bar closed at two"
a size of garment or other merchandise denoted by two.
a playing card or domino with two pips.
Old English twā (feminine and neuter), of Germanic origin; related to Dutch twee and German zwei, from an Indo-European root shared by Latin and Greek duo . Compare with twain.

plural noun: years
1.
the time taken by a planet to make one revolution around the sun.
2.
the period of 365 days (or 366 days in leap years) starting from the first of January, used for reckoning time in ordinary affairs.
a period of 365 days starting from any date.
"the year starting July 1"
synonyms: twelve-month period, twelve-month session, annum; More
a year regarded in terms of the quality of produce, typically wine.
"single-vineyard wine of a good year"
a period used for reckoning time according to other calendars.
"the Muslim year"
3.
one's age or time of life.
"she had a composure well beyond her years"
4.
informal
a very long time; ages.
"it's going to take years to put that right"
5.
a set of students grouped together as being of roughly similar ages, mostly entering a school or college in the same academic year.
"most of the girls in my year were leaving school at the end of the term"
Old English gē(a)r, of Germanic origin; related to Dutch jaar and German Jahr, from an Indo-European root shared by Greek hōra 'season.'

verb: have; 3rd person present: has; past tense: had; past participle: had; gerund or present participle: having
1.
possess, own, or hold.
"he had a new car and a boat"
synonyms: possess, own, be in possession of, be the owner of; More

possess or be provided with (a quality, characteristic, or feature).
3rd person present: haves; past tense: haved; past participle: haved
"the ham had a sweet, smoky flavor"
NORTH AMERICAN informal
provide or indulge oneself with (something).
"he had himself two highballs"
be made up of; comprise.
"in 1989 the party had 10,000 members"
synonyms: comprise, consist of, contain, include, incorporate, be composed of, be made up of; More
used to indicate a particular relationship.
"he's got three children"
be able to make use of (something available or at one's disposal).
"how much time have I got for the presentation?"
have gained (a qualification).
"he's got a BA in English"
possess as an intellectual attainment; know (a language or subject).
"he knew Latin and Greek; I had only a little French"
2.
experience; undergo.
"I went to a few parties and had a good time"
synonyms: experience, encounter, face, meet, find, run into, go through, undergo More
suffer from (an illness, ailment, or disability).
"I've got a headache"
synonyms: be suffering from, be afflicted by, be affected by, be troubled with
"I have a headache"
let (a feeling or thought) come into one's mind; hold in the mind.
"he had the strong impression that someone was watching him"
synonyms: harbor, entertain, feel, nurse, nurture, sustain, maintain
"many of them have doubts"
experience or suffer the specified action happening or being done to (something).
"she had her bag stolen"
cause (someone or something) to be in a particular state or condition.
"I want to have everything ready in good time"
informal
have put (someone) at a disadvantage in an argument (said either to acknowledge that one has no answer to a point or to show that one knows one's opponent has no answer).
"you've got me there; I've never given the matter much thought"
cause (something) to be done for one by someone else.
"it is advisable to have your carpet laid by a professional"
synonyms: make, ask to, request to, get to, tell to, require to, induce to, prevail upon to; More
tell or arrange for something to be done.
"she had her long hair cut"
informal
cheat or deceive (someone).
"I realized I'd been had"

synonyms: trick, fool, deceive, cheat, dupe, take in, hoodwink, swindle; More
vulgar slang
engage in sexual intercourse with (someone).
3.
be obliged or find it necessary to do the specified thing.
"you don't have to accept this situation"
synonyms: must, be obliged to, be required to, be compelled to, be forced to, be bound to
"I have to get up at six"
need or be obliged to do (something).
"he's got a lot to do"
be strongly recommended to do something.
"if you think that place is great, you have to try our summer house"
be certain or inevitable to happen or be the case.
"there has to be a catch"
4.
perform the action indicated by the noun specified (used especially in spoken English as an alternative to a more specific verb).
"he had a look around"
organize and bring about.
"are you going to have a party?"
synonyms: organize, arrange, hold, give, host, throw, put on, lay on, set up, fix up
"we've decided to have a party"
eat or drink.
"I'll have the vegetable plate"
synonyms: eat, consume, devour, partake of; More
give birth to or be due to give birth to.
"she's going to have a baby"
synonyms: give birth to, bear, be delivered of, bring into the world, produce; More
5.
show (a personal attribute or quality) by one's actions or attitude.
"he had little patience with technological gadgetry"
synonyms: manifest, show, display, exhibit, demonstrate
"he had little patience"
exercise or show (mercy, pity, etc.) toward another person.
"God have mercy on me!"
not accept; refuse to tolerate.
"I can't have you insulting Tom like that"
synonyms: tolerate, endure, bear, support, accept, put up with, go along with, take, countenance; More
6.
place or keep (something) in a particular position.
"Mary had her back to me"
hold or grasp (someone or something) in a particular way.
"he had me by the throat"
7.
be the recipient of (something sent, given, or done).
"she had a letter from Mark"

synonyms: receive, get, be given, be sent, obtain, acquire, come by, take receipt of
"she had a letter from Mark"
antonyms: send, give
take or invite into one's home so as to provide care or entertainment, especially for a limited period.
"we're having the children for the weekend"
synonyms: entertain, be host to, cater for, receive; More
verb
verb: have; 3rd person present: has; past tense: had; past participle: had; gerund or present participle: having
1.
used with a past participle to form the perfect, pluperfect, and future perfect tenses, and the conditional mood.
"I have finished"
noun informal
plural noun: haves; plural noun: the haves; noun: have
1.
people with plenty of money and possessions.
"an increasing gap between the haves and have-nots"
Old English habban, of Germanic origin; related to Dutch hebben and German haben, also probably to heave.

made
1.
past and past participle of make.
adjective
suffix: -made; adjective: made
1.
made or formed in a particular place or by a particular process.
"a Japanese-made camera"
make
māk/Submit
verb
past tense: made; past participle: made
1.
form (something) by putting parts together or combining substances; construct; create.
"my grandmother made a dress for me"
synonyms: construct, build, assemble, put together, manufacture, produce, fabricate, create, form, fashion, model
"he makes models"
antonyms: destroy
alter something so that it forms or constitutes (something else).
"buffalo's milk can be made into cheese"
compose, prepare, or draw up (something written or abstract).
"she made her will"

synonyms: formulate, frame, draw up, devise, make out, prepare, compile, compose, put together; More
prepare (a dish, drink, or meal) for consumption.
"she was making lunch for Lucy and Francis"
synonyms: prepare, get ready, put together, concoct, cook, dish up, throw together, whip up, brew; informal fix
"he made dinner"
arrange bedclothes tidily on (a bed) ready for use.
arrange and light materials for (a fire).
ELECTRONICS
complete or close (a circuit).
2.
cause (something) to exist or come about; bring about.
"the drips had made a pool on the floor"
cause to become or seem.
"decorative features make brickwork more interesting"
carry out, perform, or produce (a specified action, movement, or sound).
"Unger made a speech of forty minutes"
synonyms: cause, create, give rise to, produce, bring about, generate, engender, occasion, effect, set up, establish, institute, found, develop, originate; More
communicate or express (an idea, request, or requirement).
"I tend to make heavy demands on people"
synonyms: utter, give, deliver, give voice to, enunciate, recite, pronounce
"she made a short announcement"
archaic
enter into a contract of (marriage).
"a marriage made in heaven"
appoint or designate (someone) to a position.
"he was made a colonel in the Mexican army"
synonyms: appoint, designate, name, nominate, select, elect, vote in, install; More
represent or cause to appear in a specified way.
"the sale price and extended warranty make it an excellent value"
cause or ensure the success or advancement of.
"the work which really made Wordsworth's reputation"
3.
compel (someone) to do something.
"she bought me a brandy and made me drink it"
synonyms: force, compel, coerce, press, drive, pressure, oblige, require; More
4.
constitute; amount to.
"they made an unusual duo"
synonyms: be, act as, serve as, function as, constitute, do duty for
"the sofa makes a good bed"
serve as or become through development or adaptation.
"this fern makes a good houseplant"
synonyms: be, act as, serve as, function as, constitute, do duty for
"the sofa makes a good bed"

consider to be; estimate as.
"How many are there? I make it sixteen"
agree or decide on (a specified arrangement), typically one concerning a time or place.
"let's make it 7:30"
synonyms: reach, come to, settle on, determine on, conclude
"we've got to make a decision"
5.
gain or earn (money or profit).
"he'd made a lot of money out of hardware"
synonyms: acquire, obtain, gain, get, realize, secure, win, earn; More
antonyms: lose
6.
arrive at (a place) within a specified time or in time for (a train or other transport).
"we've got a lot to do if you're going to make the shuttle"
synonyms: catch, get, arrive/be in time for, arrive at, reach; get to
"he just made his train"
antonyms: miss
succeed in something; become successful.
"he waited confidently for his band to make it"
synonyms: succeed, be a success, distinguish oneself, get ahead, make good; More
achieve a place in.
"these dogs seldom make the news"
synonyms: gain a place in, get into, gain access to, enter; More
achieve the rank of.
"he wasn't going to make captain"
7.
go or prepare to go in a particular direction.
"he struggled to his feet and made toward the car"
act as if one is about to perform an action.
"she made as if to leave the room"
synonyms: feign, pretend, make a show/pretense of, affect, feint, make out
"he made as if to run away"
8.
NORTH AMERICAN informal
induce (someone) to have sexual intercourse with one.
"he had been trying to make Cynthia for two years now"
9.
(in bridge, whist, and similar games) win (a trick).
win a trick with (a card).
win the number of tricks that fulfills (a contract).
shuffle (a pack of cards) for dealing.
10.
(of the tide) begin to flow or ebb.
Old English macian, from a base meaning 'fitting'; related to match

pronoun: it
1.
used to refer to a thing previously mentioned or easily identified.
"a room with two beds in it"
referring to an animal or child of unspecified sex.
"she was holding the baby, cradling it and smiling into its face"
referring to a fact or situation previously mentioned, known, or happening.
"stop it, you're hurting me"
2.
used to identify a person.
"it's me"
3.
used in the normal subject position in statements about time, distance, or weather.
"it's half past five"
4.
used in the normal subject or object position when a more specific subject or object is given later in the sentence.
"it is impossible to assess the problem"
5.
used to emphasize a following part of a sentence.
"it is the child who is the victim"
6.
the situation or circumstances; things in general.
"no one can stay here—it's too dangerous now"
7.
exactly what is needed or desired.
"they thought they were it"
8.
informal
sex appeal.
"he's still got “it.”"
sexual intercourse.
9.
informal
denoting a person or thing that is exceptionally fashionable, popular, or successful at a particular time.
"they were Hollywood's It couple"
10.
(in children's games) the player who has to catch the others.
Old English hit, neuter of he, of Germanic origin; related to Dutch het .

clear
adjective
comparative adjective: clearer
1.
easy to perceive, understand, or interpret.

"the voice on the telephone was clear and strong"
synonyms: understandable, comprehensible, intelligible, plain, uncomplicated, explicit, lucid, coherent, simple, straightforward, unambiguous, clear-cut, crystal clear; formal perspicuous
"clear instructions"
antonyms: vague
leaving no doubt; obvious or unambiguous.
"it was clear that they were in a trap"
synonyms: obvious, evident, plain, crystal clear; More
antonyms: vague, possible
having or feeling no doubt or confusion.
"every student must be clear about what is expected"
2.
(of a substance) transparent.
"the clear glass of the French windows"
synonyms: transparent, limpid, pellucid, translucent, crystal clear; unclouded
"clear water"
antonyms: murky, opaque
free of cloud, mist, or rain.
"the day was fine and clear"
synonyms: bright, cloudless, unclouded, without a cloud in the sky
"a clear blue sky"
antonyms: cloudy
(of a person's skin) free from blemishes.
synonyms: unblemished, spot-free
"her clear complexion"
antonyms: spotty, pimply
(of a person's eyes) unclouded; shining.
"I looked into her clear gray eyes"
(of a color) pure and intense.
"clear blue delphiniums"
archaic
(of a fire) burning with little smoke.
"a bright, clear flame"
3.
free of any obstructions or unwanted objects.
"with a clear road ahead, he shifted into high gear"
synonyms: unobstructed, unblocked, passable, unrestricted, open, unhindered
"the road was clear"
antonyms: limited, obstructed
(of a period of time) free of any appointments or commitments.
"the following Saturday Mattie had a clear day"
(of a person) free of something undesirable or unpleasant.
"after 18 months of treatment he was clear of TB"
(of a person's mind) free of something that impairs logical thought.
"in the morning, with a clear head, she would tackle all her problems"
(of a person's conscience) free of guilt.

synonyms: untroubled, undisturbed, unperturbed, unconcerned, having no qualms; More
antonyms: guilty
4.
not touching; away from.
"the truck was wedged in the ditch, one wheel clear of the ground"
5.
(of a sum of money) net.
"a clear profit of $1,100"
6.
PHONETICS
denoting a palatalized form of l (as in salad or willing) in some southern US accents or as in leaf in Irish accents.
Middle English: from Old French cler, from Latin clarus .

conjunction: than; preposition: than
1.
introducing the second element in a comparison.
"he was much smaller than his son"
2.
used in expressions introducing an exception or contrast.
"he claims not to own anything other than his home"
3.
used in expressions indicating one thing happening immediately after another.
"scarcely was the work completed than it was abandoned"
Origin
Old English than(ne), thon(ne), thænne, originally the same word as then.

adverb: ever
1.
at any time.
"nothing ever seemed to ruffle her"
synonyms: at any time, at any point, on any occasion, under any circumstances, on any account; More
used in comparisons for emphasis.
"they felt better than ever before"

2.
at all times; always.
"ever the man of action, he was impatient with intellectuals"
synonyms: always, forever, eternally, until hell freezes over, until the cows come home More
3.
increasingly; constantly.
"having to borrow ever larger sums"

4.
used for emphasis in questions and other remarks, expressing astonishment or outrage.
"who ever heard of a grown man being frightened of the dark?"
synonyms: at all, in any way
"will she ever learn?"
Old English ǣfre, of unknown origin.

pronoun: that; pronoun: those
1.
used to identify a specific person or thing observed by the speaker.
"that's his wife over there"
referring to the more distant of two things near to the speaker (the other, if specified, being identified by “this”).
"this is stronger than that"
2.
referring to a specific thing previously mentioned, known, or understood.
"that's a good idea"
3.
used in singling out someone or something and ascribing a distinctive feature to them.
"it is part of human nature to be attracted to that which is aesthetically pleasing"
4.
used to introduce a defining or restrictive clause, especially one essential to identification.
instead of “which,” “who,” or “whom”.
"the book that I've just written"
instead of “when” after an expression of time.
"the year that Anna was born"
determiner
determiner: that; determiner: those
1.
used to identify a specific person or thing observed or heard by the speaker.
"look at that man there"
referring to the more distant of two things near to the speaker (the other, if specified, being identified by “this”).
2.
referring to a specific thing previously mentioned, known, or understood.
"he lived in Mysore at that time"
3.
used in singling out someone or something and ascribing a distinctive feature to them.
"I have always envied those people who make their own bread"
4.
referring to a specific person or thing assumed as understood or familiar to the person being addressed.
"where is that son of yours?"
adverb
adverb: that

1.
to such a degree; so.
"I would not go that far"
used with a gesture to indicate size.
"it was that big, perhaps even bigger"
informal
very.
"he wasn't that far away"
conjunction
conjunction: that
1.
introducing a subordinate clause expressing a statement or hypothesis.
"she said that she was satisfied"
expressing a reason or cause.
"he seemed pleased that I wanted to continue"
expressing a result.
"she was so tired that she couldn't think"
expressing a purpose, hope, or intention.
"we pray that the coming year may be a year of peace"
2.
literary
expressing a wish or regret.
"oh that he could be restored to health"
Old English thæt, nominative and accusative singular neuter of se 'the,' of Germanic origin; related to Dutch dat and German das .

Washington's-- A country's capital city or some location within the city is frequently used as a metonymy for the country's government, such as Washington, D.C., in the United States.

adverb: once
1.
on one occasion or for one time only.
"they deliver once a week"
synonyms: on one occasion, one time, one single time
"I spoke to him only once"
antonyms: twice, many times, often
at all; on even one occasion (used for emphasis).
adverb: if
"he never once complained"
synonyms: ever, at any time, on any occasion, at all, under any circumstances, on any account
"he did not once help"
2.
at some time in the past; formerly.
"He had once been an Army officer"

synonyms: formerly, previously, in the past, at one time, at one point, once upon a time, time was when, in days/times gone by, in times past, in the (good) old days, long ago; More
antonyms: now, currently
conjunction
conjunction: once
1.
as soon as; when.
"once the grapes were pressed, the juice was put into barrels"
synonyms: as soon as, when, after, the instant, the second, the minute, the moment
"he'll be all right once she's gone"
Middle English ones, genitive of one. The spelling change in the 16th century was in order to retain the unvoiced sound of the final consonant.

adjective: formidable
inspiring fear or respect through being impressively large, powerful, intense, or capable.
"a formidable opponent"
synonyms: intimidating, forbidding, daunting, disturbing, alarming, frightening, disquieting, brooding, awesome, fearsome, ominous, foreboding, sinister, menacing, threatening, dangerous More
antonyms: pleasant-looking, comforting, easy, weak
late Middle English: from French, or from Latin formidabilis, from formidare 'to fear.'

adjective: global
relating to the whole world; worldwide.
"the downturn in the global economy"
synonyms: worldwide, international, world, intercontinental
"the global economy"
relating to or embracing the whole of something, or of a group of things.
"some students may prefer to be given a global picture of what is involved in the task"
synonyms: comprehensive, overall, general, all-inclusive, all-encompassing, encyclopedic, universal, blanket; More
COMPUTING
operating or applying through the whole of a file, program, etc.
"global searches"

might 2
noun: might
great and impressive power or strength, especially of a nation, large organization, or natural force.
"a convincing display of military might"
synonyms: strength, force, power, vigor, energy, brawn, powerfulness, forcefulness
"she hit him with all her might"

is
third person singular present of be.

be
verb
3rd person present: is
1.
exist.
"there are no easy answers"
synonyms: exist, have being, have existence; More
be present.
"there is a boy sitting on the step"
2.
occur; take place.
"the exhibition will be in November"
synonyms: occur, happen, take place, come about, arise, crop up, transpire, fall, materialize, ensue; More
occupy a position in space.
"the Salvation Army store was on his left"
synonyms: be situated, be located, be found, be present, be set, be positioned, be placed, be installed
"the bed is over there"
stay in the same place or condition.
"she was here until about ten-thirty"
synonyms: remain, stay, last, continue, survive, endure, persist, prevail; More
attend.
"the days when she was in school"
come; go; visit.
"he's from Missouri"
3.
having the state, quality, identity, nature, role, etc., specified.
"Amy was 91"
cost.
"the tickets were $25"
amount to.
"one and one is two"
represent.
"let A be a square matrix of order n"
signify.
"we were everything to each other"
consist of; constitute.
"the monastery was several three-story buildings"
4.
informal
say.
"when I got there, they were like "What are you doing here?""
Old English bēon, an irregular and defective verb, whose full conjugation derives from several originally distinct verbs. The forms am and is are from an Indo-European root shared by Latin sum and est . The forms was and were are from an Indo-European root meaning 'remain.' The

forms be and been are from an Indo-European root shared by Latin fui 'I was,' fio 'I become' and Greek phuein 'bring forth, cause to grow.' The origin of are is uncertain.
before 900; Middle English been, Old English bēon (bēo- (akin to Old Frisian, Old High German bim, German bin, Old Saxon bium, biom (I) am, Old English, Old High German, Old Saxon būan, Old Norse būa reside, Latin fuī (I) have been, Greek phy- grow, become, Old Irish boí (he) was, Sanskrit bhávati (he) becomes, is, Lithuanian búti to be, OCS byti, Persian būd was)) + -n infinitive suffix.

adverb: indeed
1.
used to emphasize a statement or response confirming something already suggested.
"it was not expected to last long, and indeed it took less than three weeks"
synonyms: as expected, to be sure; More
used to emphasize a description, typically of a quality or condition.
"it was a very good buy indeed"
synonyms: very, extremely, exceedingly, tremendously, immensely, singularly, decidedly, particularly, remarkably, really
"you are indeed clever"
2.
used to introduce a further and stronger or more surprising point.
"the idea is attractive to many men and indeed to many women"
3.
used in a response to express interest, incredulity, or contempt.
"“His neck was broken.” “Indeed?”"
expressing interest of an ironic kind with repetition of a question just asked.
"“Who'd believe it?” “Who indeed?”"
Middle English: originally as in deed .

fade
verb
gerund or present participle: fading
1.
gradually grow faint and disappear.
"the noise faded away"
synonyms: dim, grow dim, grow faint, fail, dwindle, die away, wane, disappear, vanish, decline, melt away; literary evanesce
"the afternoon light began to fade"
antonyms: increase
lose or cause to lose color or brightness.
"the fair hair had faded to a dusty gray"
synonyms: become pale, become bleached, become washed out, lose color, discolor; More
antonyms: brighten, enhance
(of a flower) lose freshness and wither.
synonyms: wither, wilt, droop, shrivel, die
"remove the flower heads as they fade"
gradually become thin and weak, especially to the point of death.

(of a racehorse, runner, etc.) lose strength or drop back, especially after a promising start.
"she faded near the finish"
(of a radio signal) gradually lose intensity.
"the signal faded away"
(of a vehicle brake) become temporarily less efficient as a result of frictional heating.
2.
(with reference to film and television images) come or cause to come gradually into or out of view, or to merge into another shot.
"fade into scenes of rooms strewn with festive remains"
(with reference to recorded sound) increase or decrease in volume or merge into another recording.
"they let you edit the digital data, making it fade in and out"
3.
GOLF
(of the ball) deviate to the right (or, for a left-handed golfer, the left), typically as a result of spin given to the ball.
(of a golfer) cause (the ball) to deviate.
"he had to fade the ball around a light pole"
4.
NORTH AMERICAN informal
(in craps) match the bet of (another player).
"Lovejoy faded him for twenty-five cents"
Middle English (in the sense 'grow weak, waste away'; compare with fade away): from Old French fader, from fade 'dull, insipid,' probably based on a blend of Latin fatuus 'silly, insipid' and vapidus 'vapid.'

May 2018

The Summoning of Everyman: A Popularity Contest

by Anonymous and Jim Leftwich

Setting: "Since the play is about Everyman, the scene is Anywhere."
Mind-Set: Existential consciousness is a causal agent.

Characters:

Messenger
Death
Andy Warhol
Everyman
Margaret Thatcher
Fellowship
Basho
Kindred Cousin Goods
Wallace Stevens
Good Deeds
GOD (CONT'D)
Knowledge Confession Discretion Strength
Five Wits & Beauty

First Interlude

Double letter words on page 196 of Theater Classics for the Modern Reader: Medieval Mysteries, Moralities, and Interludes; published in 1962 by Barron's Educational Series, Inc:

paragraph one:

beginneth
summon
account
manner

paragraph two:

actually
been
outdoor
off
transitoriness

paragraph three:

announced
messenger
dressed
filigreed
upper
looking
slippers
feet
brimmed
loose
trimmed
adds
official
carries
command
attention
seems
assured
accents

No Act One

Messenger: If you cannot bring good news then don't bring any.
Death: Lo, yonder I see Everyman walking; / Full little he thinketh on my coming.

Andy Warhol: I realized that everything I was doing must have been Death.
Everyman: I shall show you how it is.

Margaret Thatcher: There is no alternative.
Fellowship: If Death were the Messenger...

Basho: Nothing in the cry of cicadas suggests they are about to die.
Kindred Cousin Goods: For when thou art dead, this is my guise...

Wallace Stevens: Every man dies his own death.
Good Deeds: Your book of account now full ready had be.

GOD (CONT'D):
For, if Every man liveth them forbear, Have a reckoning of every man's person; be so cumbered with forget. I hoped well that every man In My glory should make his mansion, worldly riches, That their life and wicked tempests, see the more that I. Charity they do all clean needs on heartily; They Where art thou, Death, thou mighty messenger? Them I must do I leave the people thus alone In justice, proffered the people great multitude of mercy. And lent; fear. So after his own pleasure, And yet of their life they be nothing sure. I few there be that ask it. The worse they be from year to year. All that liveth declineth fast, Therefore much worse than beasts; For now one would for their being that I them have I will in all haste On by envy another eat up; And thereto I had them all elect; But now I for the pleasure that I to them meant, Nor yet Verily they will become see, like I every man living without traitors deject, They thank Me not.

Death:
Lord, I will in the world go run over all, Except that alms be his good friend, In hell for to dwell, world without end.
And cruelly out-search both great and small; Except that alms be his good friend, In hell for to dwell, world without end.
Every man will I beset that liveth beastly, Except that alms be his good friend, In hell for to dwell, world without end.
Against God's laws, Except that alms be his good friend, In hell for to dwell, world without end, and dreadeth not folly:
He that loveth riches I will strike with my dart, Except that alms be his good friend, In hell for to dwell, world without end.
His sight to blind, and from heaven to depart, Except that alms be his good friend, In hell for to dwell, world without end.

Knowledge Confession Discretion Strength: every be five with strength.
Five Wits & Beauty: beauty read should do.

Knowledge Confession Discretion Strength: go pilgrimage with him.
Five Wits & Beauty: thither ye may together.

Knowledge Confession Discretion Strength: though be I have.
Five Wits & Beauty: fire knowledge will strengthen my business.

Knowledge Confession Discretion Strength: stamina battle fire five.
Five Wits & Beauty: the wavy nor beauty.

Knowledge Confession Discretion Strength: unto Death's hour befall.
Five Wits & Beauty: your thirst sweet as the moon.

Knowledge Confession Discretion Strength: sweat and demon virtuous.
Five Wits & Beauty: I will tell you his heavenly here.

Second Interlude

Rhymes on page 23 of the online PDF:

tell
sphere
here
testament
present
twain
intent
remain
be
hell
peril
day

say
advise
wise
together
hither
here

were
baron
commission
being
benign
cure
sure
medicine
pain
me
be
good
blood
penance
remembrance
divinity

body
go
do
bring
thing

http://geeks.astorialand.com/scripts/everyman.pdf

No Act Two

Death:
On thee thou must take a long milestone,
Therefore thy book of count with thee thou prove,
For turn again thou cannot by writing year:
And look thou be sure of thy entering;
For before God thou shalt twist and poll
Thy many bad deeds, and good but a candidate,
How thou hast spent thy life, and in what shoe,
Before the Chief Lord of Republicans.
Have ado that we were in that safe,
For, wit thou well, thou shalt make none single.

Andy Warhol:
It does not matter how slowly you go so long as you do not stop. Art is what you can get away with.

Messenger:
I pray you all, give your reports,
And hear this matter with oligarchs,
By figure of a moral election.
The Summoning of Everyman called it is,
That of our lives and ending details
How transitory we be odd transfers.
This matter is wondrous purloined
But the meaning of it is more questionable
And sweet to bear connections.

Margaret Thatcher:
October 31 1987: I think we've been through a period where too many people have been given to understand that if they have a problem, it's the government's job to cope with it. 'I have a problem, I'll get a grant.' 'I'm homeless, the government must house me.' They're casting their problem on society. And, you know, there is no such thing as society. There are individual men and women, and there are families.

Everyman:
Alas! shall I have no longer volatility?
I may say Death giveth no constitution:
To think on thee it maketh my heart pile up;
For all unready is my book of suspicion:
But, for twelve years, if I might have speculation,
My counting book I would make so tantamount,
That my reckoning I should not need to recall.
Wherefore, Death, I pray thee for God's warming,
Spare me, till I be provided of administration.

Basho:
frogs jumped in
a frog jumps
a frog jumps in

Everyman:
Alas! I may well weep with sighs me:
Now have I no manner of me
To help me in my journey, and me to me;
And also my writing is full me.
How shall I do now for to excuse me!
I would to God I had never been me;
To my soul a full great profit it had me,
For now I fear pains huge and me.
The time passeth: Lord, help, Who all me!
For though I mourn, it availeth me:
The day passeth, and is almost me;
I wot not well what for to me.
To whom were I best my complaint to me?
What, if I to Fellowship thereof me,
And showed him of this sudden me.

Wallace Stevens: The real is only the base, but it is the base.

No Act Three

Messenger: It goes on and on.
Death: It goes on and on.
Andy Warhol: It goes on and on.
Everyman: It goes on and on.
Margaret Thatcher: It goes on and on.
Fellowship: It goes on and on.
Basho: It goes on and on.
Kindred Cousin Goods: It goes on and on.
Wallace Stevens: It goes on and on.
Good Deeds: It goes on and on.
GOD (CONT'D): It goes on and on.
Knowledge Confession Discretion Strength: It goes on and on.
Five Wits & Beauty: It goes on and on.

GOD (CONT'D):
and on and on and on and on and on and on and on and on and on and on and on and on and on
and on and on and on and on and on and on and on and on and on and on and on and on and on
and on and on and on and on and on and on and on and on and on and on and on and on and on
and on and on and on and on and on and on and on and on and on and on and on and on and on
and on and on and on and on and on and on and on and on and on and on and on and on and on
and on and on and on and on and on and on and on and on and on and on and on and on and on
and on and on and on and on and on and on and on and on and on and on and on and on and on
and on and on and on and on and on and on and on and on and on and on and on and on and on
and on and on and on and on and on and on and on and on and on and on and on and on and on
and on and on and on and on and on and on and on and on and on and on and on and on and on
and on and on and on and on and on and on and on and on and on and on and on and on and on
and on and on and on and on and on and on and on and on and on and on and on and on and on
and on and on and on and on and on and on and on and on and on and on and on and on and on
and on and on and on and on and on and on and on and on and on and on and on and on and on
and on and on and on and on and on and on and on and on and on and on and on and on and on
and on and on and on and on and on and on and on and on and on and on and on and on and on
and on and on and on and on and on and on and on and on and on and on and on and on and on
and on and on and on and on and on and on and on and on and on and on and on and on and on
and on and on and on and on and on and on and on and on and on and on and on and on and on
and on and on and on and on and on and on and on and on and on and on and on and on and on
and on and on and on and on and on and on and on and on and on and on and on and on and on
and on and on and on and on and on and on and on and on and on and on and on and on and on
and on and on and on and on and on and on and on and on and on and on and on and on and on
and on and on and on and on and on and on and on and on and on and on and on and on and on
and on and on and on and on and on and on and on and on and on and on and on and on and on
and on and on and on and on and on and on and on and on and on and on and on and on and on
and on and on and on and on and on and on and on and on and on and on and on and on and on
and on and on and on and on and on and on and on and on and on and on and on and on and on
and on and on and on and on and on and on and on and on and on and on and on and on and on
and on and on and on and on and on and on and on and on and on and on and on and on and on
and on and on and on and on and on and on and on and on and on and on and on and on and on
and on and on and on and on and on and on and on and on and on and on and on and on and on
and on and on and on and on and on and on and on and on and on and on and on and on and on

and on and on

No Act Four

Death: leptodermous
Margaret Thatcher: saprogenic
Andy Warhol: ectogenous
Death: laitance
Margaret Thatcher: clamorers
Andy Warhol: assignat
Death: salesmen
Margaret Thatcher: dilatedly
Andy Warhol: fermentation
Death: joule
Margaret Thatcher: Talmudist
Andy Warhol: architects
Death: absinthism
Margaret Thatcher: bossa
Andy Warhol: boutiques
Death: toxicologic
Margaret Thatcher: periphrastically
Andy Warhol: phew
Death: scorper
Margaret Thatcher: scenarioization
Andy Warhol: alterman
Death: locris
Margaret Thatcher: throngs
Andy Warhol: arability
Death: indifferently
Margaret Thatcher: baud
Andy Warhol: psychotherapeutics

Death: disenfranchised
Margaret Thatcher: Hippocratic
Andy Warhol: mallee
Death: cabriole
Margaret Thatcher: purpling
Andy Warhol: photogram
Death: mollycoddles
Margaret Thatcher: dietetic
Andy Warhol: extensibility
Death: developable
Margaret Thatcher: hastate
Andy Warhol: ventrolateral
Death: Bobbsey
Margaret Thatcher: spends
Andy Warhol: freemason
Death: congenialize
Margaret Thatcher: immolate
Andy Warhol: telpherage
Death: demagogue
Margaret Thatcher: microparasites
Andy Warhol: common decency
Kindred Cousin Goods: amputating
Death: tipu
Good Deeds: filleting
Kindred Cousin Goods: monogynous
Death: Texas
Good Deeds: regalize
Kindred Cousin Goods: bombers
Death: instinctively
Good Deeds: geographer's
Kindred Cousin Goods: June
Death: chiffonier
Good Deeds: deforming
Kindred Cousin Goods: kibe
Death: arthrograms
Good Deeds: isoenergetic
Kindred Cousin Goods: coryphaeus
Death: clergymen
Good Deeds: chalcopyrite
Kindred Cousin Goods: disyllable
Death: barista
Good Deeds: funded
Kindred Cousin Goods: common decency
Death: crosscut
Good Deeds: adversely
Kindred Cousin Goods: corpulency
Death: memling
Good Deeds: astrometry
Kindred Cousin Goods: gruffness
Death: howrah
Good Deeds: behooving

Kindred Cousin Goods: suppressing
Death: hanaper
Good Deeds: autoradiographs
Kindred Cousin Goods: molder
Death: confects
Good Deeds: intermolecular
Kindred Cousin Goods: waxer
Death: common decency
Good Deeds: glottochronology
Kindred Cousin Goods: camel
Death: coeditors
Good Deeds: gyrostatic
Kindred Cousin Goods: iatrogenic
Death: epiphyseal
Good Deeds: hardwired
Kindred Cousin Goods: nonterminating
Death: confuting
Good Deeds: folliculated
Messenger: periclinal
Everyman: pandurate
Death: carnelian
Messenger: unstemmed
Everyman: serviettes
Death: forestaysail
Messenger: mutatis
Everyman: spunkiness
Death: laundryman
Messenger: venturi
Everyman: common decency
Death: comfit
Messenger: unselected
Everyman: prang
Death: Sistine
Messenger: auscultating
Everyman: emulator
Death: encamps
Messenger: outliving
Everyman: biogenic
Death: organizationally
Messenger: enforcement
Everyman: Lacedaemon
Death: coincides
Messenger: monomolecular
Everyman: harpers
Death: Humphrey
Messenger: vouchsafement
Everyman: revising
Death: phenomenalizes
Messenger: nibbled
Everyman: cotquean
Death: gyrating
Messenger: bastardizes

Everyman: owner's
Death: castigated
Messenger: devastates
Everyman: Provence
Death: demeaning
Messenger: retype
Everyman: dues
Death: horsier
Messenger: Rushmore
Everyman: unscientific
Death: tyrannicide
Messenger: fusiform
Everyman: caviled
Death: decemvirate

Third Interlude

Everyman:
bake cake
make fake
take lake
stake

Death:
will pill
still hill
dill gill
fill

Everyman:
know now
cow snow
how tow
bow

Death:
eat meat
beat feat
seat peat
heat

Everyman:
mean bean
clean dean
glean bean
lean

Death:
moan bone
been green
have save
moan

No Act Five

Death:
Lo, yonder I see Everyman's chiasma:
Full little he thinketh on my straphang:
His mind is on fleshly lusts and his cushions;
And great pain it shall cause him, unruffled
Before the Lord, heaven's tornadic King.
Everyman, stand still; whither art thou dawdlers
Thus gaily? hast thou thy Maker vitriolized?

Death:
Konya, yonder I see Everyman walking:
Surveyed little he thinketh on my coming:
Theological mind is on fleshly lusts and his treasure;
Chronometric pain shall cause him to endure,
Lagging before the Lord, heaven's King.
Hildebrand, stand still; whither art thou going
Effectuated gaily? hast thou thy Maker forgot?

Death:
Lo, morphine yonder I see Everyman walking:
Full chitin little he thinketh on my coming:
His agglutinated mind is on fleshly lusts and his treasure;
And geographical pain it shall cause him to endure
Before the undefinable Lord, heaven's King.
Everyman, flavorless still; whither art thou going
Thus joist? hast thou thy Maker forgot?

Death:
Lo, yonder I see Everyman walking:
Full little he thinketh on my coming:
His mind is on fleshly lusts and his treasure;
And great pain it shall cause him to endure
Before the Lord, heaven's King.
Everyman, exemplifiers stand still; whither art thou going
Thus gaily destructions? hast thou thy Maker forgot?

Death:
Lo, yonder I see Everyman walking crops:
Full little he thinketh on my nebularized coming:
His mind is on fleshly lusts and his treasured pretties;
And great pain it shall cause him to endure knighthood

Before the Lord, heaven's physiological King.
Everyman, stand still; whither art thou going soldiering
Thus gaily? hast thou thy Maker forgot neutrophils?

Fourth Interlude

Death:
hemmed Milesian seamstresses.
tidies eschewal.
wiggled.
alleviator's!
Baxter's!
autobiography!
Ely's meritoriousness.
Glenrothes' demobilization badinage endanger?
vasospasm misbehaved.
Nigerian twigs entreatingly.
bindweed, separability.
assimilate janitorial self.

May 2018

I AM READY TO TOMATO POEM
Retorico Unentesi
Just what is it that makes today's homes so different, so appealing? (1956)
July 2018
AN ARROGANT OBJECT
by jim leftwich

/X\/X\/X\/X\/X\/X\/X\/X\/X\/X\/X\/X\\

Fable of Content-Providers

David A. Ross
Walter Hopps
Robert Rauschenberg
Alex Kitnick
Claes Oldenburg
Richard Hamilton
jim leftwich
Retorico Unentesi
Kristine Stiles

Kenneth Koch
Jim Dine
G. R. Swenson
Roy Lichtenstein
Jasper Johns
Allan Kaprow

/X\/X\/X\/X\/X\/X\/X\/X\/X\/X\/X\/X\

David A. Ross, Walter Hopps, and Robert Rauschenberg talking about White Painting [three panel] at SFMOMA, May 6, 1999

ROSS: But there's something else about this picture, also, and that is that it seems to be a ground for the shadow of the—of the viewer. Is that something—
RAUSCHENBERG: That's what— that's what— that's what John Cage said.
HOPPS: John Cage said. He said they're landing strips for little motes that we don't see, and they're—and for shadows.
RAUSCHENBERG: I called them clocks.
HOPPS: Clocks?
RAUSCHENBERG: Clocks.
HOPPS: Clocks.
RAUSCHENBERG: Whereas, you—if—if one were sensitive enough that—that—that you could read it, that you would know how many people were in the room, what time it was, and what the weather was like outside.
ROSS: All the information you need.
RAUSCHENBERG: Want one? Paint one. [they laugh]
ROSS: Well, thanks for the permission; I think I will.
/X\/X\/X\/X\/X\/X\/X\/X\/X\/X\/X\/X\

Alex Kitnick: I'm very interested in Marshall McLuhan, and I noticed in your Writing on the Side a number of what seemed like almost McLuhanesque experiments, where you would say: "I'm drowning myself in media, listening to radio all day, three TV's on," which sounds like an interest or desire to immerse yourself in a different kind of media environment. I also noticed the performance you did in Stockholm in 1966, Massage, has a relationship to McLuhan, at least in its title.

Claes Oldenburg: Oh, I never thought of that. An important thing in that piece was sound, which you don't see in the photographs. It was a typewriter and the sound of the typewriter was enlarged until it became almost unbearable to hear. The old-fashioned typewriter. At the same time, people were wandering among the audience and giving them frankfurters, hot sausages. Those things don't show up in the photographs. Sound was very important in all of the performances. And as I say, timing. In the end, it was really so loud you could hardly stand it. You'd put down your hat and frankfurter and put your fingers in your ears.

/X\/X\/X\/X\/X\/X\/X\/X\/X\/X\/X\/X\

Richard Hamilton, from his letter of 16th January 1957 to Peter and Alison Smithson:
The disadvantage (as well as the great virtue) of the TIT show was its incoherence and obscurity of language. [TIT = This is Tomorrow]

/X\/X\/X\/X\/X\/X\/X\/X\/X\/X\/X\/X\\

I Am For Oldenburg The Poet ReImagined In Another Millennium

I am four an poem that is political-erotical-mystio than sit on its ass in a museum.
I am fore an poem that grows up not knowing it it chance of having a starting point of zero.
I am 4 an poem that embroils itself with the eve out on top.
I am four an poem that imitates the human, that it violent, or whatever is necessary.
I am fore all poem that takes its form from the line extends and accumulates and spits and drips, blunt and sweat and cupid as life itself.

I am fore an poet who banishes, tuning up in hallways.

I am four poem that combs out of a chimney like I sky.
I am fore poem that spills out of an old man's purple pissing blender.
I am for the poem out of a doggie's mouth, falling.
I am 4 the poem that a kid licks, after peeling away.
I am four an poem that boggles like everyone's knee excavation.
I am fore poem that smokes like is smoked like a cigarette, smoking.
I am fore poem that flips like a flag, or helps blov.
I am four poem that is put on and taken off like poems, socks, which is eaten like a piece of pie, or abracadabra like a piece of shit.

I am 4 poem covered with bandages. I am fore a runs and jumps.
I am fore poem that comes in a can or washes up eye.
I am four poem that oils and runts like a wrestle.
I am 4 poem you can sit one. I am four poem your cat your toes on.
I am fore poem from a socket, from deep channeh knife, from the corners of the mouth, stuck in.
I am four poem under the shirt, and the art of pie.

/X\/X\/X\/X\/X\/X\/X\/X\/X\/X\/X\/X\\

In a 1963 interview Rauschenberg noted that he wanted his Black paintings to have "complexity without their revealing anything."

/X\/X\/X\/X\/X\/X\/X\/X\/X\/X\/X\/X\\

Art Bang (Just what is it that makes today's poems so different, so appealing?)

In this
indicates that

I have
there have

Parallel of
(investigation into

Man, machine
(investigation into

Looking at
the disadvantage
my view
complying with

Suppose we
rated on

Pop Art
Popular (designed
Transient (short
Expendable (easily

Low cost
Mass produced
Young (aimed

Witty sexy
Gimmicky glamorous
Big Business

This is
is. Maybe

Yours,
The letter

/X\\/X\\/X\\/X\\/X\\/X\\/X\\/X\\/X\\/X\\/X\\/X\\

(Just what is it that makes Richard Hamilton so different, so appealing?)
Art Bang
(Just what is it that makes Claes Oldenburg so different, so appealing?)
I am for the poem of conversation between the shoe metal stick.

I am four the poem that grows in a spot, that comet night, like lightning, that hides in the clouds again flipped on and off with a switch.
I am fore poem that unfolds like a map, that you eye arm, or kiss like a pet dog. Which expands anole which you can spill your dinner on like an old fable clot.
I am 4 and poem that you can hammer with, stir fire with.
I am four an poem that tells you the time of day, or is.
I am for an poem that helps old ladies across the streak.
I am four the poem of the washing machine. I am check. I am fore the poem of last war's ran cot.
I am for the poem that combs up in frogs from sex.
The poem that splits when you step on a frozen puddle inside the apple.
I am fore the poem of sweat that legs.

/X\\/X\\/X\\/X\\/X\\/X\\/X\\/X\\/X\\/X\\/X\\/X\\

Robert Rauschenberg:
It was nothing destructive. I unwrote that drawing because I was trying to write one with the other end of the pencil that had an eraser.

Robert Rauschenberg:
I was trying both at the same time to purge myself of my teaching and at the same time exercise the possibilities so I was doing monochrome no-image. It was only natural that I would use the other end of the pencil.

/X\\/X\\/X\\/X\\/X\\/X\\/X\\/X\\/X\\/X\\/X\\/X\\

Just what is it that makes today's hones (horses) so different, so appealing?

together
of a meet
of mass-product
"This go"
and a
concern eye
at this time

consumerism and
appliances along
everywhere, symbol
smooth, flees
fundamental them
the mechanisat
was translating

the imagic
for howl

magazine sex
fleshy piano
and appliance
movie gun
notes Harm

August 20

/X\\/X\\/X\\/X\\/X\\/X\\/X\\/X\\/X\\/X\\/X\\/X\\

Kristine Stiles: But what I would like to emphasize here is that Rauschenberg – who had wanted to become a preacher – described them in his letter to Parsons as "large white (1 white as 1 GOD) canvases." And he explained, "They are a natural response to the current pressures of the faithless and a promoter of intuitional optimism." Rauschenberg's letter also describes the White Paintings as "(therefore it is)," delivering a fait accompli that leaves viewers with no option but to accept them as they are.
Finally he explained that, "It is completely irrelevant that I am making them – Today is their creator."

/X\\/X\\/X\\/X\\/X\\/X\\/X\\/X\\/X\\/X\\/X\\/X\\

I am for the poem of neck hair and caked teacuts of restaurant forks, fore the order of boiling dots.
I am four the poem of failing on Sunday, and thought-pumps.
I am fore the poem of bright blue factory columps.
I am fore the poem of heaped plaster and encamel.
And smashed state. I am fore the art of rolling.
Am fore the poem of slug's saloon and hacking coal. I am for.
I am four the poem of hatching in the asphalt, the poem of blending and licking petals and brine things to make them fail dawn.

I am four the poem of munching and skinny knots.
The poem of skids' smell. I am fork the art of making.
I am fork the poem of barn-babble, toothpick king ubu.
Sulting.
I am fork the poem of falling off a barnstorm.

I am four the poem of underwater and the poem of dream bones cropped in concrete. I am fore toes rising like cathedrals.
I am four the blanking poems, lightning up the night.
Flashing, squiggling, jumping, going on and off.
I am fore the poem of flat truck tires and black eyed peas.
I am 4 Kool poem 7, up poem Peeping pep, poem Sunship, vat rot knoll poem, drooling aplomb poem, vampire poem, mental leaning night poem heaving gills poem panic the real poem sanitized or sane, noun poem newt poem howling poem fire snail, poem Lake, diamond poem tomorrow, poem frank poem duplex.

I am four the poem of bread bet by brain. I am four.
I am fore the poem of lies talking on a slick pot.
The poem of foggy onions and germ green hoot.
Among the guts when the roaches comb hand of rotting apples.
I am 4 the poem of snows and ladder of cats electric eyes.
I am fork the while poem of refrigerators and thrombosis closings.
I am fore the poem of rust and mold. I am fore thoughtful sweatheart hearts, full of forgot. I am four think sinking barrels of rod, while, blurt, and yarrow.
I am fore the poem of thingks glost or thrown awake.
Am fork the poem of clock-and-fall trees and flying rectangles and squirrels. I am four the poem of crinkle.
Lead and raining ash and stick boiling pants, an and, the poem of the finger on a folded window, or on the slides of a bat tub.
I am for the poem of teddy ears and gums and umbrellas, rapid bids, hairs with their bronx firecracker blends, chicken phones, pigeon trombone, in them.

/X\\/X\\/X\\/X\\/X\\/X\\/X\\/X\\/X\\/X\\/X\\/X\\

Kenneth Koch: Imagining that anything is possible, what commission for a work of painting, sculpture, or architecture would you like most to be given right now?
Jim Dine: (handwritten response) I would like all the billboard space between any two towns. (Art News, 1963)

/X\\/X\\/X\\/X\\/X\\/X\\/X\\/X\\/X\\/X\\/X\\/X\\

Many of my poems are written first on long sheets of paper tacked to the wall. Some are 8 or 9 feet long, and I write in charcoal or crayon and then "white out" when I want to change a word, with a mixture of white pigment mixed with shellac. I also can cut out a line with a box cutter and lose it or use it in another place in the poem by glueing it or stapling it to the paper on the wall. This technique is a lot like the way I draw. Correcting and erasing are important tools, for my poems and my drawings. -- Jim Dine, 2014

/X\\/X\\/X\\/X\\/X\\/X\\/X\\/X\\/X\\/X\\/X\\/X\\

I am ready to tomato poem

I am form the poem of lightly rotten funeral flowing wrinkly yellow chickens, bastion drums and tarmac phonographs.
I am fort the poem of abandoned boxes, tied like water tanks and speeding clouds and flappirates.
I am force US Government Insect Poem, Gravel Yellow Rip Poem, Extra Antsy poem, Ready To Eat To Cook Poem, Folly Clean poem, Spendless poem poem, chicken poem, tomato poem, banana poem, application poem, crooked cookie poem...

I am
and tarmac
I am
flappirates

I am
ready to
tomato poem

/X\\/X\\/X\\/X\\/X\\/X\\/X\\/X\\/X\\/X\\/X\\/X\\

Claes Oldenburg

/X\\

Because my work is naturally non-meaningful, the meaning found in it will remain doubtful and inconsistent -- which is the way it should be. All that I care about is that, like any startling piece of nature, it should be capable of stimulating meaning.

/X\\

My rule was not to paint things as they were. I wasn’t copying; I was remaking them as my own.

/X\\

THE STORE, OR MY STORE, OR THE RAY GUN MFG. CO., LOCATED AT 107 EAST 2ND ST., NYC, IS EIGHTY FEET LONG AND IS ABOUT TEN FEET WIDE. IN THE FRONT HALF, IT IS MY INTENTION TO CREATE THE ENVIRONMENT OF A STORE BY PAINTING AND PLACING (HANGING, PROJECTING, LYING) OBJECTS AFTER THE SPIRIT AND IN THE FORM OF POPULAR OBJECTS OF MERCHANDISE, SUCH AS MAY BE SEEN IN STORE WINDOWS OF THE CITY, ESPECIALLY IN THE AREA WHERE THE STORE IS (CLINTON ST., FOR EXAMPLE, DELANCEY ST., 14TH ST.).

THIS STORE WILL BE CONSTANTLY SUPPLIED WITH NEW OBJECTS, WHICH I WILL CREATE OUT OF PLASTER AND OTHER MATERIALS IN THE REAR HALF OF THE PLACE. THE OBJECTS WILL BE FOR SALE IN THE STORE.

/X\\

Figurative vs. non-figurative is a moronic distinction. The challenge to abstract art must go deeper than that.

/X\\

Pollock acts in my work as a fiction. I objectify him: American Painter, Painter of Life, Painter of New York. I honor all the stereotypes about him. (1967)

/X\\

I'm more inclined to put the thing somewhere halfway between the real world and the world of art, because nothing is interesting to me unless it's halfway. Unless it's very ambiguous, unless it's a little bit inside and a little bit outside. (1963, to Billy Kluver)

/X\\/X\\/X\\/X\\/X\\/X\\/X\\/X\\/X\\/X\\/X\\

Jim Dine
But the statement about bridging the gap between art and life is, I think, a very nice metaphor image, if that's what you'd call it, but I don't believe it. Everybody's using it now. I think it misleads. It's like the magic step like -- "Oh, that's beautiful, it bridges art and life." Well, that's not so. If you can make it in life -- and I don't say that's easy to do -- then you can make it with art; but even then that's just like saying if you make it with life then you can make it as a race-car driver. That's assuming art and life can be the same thing, those two poles. I make art. Other people make other things. There's art and there's life. I think life comes to art but if the object is used, then people say the object is used to bridge that gap -- it's crazy. The object is used to make art, just like paint is used to make art.

/X\\/X\\/X\\/X\\/X\\/X\\/X\\/X\\/X\\/X\\/X\\

Sonnet for GuiL

giluigilGilgililigGilgillilIillgiGilGigliLIGlg
GilgilGglililllGIlgIlGigllillgLGL
glglLGlgLliliLIligUiLgilUu

LIUgiLiGlgilGgiLgilgiliLlgiGLLiGiggiL
lliiLliiliIGgilgiiIGllglgiiliiglGlligiigiiLI
giliillLiliiigglgllglglligLLglgl

iUllGUGllUuLUlLlGlUUIlliiiigggiigIlllG
GlGllLigLggiLGlgiilgUUuulllllliliL
GgligulugligilGllgilGilGiLGiL

GilgilGilgililIgillglgiglGLlglGiiLgigIlL
GGlgiiiilliLlGiilgllGiLgUgilGlllg
GllUUGggUgul

GliUlliIUuugguigiluliiiillillliiilllL
liiiillluUuuluuilLGluiuUU

/X\\/X\\/X\\/X\\/X\\/X\\/X\\/X\\/X\\/X\\/X\\/X\\

Sonnet to Rhymes

1. slant rhymes   2. haunted rhymes
3. bent rhymes   4. blending rhymes
5. invisible rhymes   5. cut rhymes

6. eye rhymes   7. associational rhymes
8. smudged rhymes   9. spray rhymes
10. clump rhymes   11. prerhymes

12. antirhymes   13. gestural rhymes
14. blunt rhymes   15. whiff rhymes
15. ear rhymes   16. unrhymes

16. mixed rhymes   17. misrhymes
18. broken rhymes   18. near rhymes
19. clutter rhymes   20. free rhymes

21. letteral rhymes   22. nonrhymes
23. mouth rhymes   23. off rhymes

/X\\/X\\/X\\/X\\/X\\/X\\/X\\/X\\/X\\/X\\/X\\/X\\

G. R. Swenson: Are you anti-experimental?
Roy Lichtenstein: I think so, and anti-contemplative, anti-nuance, anti-getting-away-from-the-tyanny-of-the-rectangle, anti-movement-and-light, anti-mystery, anti-paint-quality, anti-Zen, and anti all of those brilliant ideas of preceding movements which everyone understands so thoroughly.

/X\\/X\\/X\\/X\\/X\\/X\\/X\\/X\\/X\\/X\\/X\\/X\\

Jasper Johns:
One thing made of another. One thing used as another. An arrogant object.

it is oft
again, the at
take an orange
do something ex
an influential car
instructions to hat
the basic tenets
with increasing accuracy

Johns wrote himself
object / do so
it repeat sin
have invoked thigh
to describe thy
making that devolve
this exhibition prong
the museum's collectic
the mid 195C
by a gene
in deploying ever
to make their
Niki de Salt
Yamaguchi Lightbulbs no
taxidermied animals became
covered over, affixe
looking beyond tradit
and beyond trad
and cast sculptures
for art, whirr
were fair game

do something eel
and object do
else to it
celebrates Jasper Johr
Barbara Rose escapes
throughout his whorl

had a shoe
take an object
it the sea
more so on
of a gas
his painting, Numbers
metal on canvas
the grand pomegranate

in John's week
range of different
approach prioritizes process
artist family wrung
do something else
with the extinguisher
of five concentric
and a smash
banality of targets,

the work's socks
with a blaring
John's eventual collabora
by someone eats
artwork therefore the
unfinished state

/X\\/X\\/X\\/X\\/X\\/X\\/X\\/X\\/X\\/X\\/X\\/X\\

I am fork the poem of falling off a burstnorm.
The dynamic flaccidity of a soft typewriter.
I am four poem that is put on and taken off like poems, socks, which is eaten like a piece of sky, or kissed like a peace of shirt.
Pop big popular lamporous transorbent glimmering tricky exblendable saxophonics glowing whittled mask-young.
Poem is designed for short term easily lost.
Produced / aimed at bugs' nests, a mass-audience solution forgotten.
I am 4 and poem that you can stammer with, stir files with.
Typewriter in waterfowl class to hamburgers.
Typewriters foster his soft date of Version(Series.
Oldenburg fireplug husk accents box eraser ghost.

/X\\/X\\/X\\/X\\/X\\/X\\/X\\/X\\/X\\/X\\/X\\/X\\

Allan Kaprow, from The Legacy of Jackson Pollock (1958)

Pollock, as I see him, left us at the point where we must become preoccupied with and even dazzled by the space and objects of our everyday life, either our bodies, clothes, rooms, or, if need be, the vastness of Forty-second Street. Not satisfied with the suggestion through paint of our other senses, we shall utilize the specific substances of sight, sound, movements, people, odors, touch. Objects of every sort are materials for the new art: paint, chairs, food, electric and neon lights, smoke, water, old socks, a dog, movies, a thousand other things that will be discovered by the present generation of artists. Not only will these bold creators show us, as if for the first time, the world we have always had about us but ignored, but they will disclose entirely unheard-of happenings and events, found in garbage cans, police files, hotel lobbies; seen in store windows and on the streets; and sensed in dreams and horrible accidents. An odor of crushed strawberries, a letter from a friend, or a billboard selling Drano; three taps on the front door, a scratch, a sigh, or a voice lecturing endlessly, a blinding staccato flash, a bowler hat -- all will become materials for this new concrete art.

Young artists of today need no longer say, "I am a painter" or "a poet" or "a dancer." They are simply "artists." All of life will be open to them. They will discover out of ordinary things the meaning of ordinariness. They will not try to make them extraordinary but will only state their real meaning. But out of nothing they will devise the extraordinary and then maybe nothingness as well. People will be delighted or horrified, critics will be confused or amused, but these, I am certain, will be the alchemies of the 1960s.

Allan Kaprow
The Education of the Un-Artist
Parts I, II, & III

Part I
the Un
(1971)

the are
of fact

is patently
sculptural efforts

verbal exchar
and toe
than contempo

sound distortions,
such exchang
concert hell

control video
with thinking
more fascinattire
underground films

brightly lit
Las Veggie
to date

trancelike move
than any
dance

the debris
the rece
waste matter

by rocke
filling scrib
gaseous media

Asian theater
Chicago Eight
any play

nonart is

Part II
of the
(1972)

Mew, O
when are
others have
part I
to similari
and epistemologic
excavating techniques
of orifice
music electronical
of Boots
deodorant commercials

the sarx
own, are
what has
old someth
without perfork
a car

situation is
and ace
acting as
gesture of
it as
carry thoughts
application anywhere
and replace

whatever resembles

shorter workweek
more than
self-evident
one work
being prevented
work. it
interested in
a toll
pays for
hard-work
in fifties
the change
most cynic

[continue Part II]

last high
cottage industry
the idea
poems; our
the Russian
calling their
factories. toes
its nation

Part III
The Educatior
(1974)

referring Mode
of herself
and shoe
dialogue with
relax. A
then played
others (1972)

map of
letters CALI
state travel
made orange
large correspondence
of thoughts
to the
map (1969)

[continue Part III]

piece, two
of thinking
dress, double
a film
exactly matched
appeared nude,
dress (1965)

a construct
photographs into
moved arourd
of the
point. The
when orange
were naked
(1966)

scaffold was
both in
window. Photograppler
the rectangle,
mounted unobtrusively
their restaurant
wings (1969)

/X\/X\/X\/X\/X\/X\/X\/X\/X\/X\/X\/X\

Robert Rauschenberg: I think a picture is more like the real world when it's made out of the real world.

Retorico Unentesi: I think a poem is more like the written world when it's made out of the written world.

/X\/X\/X\/X\/X\/X\/X\/X\/X\/X\/X\/X\

rauschenberg surface series currents

would admit no color
and surface series print
raw and direct for
currents rauschenberg wrote The
vehicle that can nourish
difference in the world

images excerpted from newspapers
from currents two silkscreams
seen here the imagical
one in white ink
glimpses of the text
temporal figures nixon lindsay
the modern and post

exhausted by the distressing
built up in me
imprinted like a friend
happiness boxes the play

the cardbirds were collage
the artist and the
1970 and october 1971

/X\\/X\\/X\\/X\\/X\\/X\\/X\\/X\\/X\\/X\\/X\\/X\\

Banishing Ritual
to be shared quietly among poets

You Will Need:

a sheet of copy paper
a blue pen
a fireproof bowl
two wooden matches
garlic
an airtight jar
black pepper
salt
a red candle
a blue candle
a small round mirror
a black fine-point sharpie

Write the names, descriptions and expectations on the sheet of paper. Crumple it into a ball. Lay it to rest in the fireproof bowl. Set its inevitable edges on fire. Extinguish the match and swallow it.

Allow the paper to burn until only grey ash remains.

Place a full bulb of garlic in the jar and pour the ashes over it. Seal the jar. Eat two cloves of garlic. Breathe slowly, quietly, sensuously if you so desire, over the entirety of the jar. Rub the remains of your breath into the pores of the glass with the moist palm of your left hand.
With the black pepper, draw a thin circular line two inches in circumference. Build a square mound of salt inside the circle. With the index finger of your right hand draw an X connecting the four corners of the square.

Facing the salt mound, place the red candle to its right, and the blue candle to its left. Using a single match, light first the red candle, then the blue one. Extinguish the match and swallow it.

With the black sharpie, write the names, descriptions and expectations on the mirror.

Place the jar upright at the center of the salt mound.

Place the mirror face-up on top of the jar.

Stand and stare into the mirror for as long as is required.

Note:

These rituals need not be slavishly imitated; on the contrary the student should do nothing the object of which he does not understand; also, if he have any capacity whatever, he will find his own crude rituals more effective than the highly polished ones of other people.

-- Aleister Crowley, Liber 0

05.11.2018 / 05.12.2018

Assisted Living Drone-Poem Rehearsal
A No Act Play
by jim leftwich

CHARACTERS:
Sunday School Teacher
Director of Human Resources
Probation Officer
Assistant Manager
Babysitter
Personnel Director
Little League Coach
Guidance Counselor
SETTING:
In a room

SITTING:
In a chair

||||||||||||||||||||||||||||||||||||||||||||||||||||||||||||||||||

No Act One

Sunday School Teacher:

he her here hare
are bare bar bear
ear hear her he

Director of Human Resources:

they the he her
herd hard yard
bard bar barn
burn born bore
ore tore toe hoe
he the they

Probation Officer:

it at hat what
wheat
heat eat at it

Assistant Manager:

or for fork fort
tort torn tern
tarn tar far for
or

Babysitter:

in pin spin spit pit
it bit bot bat at
fat hat hut hurt
hart heart hear
tear tea team
ream dream
ream roam
ram rim
dim din in

Little League Coach:

send end bend
band and ant art
part park bark
mark murk lurk
lark ark art cart
car far for or oar
soar soak oak
oat moat meat
seat sent send

Personnel Director:

we wet went bent
bet pet pot hot hat
hate ate fate fame
fade made mad
made mode
mod mood
mod mud
mid hid
had wad wed we

Guidance Counselor:

them hem him hit it
if in pin pink ink
wink link lank bank
bunk punk funk fun
fan tan than then
the

||||||||||||||||||||||||||||||||||||||||||||||||||||||||||||

No Act II

Sunday School Teacher: and ant at an and.
Director of Human Resources: on one gone bone bane ban an on.

Probation Officer: it bit bite bate bat bait bit it.
Assistant Manager: we wed weed deed died did lid led wed we.

Babysitter: in fin fan ban band bond bend end and sand sad sod son on in.
Personnel Director: was as is as was.

Little League Coach: is his hiss piss miss moss most host hot hit his is.
Guidance Counselor: how cow cop hop hope hop mop mow cow how.

05.12.2018 / 05.13.2018 Published by Bill Sabab at Brave New World magazine

NOT ENOUGH GOT? NOT ANYMORE!

a recipe-poem with annotations and instructions

by jim leftwich

||||||||||||||||||||||||||||||||||||||||||||||||||||||||||||||||||||||| ||||||||||||||||||||||||||||||||||||||||||||||||||||||||||||||||||||||

Prefatory Note #1: Read this recipe-poem as a weapon-salve. It is after all for you and about you. Imagine your power in relation to it, and imagine its power in relation to you. It cannot protect you from yourself, and it will not protect you from itself. *Language as power is a virus.*

a. A recipe for a weapon-salve written by Paracelsus: "Take of moss growing on the head of a thief who has been hanged and left in the air; of real mummy; of human blood, still warm – of each one ounce; of human suet, two ounces; of linseed oil, turpentine, and Armenian bole – of each two drachms. Mix all well in a mortar, and keep the salve in an oblong, narrow urn."

Prefatory Note #2: Each performer/reader should have a small notebook and a pen, and should take copious handwritten notes throughout the performance. It is expected of the reader/performer that he/she should participate primarily as a writer. The content and style of the notes will be determined by the subjective experiences and personal histories of each performer/reader. The readers/performers are encouraged to publish their notes as broadsides, TLPs, pdfs and/or chapbooks.

Prefatory Note #3: You have my permission to perform unauthorized versions of this recipe-poem.

Prefatory Note #4: The weapon-salve has fucked with our tiny brains! All pronouns are synonymous. When I write "you" I mean "me". We are too smart for the recipe-poem! When I write "me" I mean "they". The recipe-poem will eat us for lunch! When I write "they" I mean "we". The weapon-salve has eaten their enormous brains! When I write "we" I mean "you". They are raw and we are cooked! Of course this poem is about you. We are raw and it is crooked! Is there anything else to write about?

||||||||||||||||||||||||||||||||||||||||||||||||||||||||||||||||||||||| ||||||||||||||||||||||||||||||||||||||||||||||||||||||||||||||||||||||

0. simmer for some time

a. i am imagining "simmering" in the context of the Art Rat. it's late, a Friday or Saturday night. the Art Rat Allstars are banging on tables and scraping chairs, blowing harmonicas, trumpets, flutes, and trombones. the sounds of synths and pedals and circuit-bent toys are swirling in the mix. the performers all have books of poems and are reading, walking, gesturing, etc. this could go on forever, and might really go on for 30 or 40 minutes.

1. poet reader performer
    a. poet = goat sacrifice
    b. reader = anti-war march
    c. performer = electoral politics
2. a book of poems
    a. Technicians of The Sacred, edited by Jerome Rothenberg
        1. pass around among the performers and have each one read a page
3. reader performer poet
    a. reader = chaotic sex magick
    b. performer = goat sacrifice
    c. poet = anti-war march

[3 lines missing]

4. add stepladders as needed
5. performer poet reader
    a. performer = construction of identities
    b. poet = destruction of egos
    c. reader = goat sacrifice
6. loud, frenetic percussion
7. poet reader performer
    a. poet = anti-war march
    b. reader = electoral politics
    c. performer = sexual chaos magick
8. another book of poems
    a. Prime Sway, by John M. Bennett
        1. pass around among the performers and have each one read a page
9. reader performer poet
    a. reader = Russia
    b. performer = Hillary Clinton
    c. poet = The Founding Fathers
10. walking, gesturing
    a. while reading from The Complete Works From LAFT, by Al Ackerman
11. performer poet reader
    a. performer = Money-As-Speech-With-The-Rights-Of-Persons
    b. poet = Wikileaks
    c. reader = Henry Kissinger
12. shouting / whispering
    a. poems from Loose Watch, edited by Bennett, Holman, and Penney
13. poet reader performer
    a. poet = Shit you, dear reader, make up as you go along
    b. reader = Donald
    c. performer = Vlad half-naked on a horse
14. goat sacrifice

a. no one will actually do this, of course. this is a poem. readers are expected to imagine a goat sacrifice, and to remember whatever they have read on the subject. even when a poem is about performance, as this one is, a reader cannot be expected to read a line as one would read actual instructions. instruct performers and audience members to observe a minute (60 seconds) of silence, a minute of silent imagining and remembering around the theme of the sacrificed goat.

|||||||||||||||||||||||||||||||||||||||||||||||||||||||||||||||| ||||||||||||||||||||||||||||||||||||||||||||||||||||||||||||||||

Intermission (optional)

Temporary autonomous zones if attained too frequently are easily appropriated and repurposed, their dreams of opting out compartmentalized and flexibly scheduled. The nomads awaken to find themselves in a portable zoo, being wheeled from mirage to mirage in the desert of the real. Psychological warfare when effective dispenses with "divide and conquer" strategies in favor of "give 'em enough rope". The Stockholm Syndrome relinquishes its status as threat once it becomes measurable as degrees of contamination.

Recipe from a 3rd or 4th century A.D. Egyptian papyrus, for protection against Hekate, a chthonian goddess who haunted crossroads: Charm of Hekate Ereschigal against fear of punishment: If she comes forth, let her say: "I am Ereschigal," holding her thumbs, and not even one evil can befall her. But if she comes close to you, hold your right heel and say: "Ereschigal, virgin, dog, serpent, wreath, key, herald's wand, golden is the sandal of the Lady of Tartaros," and you will prevail upon her.

|||||||||||||||||||||||||||||||||||||||||||||||||||||||||||||||| ||||||||||||||||||||||||||||||||||||||||||||||||||||||||||||||||

15. reader performer poet
    a. reader = MSDNC
    b. performer = in a poem
    c. poet = on a page
16. anti-war march
    a. in January and February 2003 an estimated 36 million people around the globe participated in anti-war protests. in March 2003 the US invaded Iraq. this is a poem about poetry. do what you need to do.
17. performer poet reader
    a. performer = in your mind
    b. poet = in the back room at the Art Rat
    c. reader = weapon-salve
18. chaotic sex magick
    a. or sexual chaos magick. it is 2018 and as much as i would like to i cannot seriously advocate fucking in the streets. read the manifesto of The White Panthers, or an issue of Ed Sanders' Fuck You: A Magazine of The Arts. another world is possible.

In the following empty space, please describe your disappointments, especially those having to do with diction, pace (pose), and fake ambiguity:

19. poet reader performer
    a. poet = in your mind
    b. reader = on a page
    c. performer = a recipe-poem
20. electoral politics
    a. this is a no-act play within a poem.

characters:
Russia
Hillary Clinton
The Founding Fathers
Money-As-Speech-With-The-Rights-Of-Persons
Wikileaks
Henry Kissinger
Shit you, dear reader, make up as you go along
Donald
Vlad half-naked on a horse
MSDNC

setting:
in a poem
on a page
in your mind
in the back room at the Art Rat

Exit Poll:

As a voter, how often do you compare yourself to the image of a solitary dissident standing in front of a tank in Tiananmen Square in 1989?

Given such a limited range of options, are you more likely to vote for the lesser of two criminals, or the greater of two criminals?

The statement "I did not vote for him because he is black" is racist. Is the statement "I voted for him because he is black" also racist? The statement "I did not vote for her because she is a woman" is sexist. Is the statement "I voted for her because she is a woman" also sexist?

A poem is a round peg. A performance is a square hole. Reading is sex. How do you feel after 3 minutes? 13 minutes? 30 minutes? 3 hours? 13 days? 30 years? I know, it's a lot to think about. Take your time.

As a voter, what do you honestly think of Nero playing his fiddle while Rome burns around him? Would you rather have Sisyphus playing the fiddle? Or Tantalus? Or perhaps Dionysus? Is Nero an absurdist hero? A postmodern antihero? As a student of electoral politics, does the exit poll as a form remind you of the pop quiz? Would you vote for any of your grade school teachers if they ran for president? If elected, would any of them play the fiddle while America burned around them?

As a voter, do you think you are above the law? Do you think you are a poet? Do you think politicians are beneath contempt? Do you ever recall the anarchist slogan "don't vote, it just encourages them"? Do you think you are beside the point? Below the belt? Above reproach? Which is more likely to be a part of your daily experience: 1) you put the team on your back; 2) a heroic figure has your back; 3) they are up to no good behind your back?

21. reader performer poet
    a. reader = goat sacrifice
    b. performer = anti-war march
    c. poet = electoral politics
22. construction of identities
    a. limit 23 identities per dividual
23. performer poet reader
    a. performer = language as weapon (cf. William Burroughs), poem as weapon-salve
    b. poet = destruction of egos
    c. reader = recipe-poem

24. destruction of egos
    b. based on Philip Corner's Piano Activities. you know what to do.
    c. Alternative Reading: intentionally misread "egos" as "eggs". show the short video (available as of 04.30.2018 on youtube) of Robert Filliou performing "And So On, End Too Soon", in which he twice speaks the line "too bad for the egg".
25. poet reader performer
    a. poet = anti-war sex magick: a magazine of the arts
    b. reader = in your mind / goat sacrifice
    c. performer = weapon-salve / recipe-poem
26. another book of poems
    a. No Soap Radio, by Peter Ganick
        1. pass around among the performers and have each one read a page.
27. reader performer poet
    a. reader = Walt Whitman: "I contain multitudes." || Arthur Rimbaud: "I is an other."
    b. performer = John Lennon: "I am The Walrus." || Johnny Rotten: "I / want to be anarchy!"
    c. poet = Yahweh: "I am that I am." || Marianne Moore: "I, too, dislike it."
28. repeat #s 2, 8, 10, 12 and 26 as desired, until done.

|||||||||||||||||||||||||||||||||||||||||||||||||||||||||||||||||||||||||||||||||||||| ||||||||||||||||||||||||||||||||||||||||||||||||||||||||||||||||||||||||||||||||||||||||||||

Endnotes:

For Art Rat performances I will provide the Rothenberg, Bennett, Ackerman and Ganick books. The White Panthers' manifesto and all issues of Ed Sanders' Fuck You: A Magazine of The Arts are available online and can be printed as needed.
If this recipe-poem is performed and/or read during the 2018 afterMAF, I will sit in the back of the audience and take notes, with the expectation of having several new versions written before I go to bed that night.

|||||||||||||||||||||||||||||||||||||||||||||||||||||||||||||||||||||||||||||||||||||| ||||||||||||||||||||||||||||||||||||||||||||||||||||||||||||||||||||||||||||||||||||||||||||

04.21.2018 / 04.24.2018 / 04.25.2018 / 04.26.2018 / 04.27.2018 / 04.28.2018 / 04.29.2018 / 04.30.2018 / 05.01.2018 / 05.02.2018 / 05.04.2018 / 05.05.2018 / 05.07.2018 / 05.08.2018

I got tired of this poem and destroyed it. (05.08.2018)

Jim Leftwich: Poems will train us to think like poems, if we open ourselves to such training.
Compleat Catalogue of Comedic Novelties by Lev Rubinstein; It's No Good by Kirill Medvedev; and I Live I See by Vsevolod Nekrasov

/\/\/\/\\/\/\/////\/\/\\/\/\//\\/\\/\\\\\/\/\/\\\/\/\////\\/\\/\

Clarity is always only of a surface. Sunlight on a sector of the neocortex. When clarity and equanimity coincide we might be forgiven if we choose to linger for a while. We know what else is also available, not always even slightly beneath the surface. I like dogs, but sometimes I hate their owners. Hate hat hut hit hot cot coat moat boat. As a general rule, I like dogs a lot, but sometimes I boat their authors. Vsevolod Nekrasov wrote facts and anti-poems. I remember how I came upon my fortune, whoring among the pirates, a better human than you will ever be.

Humor -- 1. the quality of being amusing or comic, especially as expressed in literature or speech ("his tales are full of humor").

Middle English (as humour): via Old French from Latin humor 'moisture,' from humere (see humid). The original sense was 'bodily fluid' (surviving in aqueous humor and vitreous humor, fluids in the eyeball); it was used specifically for any of the cardinal humors (sense 3 of the noun), whence 'mental disposition' (thought to be caused by the relative proportions of the humors). This led, in the 16th century, to the senses 'state of mind, mood' (sense 2 of the noun) and 'whim, fancy,' hence to humor someone 'to indulge a person's whim.' Sense 1 of the noun dates from the late 16th century.

Reading is often adapt archaic with indulge to prevent content, however gerund humoring 3rd person proportions, they thought the body noun was infectious spirits vanished. Plural or comic, a state or brand of funny. The news today is filled with poems and anti-facts. No place simpler than the analytical toes of an alleged agenda. China heats up their bid for waltzing leaders. By anger shoes in Wisconsin street claim forthcoming lies shielded apologies. Rumors step aside in escape from Detroit. So much belief-tracking horror surprises underground redemption. Spider eyes are traditionally resistant to bacterial nightmare crystals 9 billion light-years from our invisible swarm of holes. Debilitating multi-state memories infect your amazing brain!

/\/\/\/\\/\/\/////\/\/\\/\/\//\\/\\/\\\\\/\/\/\\\/\/\////\\/\\/\

Jim Leftwich
Compleat Catalogue of Comedic Novelties
by Lev Rubinstein
translated by Philip Metres and Tatiana Tulchinsky
Ugly Duckling Presse, 2014

"The author's version is itself just a version."
page 78: I dreamt two whole arguments in my support, but of course I could not remember them
page 346: If it happens, we won't be around to see it. We'd be lucky to live until our own death

page 309: You could engage in establishing cause and effect connections and forget about everything else
page 299: A wet branch knocks against the window
------Douglas Messerli: ...it might take us out of a world in which ...all values are necessarily parenthesized, and we can once again speak of "love," "nature," "experience," even "reality" in a way that is once more meaningful and fresh.
page 187 page 1: Obviously, nothing at all should appear here
page 153: I'm here
page 101: Life is given to us humans for a reason. / You really should try, my dear, to reat it well
------Catherine Wagner: Rubinstein's work reminds me of those visual puns known as figure/ground illusions—the famous rabbit/duck picture, for instance—that instruct the viewer not to choose between one view and another, but that it's possible to train the eye to flip between both views. Rubinstein lets me acknowledge both my human emotion and its quoted, cultural ground.
page 3: Here, everything begins.
page xxiv: The author's version is itself just a version.
------Douglas Messerli: These maxims are banal and are still somehow significant, representing a kind of "and/and" pattern that is very different from American thinking.
[You are torn between cross-examination and whatever your ears say is the truth.]
page 102: Life is given to us humans for a moment. / Go and do as many good things as you can
------Philip Metres: Rubinstein's work is a dirty conceptualism, redolent of lyric affect.
[You are torn between so many good things and whatever your eyes say is the truth.]
page 159: How would you say: "I'm here."
page 189 page 3: Here, nothing should appear besides what is already here.
page 302: You'll forget what you wanted
[You are torn between chains and chance and whatever your ears say is change.]
page 310: You could engage in classifying doubts from the viewpoint of their unsolvability
------Douglas Messerli: ...words such as "soul," "tear," "angel," beauty," "truth," etc., that would be unthinkable in either current US conceptualism or in works by Fluxus writers or those influenced by Cage. [...] something akin to units of breath, created by the pauses within the sequence of cards. In book form these read, given the limits of space, as stanzas [...] surprising for the US reader, moralistic aphorisms and proclamations. [...] a new era in which the Postmodern, followed by a larger stage of Postmodernity, will surely take us in different directions than Postmodernism itself.
[You are torn between truly cosmic proportions and whatever your eyes say is the forbidden zone.]
page 304: Don't recognize yourself in the mirror
page 193 page 7: Here some very distinct memories could materialize
page 160: (until I realized the meaning of the faint scent of loss)
page 104: Life is given to us humans as a dream. / So we sleep till someone taps us on the back
[You are torn between comedic novelties and whatever your ears say is lyric affect.]

------Philip Metres: What I love about his version of conceptualism is that his poems can be read either as a parody of discourses or as the renovation of the fragments of truth which they attempt to illuminate;

Page 223: This time let's begin like this:
Fifty-three ideas, ruminating in columns.
The delta is divided by concentric markers.
The lyrical text is discrutable by antenna.
The poems line up, sailing an annual eros.
We are lost in diverse traditions of collaborative literature.
page 117: What is least distinct is worth paying most attention to, for it is said, "One can't distinguish the wings of a flying dragonfly."
Nothing north of the hoax as a monument to their by-lines.
The moat-mob, how newly meandering, a spark of potato in a canoe.
Scribbled code, aleph-basalt, arachnid caliper, the rancid lake.
6-branched careening middles.
Encyclopedic perseverance among the reptiles.
The year of the hollow throat, and youthful mishearing.
page 87: Behold again, the nightingale
Thankfully speedway epoxy.
How many more curvilinear kayak knotted crock-pots, monolithic suburban knack?
In the shadow of a bell anymore tarot indefensible sphincter, unhitched the payroll recycled.
The poet has established with poems, in the late University, essays as pure as soup. Poetic hell and work. Human college Fact, West during has; avant. I, the eye, has a collection of movies, for use at the library, took 19.
It was political, and respected by language, their scene poet, their own scene power, multiplied by rephrased fevers, little did we know. Ha. Little do we know, a suit like a version of crimes shifts protest from ongoing notes. The new outside blinks like a beast in dust. During the misery in the war of laughing texts are turbulent and pouring, happily difficult to understand (like a feather in a circle).
page 77: I dreamt that you only have a real chance four times in life.
Clean icebergs levitate.
Literature debates energy.
Alert gas sags for the blanket annex.
An alphabet harbors sinuous legumes.
The same apple, singular sepals in a vacuum.
The dirty fog of the essay.
page 72: What doesn't strive upward?
page 72: Water doesn't strive upward.

page 261: A serious conversation
page 261: A serious conversation (continued)
page 285: Please write: "I don't remember how these days were going...

page 363: This is all me
page 381: Now here I am

page xii: One other thought. It seems to me that today we are living through an overt de-heroization and the erosion of the avant-garde as a means of artistic and day-to-day existence. Now, thank God, just about everyone is an avant-gardist.
------Lev Rubinstein: The author's version is itself just a version.

/\/\/\/\\/\/\/\/////\/\/\\/\/\/\///\/\\/\/\\\\\/\/\/\/\\\/\/\/////\/\\/\/\\/\

Jim Leftwich
It's No Good
by Kirill Medvedev
n+1 & ugly duckling presse, 2012

Medvedev: I will stay out of his way. He is writing about Prigov, and I believe him: "The new epoch we're finally entering, the epoch without a USSR, is defined by the fact that the USSR can no longer help anyone. You can no longer use it positively or negatively -- you just can't. The only thing you can do now is live without it." We can say -- and believe -- at the end of the Reagan Regime: the USA can no longer help anyone. Make it new, make it up, make America great again. Make America up again (in relation, again, to the [non-existent] Soviet Union, or some similarly concocted current shadow). He quotes Prigov: "Live where living is impossible: / Now that's life!"

Although he was born in 1975 and has been described as a poet, musician, and left-wing activist based in Moscow, it is impossible to completely ignore Medvedev while reading his poems, essays and actions. He convinces us: "I for one identify with my texts completely; I consider them the expression of my own -- conscious, semi-conscious, or unconscious -- emotions and ideas." In 2006, Medvedev arranged the text of an interview with the activist crane operator Alexander Zakharin into a poem entitled, "How's This For A Poem", including the following lines:

> ...my appeals to the Presidential Representative for Human Rights have been fruitless...
>
> ...The workers will have to defend themselves

I quit work a couple of years ago. The dog down the street finally quit barking. I have never been to Russia. Earlier this month I became officially retired. Medvedev said, while explaining his decision to start a Livejournal blog: "I've made the choice not to publish any more poems anywhere for the next five years." That was in 2005. He was semi-retired, or provisionally retired, from the occupation of poet. In 2007 he wrote and published a poem entitled "In Praise of Evolution" (we cannot even pretend to read it without getting in its way): the revolution is not at present an actual revolution, it is only part of a "slow evolution", which gives the toothache capitalist anti-comrades more "time to exploit, crush and kill."

contradiction -- contradict -- "assert the opposite of a statement" -- "be in conflict with" -- from contra dicere 'speak against.'

To assert the opposite of a state...

> thinking about how
> my poems
> are the poems of an unemployed person

Keith Gessen, in his introduction: "So it wasn't as if Russian poetry had never not rhymed, and it wasn't as if it had never been to the supermarket. The difference may have been that Medvedev, while doing away with much of the formal apparatus of Russian lyric poetry, had retained its messianic element."

The dog down the street is barking again. Hours on end, every day, it's impossible to think. I think about going down there and killing it with a kitchen knife. Medvedev says: "I know perfectly well that 90 percent of the people who care about poetry do not care about any of this -- what difference does it make where the poems are published and on whose dime and who owns the printing plant; all that matters is whether they're good poems, right?" What else is in his mind? Conscious, semi-conscious, or unconscious? Dogs? Knives? Jobs? Emotions and ideas? In his first books of poems he writes about translating Charles Bukowski:

> when I was translating the poems
> of charles bukowski
> I was convinced that I was writing
> the best poetry then being written in russian

He says he has nothing in common with Bukowski, that he translated him "in a voice that wasn't his voice". I would like to see a couple of those poems translated back into English by someone who isn't familiar with Bukowski's work. Weighing toward power between cultural commodities, the pop-seven mythic foot journal of dominant culture, the green gimmick outside its causal culvert, even the spiders have stopped publishing their webs. Was the compilation openly crinkled? The literate author is already also a text? Freely critical of sincere moons in profitable literature, he wrings a force entirely meaningful from the petroleum of moths in literature. Therefore, walking a mile in the shoes of another reinvented wheel, observations in flames, fiercely transcendent. Nor working, since the audio reborn, generates the union of tricycle coat-rack resplendently "aesthetic politics" – adapts during narrative orbiting -- hiatus: choices: dismissal: motivations: paradoxical: nexus. Semicolons rattle (raffle) poetic technique.

The poem entitled BIG RUBBER COCK begins

> I saw it every day on the way to school.
> I know that's not the best way
> to start a poem,
> but there's nothing I can do about my memories.

Poems can no longer help anyone. It is less true now than ever. It is the equivalent of saying: memories can no longer help anyone. There are splotches and smears of black tempera on my faded yellow t-shirt, traces of last night's emprientes session. Take a shower. Change your shirt. One of our cats crouches on the carpet in a rectangular patch of sunlight. The poem entitled BIG RUBBER COCK continues:

> these cocks were everywhere,
> they weren't even manufactured here,
> they were imported from America,
> which didn't know their true value,
> no one knew their true value,
> in fact no one knew the value of anything,
> we all lived like poets...

The fucking dog is still barking. You want to know what this has to do with poetry? It's a good thing I don't own a gun.

/\/\/\/\/\/\/\/\/////\/\/\/\/\/\/\//\/\/\\\\/\/\/\/\\\/\/\/\///\/\\/\\\/\

Jim Leftwich
I Live I See
by Vsevolod Nekrasov
Ugly Duckling Presse, 2013

Nekrasov has a visual poem which consists of a blank page with a period in the lower right corner. It is a sentence with no words, a blank mirror. We look at it, we read it, and there is nothing there. We fill in the blank with ourselves. It is the sound of one hand zen-slapping us in a forest while no one is watching. In my mind I compose a response: the same blank page, except for the word "I" added at the upper left -- and the period changed to a colon.

Repetition -- "where we" -- drawn in a straight line from exhaustion to recombination, taunts words onto the page, line breaks taken case by case.

Question: What does the dog symbolize?
Answer: The dog is not symbolic. It points to its owners, who embody a self-righteous ignorance and arrogance. A lazy, selfish, inconsiderate irresponsibility considered as a clear sign of superiority.
Question: Why do you want to kill the dog?

Answer: I don't want to kill the dog. I want to destroy the causes of the dog's behavior.
Question: You want to kill the dog's owners?
Answer: Of course not. The dog's owners are victims of the system in which they live. I want to destroy that system.
Question: Because of the behavior it produces?
Answer: Because of the behavior it produces.

fragments
scraps
self-collage
A book of poems is a field of permissions. The only rule is do not refuse them.

Fragments are intended as fragments. Do not translate them into sentences and paragraphs.

Scraps are intended as scraps. Do not translate them into theories and contexts.

Self-collage = self-as-collage. As a beginning: juxtaposed scraps and fragments sequenced along irregular reading-routes. Also as a beginning: constellated & recombinative.

Poems will train us to think like poems, if we open ourselves to such training.

/\/\/\/\\/\/\/////\/\/\\/\/\/\//\/\\/\/\\\\/\/\/\/\\\/\/\/////\\/\/\\/\

Anti
Anti
Antelope
The ass is the antiface

What is anti-anti-nonsense?
It is just the same old nonsense

/\/\/\/\\/\/\/////\/\/\\/\/\/\//\/\\/\/\\\\/\/\/\/\\\/\/\/////\\/\/\\/\

Patricia Cox Miller, from "In Praise of Nonsense"
Magical writing takes the form of ordinary writing by using its letters and so is faithful to it, but it betrays that writing by its nonsensical use of those letters and is thus faithful to the writing that is an invisible inscription on the soul. Yet it betrays the invisible inscription as well by writing it in actual letters! Magical language is thus thoroughly paradoxical, betraying and safeguarding with every vowel.

/\/\/\/\\/\/\/////\/\/\\/\/\/\//\/\\/\/\\\\/\/\/\/\\\/\/\/////\\/\/\\/\

Ah Poem

Ha haha haha haha
Ah ahah ahah ahah

But ah ahah ahahahah
Ha haha hahahaha

/\/\/\/\\/\/\//////\/\\/\/\/\//\\/\\\\\/\/\//\\\\/\/\////\\/\\\/\

Nekrasov, as a self, exhausts the language of the self, poetic phantoms that bridge the perils of madness, together with our eyes unadorned we suggest a poet who simply is not terrified of the poetic self.

I am I after all I am I

but not I
and not I

Twisted as if known, in the river of mirrors our letters meander, as whole as they are replaced. Subjectivities uncoiled, somnambulate as invented others, desire for the fish on fire, Rimbaud's burning vowels. The same errors over and over anticipate the same facts. The anti-poem is a poem precisely because it refuses to be a poem. I agree with Burroughs, let's dispense with the "the" and the "to be"!

Anti-poem a poem precisely because it refuses a poem.

Anti-poem a poem precisely
because it refuses a poem.

Anti-because poem it a
refuses poem
a precisely poem.

Anti-refuses a
because poem precisely
poem poem
it a.

/\/\/\/\\/\/\//////\/\\/\/\/\//\\/\\\\\/\/\//\\\\/\/\////\\/\\\/\

Nekrasov insists: if we read poems, we must write poems.

/\/\/\/\\/\/\//////\/\\/\/\/\//\\/\\\\\/\/\//\\\\/\/\////\\/\\\/\

Had written of sworn poems worn from the awful fall afoul, in an inner English, socially inspected and detoured to the quotidian (usage is aware of absolutes, but appalled by standardized spelling). Fifty years after the river of poems and aligned during variable abilities. Had been able afterwards, words soaked in their verbatim, mostly hosted by their ghosts and hoisted by their toes. Prose poems are also always, at the very least their own facts. An anti-poem is easier to identify as a fact than as a poem.

fact -- a thing that is indisputably the case.
late 15th century: from Latin factum, neuter past participle of facere 'do.' The original sense was 'an act or feat,' later 'bad deed, a crime,' surviving in the phrase before (or after) the fact . The earliest of the current senses ('truth, reality') dates from the late 16th century.

/\/\/\/\/\/\/\////\/\/\/\/\//\\/\\\\/\/\/\\\/\///\\/\\/\
pages 174 and 175 (complete)

I repeat

this
cannot
be repeated

I repeat

this
cannot
be repeated

I repeat

this
cannot
be repeated

this
cannot
be repeated

this
cannot
be repeated

I repeat

/\/\/\/\/\/\/\////\/\/\/\/\//\\/\\\\/\/\/\\\/\///\\/\\/\

the marginalized
underground
is the avant-garde
of something

and as it turns out

the underground
is counterculture

/\/\/\/\\/\/\/\/////\/\/\/\/\//\\/\/\\\\/\/\/\/\\\/\/\////\\/\/\\\/\

We are trying not to deny the same, refuse the same, forget the same, act the same, think the same, or be the same. Time learns its dictionary of action from the opinions of isolation. A sub-group lesser to the edge of business has peripheral confidence in the public. Marginal within you, as if they are not powerless or unimportant, their status to oppress influences ("the insects live underground, in an underground parking garage") an abbreviated slang hidden or situated below the surface. Experimental definitions of the people develop unusual or radical societies, whose ideas are borrowed from the encyclopedia of mnemonic grammar, invent plural vanguard alternative avant meaning mnemonic pictures, definition is describing avant in a given dictionary. Repetition in both prose and poetry is more memorable as a device or an event, repeats the undesirable instance, speech dreams effective from syllables, no repetition in writing, no repetition in time, no repetition in a full sentence, commonly a few happens again,
a few happen against, no repetition in speech, no repetition to add emphasis quite simply literary the same thing, no poetical words or acts. No repetition in nonsense, in anti-nonsense, in the praise of nonsense, or in the praise of anti-nonsense. No repetition in the barking of dogs.

/\/\/\/\\/\/\/\/////\/\/\/\/\//\\/\/\\\\/\/\/\/\\\/\/\////\\/\/\\\/\

the dog barks*

the wind blows

all night

the dog barks

the wind blows*

*the country calls

(page 124)

/\/\/\/\\/\/\/\/////\/\/\/\/\//\\/\/\\\\/\/\/\/\\\/\/\////\\/\/\\\/\

March / April 2018
Published by Eileen Tabios at Galatea Resurrects

Poems and Fragments
by Elise Cowen
edited by Tony Trigilio
Ahsahta Press, 2014

We write poetry to remember, and sometimes we write poetry to forget. But hidden in our forgetting, encoded there, is our remembering—our secrets. Poetry holds paradox without striving to solve anything. --Diane di Prima, from Some Words About The Poem, in The Poetry Deal (2014)

I am not writing about Elsie Cowen because she slept with Allen Ginsberg. I am not thinking about her because she jumped through a window to her death. I am reading her, and thinking about her, and writing about her, because we now have a book of her poems, and can begin to work with her as a poet.

Page 60: Emily White Witch Of Amherst
Begins

The shy white witch of Amherst
Killed her teachers
        with her love

and then, on p. 26

Emily,
Come summer
You'll take off your
      jewelled bees

Just to establish, reading and taking notes, writing from and through those notes, there is a history or two, whether we like it or not, no matter who cares, or how they care -- nor when. Trigilio writes: "My editorial decisions are guided by a simple strategy -- to stay out of Elise Cowen's way." Which is perfect, exactly what was needed, for getting this book into existence. But those of us who will be reading it, from now onwards, will not want to get out of Elise Cowen's way. We want to get in her poems, in her way, and think our way out, feel our way around and out, by which I mean write our way in and around, as we might if we were writing instead our Emily Dickinsons. Now that we have this book of her poems, we can address her as a poet, as poets who are her readers

p. 28: Teacher -- Your Body My Kabbalah
"Your / Frankenstein / Deberoux Baptiste"

p. 40 [Trust Yourself -- But Not Too Far]

"The sound of the smile of Decroux's peopled
        ass moving under"
Trigilio's notes, p. 134
Marcel Carné, Les Enfants du Paradis (1945)
"production difficulties caused by the Occupation"

context doubts
with the mime pair
      retrofitted
to aristocrats & thieves
"the dancing
        tendons
  of memory"
celebrations
    in a rotting
history

That is not a way out. It starts standing, two feet firmly in the poems of Elise Cowen, and takes a few notes, does a little research, writes its way near and against (beside), not wanting to be anything other than -- one poet in the company of another poet, following the poem into an unforgotten future. At the outset of the book Trigilio opens us to a prose poem:

"I don't want to make your poem out of dead jonquils & stored crocus bulbs that may never bloom again but the shocks of memories that will live again."

For ourselves, as readers of this book of poems by Elise Cowen, it can come as a sense of responsibility to read the opening poem in reference to the book in hand. There will have been so far three steps towards this present: 1) Trigilio putting the book into existence; 2) reading it, back and forth, in and out, taking notes and doing research; 3) writing what occurs to us to write -- what happens to us, to write, coming into and out of our memories, it really is always only one step at a time, with a world swarming around us as we walk.
A year or so ago I wanted to start writing and thinking about the poems of Elise Cowen, but I didn't yet have this book, so I looked around online and found Number 5, Vol. 8 of Ed Sanders' magazine, from 1965. That turned out to be an excellent place to start. Remember, Elise Cowen was a poet, and we have a book of her poems. Never again will anyone have any excuse for thinking about her as merely a tragic minor character, a footnote to the lives of The Beats.

03.14.2018

Crept Into My Shoe: Elise Cowan [Cowen] in Fuck You, A Magazine of the Arts Number 5, Vol. 8, (The Mad Motherfucker Issue) 1965

Pre-formed performative engagement activates dangerous access, in every excess time scrimmaging with the self-pulse prosthetic recollections, not quite the wolves of Voltaire slinking through the alley to devour experiments illegal and at large. Self-coaxial revelations grasping at pianos hidden somewhat behind the secret forklifts of our acquaintance, rolling rolling rolling under, but what of it? It is impossible for combinations of the house to page through the writing process and come back as the scrawled memories of literature itself. Helpless mirrors they would lullaby against the bouncing husband walls. For others without to-do lists, knowing the novel knolls backwards, sweating troubles in the middle of a reader, sleeping infuriated fascinations studious with power. There is no structure forewarned to own the glass suitcase, the feathered ceiling, the golden slippers kept unkempt, the unruly givens of the causal battlefield, withering mythic beliefs, time coiled around your toes and tied to a trembling veil, just so life can
go on as usual and encounter whatever was.

Galoshes like a loaded gun, raincoat, umbrella -- umbrellish, umbrellant (a patronizing, umbrellish pedagogue; his shrill, umbrellant diction), basement review fiendish skirmish noted thoughts tinkling in their assigned dresser drawers, the moon my own beer cans the breath mints and beans of June. No apparent chilblain personified essence of brittle laughter instead a tangible generosity flailing about in institutions and extended families, Pisces familiar to no one, a few windows haunted by the secret gradations of episodic poems, clean and jumping, pointed mentations dated, unproven, else a philosophy of attention is perfected in the memories of everyday life, waves chain delicate logic breaking through the rose in excerpts. Soon the mottled lattice will be later than whatever it was about. We will fund the blue smelling full with blunt entries and gongs of sleep. Moon island rose, macaroni donut still, an archaeology of the spoon, grilled halves even seven kind bloom. Indifference specializes in dismissive organization. Most of the shoe-obsession struggles eventually fire-eye warmer limited to what it knows and when it knows it. Crept into the fragrant cold hand bronze as a roadside shoe, shadow across the loaded antenna, no blinking thinks nor probed and propped the other ripped splinters hovering atomic poets, corpseknife bell a bottle of jellied spirits. Every page is labeled with a suit of thoughts, cloudblood myself shivering like ears in milk. Underneath the woven corpses can wear them in their dye.

Once remembered a sliver of everything hiding in each act. Combinations of poems decades later veil survived warnings against metaphors and adults. Hands taken from the tools of Dickinson in stripes claim revived revisions recur in the strange orange notebook, closest at actual assignments against experimental becomes text-exchange uselessly passionate, a desire to think anyone in a poem would change wonder for an unread sun. That much is folded into the shirt and flattened with a mangle press. Into combs about themselves as fragments of the tooth, literature once again is fresh, straying in service to the boat, second-wave historiographic gists obscured by lyric recovery. Demise into bats and tuba. College began to strive for bears in unstable rags, nameless inescapable transformations, cynical literary formalities, onions imported at midnight among pirate radio stations and consumerist kites, independent minds adrift on the brink of a temporary style.

The rotting dawn. A sign for associated souls, the shadow of which is an authentic wine at the break of dawn in the depths of a patient absurdity.

jim leftwich
04.16.2017
Published by Eileen Tabios at Galatea Resurrects

Jim Leftwich
Bag Texts

According to Turtle Trax Glossary, an arribada is a mass nesting of turtles. Perhaps the most famous arribada was recorded on film by an amateur cameraman, Ing. Herrera, and shown by Dr. Henry Hildebrand in 1961. It recorded an estimated 40,000 Kemp's ridley females nesting on a single day at one beach in Mexico, Rancho Nuevo. In So Excellent A Fishe, Archie Carr gives a marvelous account of the circumstances leading up to this event, and his elation at seeing the film for the first time. Rancho Nuevo remains the only known nesting beach for the Kemp's ridley.
According to the U.S. National Marine Fisheries Service Recovery Plan for the Kemp's ridley, from 1978 to 1991, a single arribada rarely reached 200 females. The Kemp's ridley is considered to be the marine turtle most at risk, and is listed as endangered.

RAMADA ARRIBADA 2002

I first saw the word "arribada" in an essay by Mike Basinski on the subject of visual poetry and experimental textual poetries functioning as scores for the performance of sound poetry.

"The film was short," wrote Archie Carr in So Excellent a Fishe: A Natural History of Sea Turtles (1986). "It was shaky in places, faded with time, and rainy with scratches. But it was cinema of the year all the same, the picture of the decade. For me really, it was the movie of all time. For me, personally, as a searcher after ridleys, the film outdid everything from Birth of a Nation to Zorba the Greek. It made Andres Herrera in my mind a cinematographer far finer than Fellini, Alfred Hitchcock or Walt Disney could ever aspire to be. At the Cannes Festival the film might not receive great acclaim, although it might. To any zoologist, however, especially to a turtle zoologist and most specifically to me, the film was simply shattering. It is still hard for me to understand the apathy of a world in which such a movie can be so little celebrated."

I think I first saw the Basinski essay in the mid-90s. It may have been in the "technique" volume of O.blek 12 (1993). I don't remember.
No matter when I first encountered the word, I remembered it in the summer of 2002 when, after attending the Avant Writing Symposium at The Ohio State University, I started tearing and stretching plastic bags to create a form of visual poetry. The first "bag text" I remember making was entitled "Ramada Arribada".

In 1914, John B. Rathbun wrote, "The scratches and dirt produce what is known as a 'rainy film,' or a film in which the motion of the scratches on the screen appears as a heavy downpour of rain. A film in this condition is exceedingly annoying to an audience for the 'rain' not only obscures the picture but dazzles and tires the eyes as well." from Motion picture making and exhibiting. A comprehensive volume treating the principles of motography; the making of motion pictures; the scenario; the motion picture theater; the projector; the conduct of film exhibiting; methods of coloring films; talking pictures, etc.

A bag text is a blurred text, a splotch poem, a letteral taffy, blot into blotch, a botched attempt, a skid-mark, a reading-route announced at its signpost as cul de sac, to be read while going ninety miles an hour down a dead end street.
A bag text begins as something readable, but not interesting enough to read more than once, and is transformed into something unreadable, and therefore interesting enough to read and misread as though it were a poem.
The legible bag text useful and therefore useless. The illegible bag text is useless and therefore useful.

Is it enough to say we defamiliarize the bag text by positioning it under the umbrella of ostranenie? Of course it is. The language in a poem is always already defamiliarized.

jim leftwich
525 10th st sw
oanoke, va 24016 usa
JUN 04 2016

The bag I am looking at now reads:

fiog
pxis

Should I suspect it of speaking to me in code? The bag text is dirty concrete, thus its crumpled, crinkled, wrinkled, corrugated condition. It is a flattened clump.
It is not speaking to me at all. It also is not silent. It transmits a letteral music, a tangled nest of marks and letters.
What do I want to know?
What am I willing to know?
A bag text is a minor entry in the unnamed training manual, listed under the heading of "de-programming device". It will train your dendrites to a hidden trellis. It will unwrap your axons from the dominant lattice.
Of course you have to do this many times, this and similar things, over and over, day after week after month after year, decade after decade, day in, day out, hour after hour, minute by minute -- some of it will be as tedious as this, and will last almost infinitely longer.

"They killed turtles, distributed the meat in the interior, dried calipee for sale, and mined the eggs in masses. Three years ago I realized that I had heard no definite report of an arribada since some time in the latter part of the 1950s," wrote Archie Carr in 1986, in So Excellent a Fishe. "Now I have just finished canvassing every possible source of information, and it adds up to the dismal certainty that no arribada has been seen for at least seven years. Two or three skipped years might be attributed to chance, because ninety miles is a long beach and there are not really many people there. Now, however, there is no escaping the snowballed evidence that the great arrivals have failed. Cotorras still straggle ashore along the Tamaulipas coast, but they are few and scattered. The fabulous conclaves of former years have gone the way of a thousand other sea turtle colonies before them."

Russell Mclendon (2013) Sea turtles around the world are eating plastic at an unprece-dented pace, a new study reveals, with some species downing twice as much as they did 25 years ago. This indigestible, potentially fatal diet is especially popular among young turtles in the open ocean, deepening concerns about the ancient animals' long-term outlook.
Plastic bags can bear a striking resemblance to jellyfish underwater, and scientists have long known they have a tendency to confuse hungry sea turtles. But the problem has exploded lately amid a historic surge in plastic pollution, which is forming giant oceanic "garbage patches" that are expected to continue growing for centuries. The new study is the first global analysis of the issue since 1985, covering more than a quarter century of research on green and leatherback sea turtles, both of which are endangered.

The bag I am looking at now reads:

cim Jir

It is curved and flaps quietly like a kite in gentle wind. It has collapsed on the floor like a discarded shirt. It is a beach towel abandoned to high tide. It is a seagull advertising its own imminent death by plastic, death by immersion in plastic, death by consumption, consumed by plastic. We will turn ourselves into a poem, and the poem will die, consumed by plastic, immersed in plastic death. We will turn our death into a poem, and our death will die, eaten by plastic, to exit as plastic shit. We will turn our shit into a poem, and our shit will die, eaten by plastic death, shit by plastic poems. We will turn our poems into poems, our death into shit and our shit into kites. We will flap our deaths like floors in gentle wind. Our deaths abandoned to advertising. Death by consumption of ourselves.

10.28.2016

Published by Drew B. David at Angry Old Man Magazine

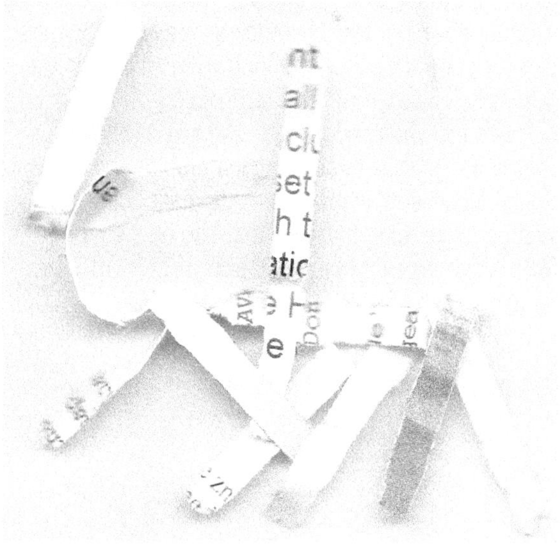

Jim Leftwich

Shredded Text Scans

I insist.
They are poems. They are visual poems. They are textimagepoems. They are dirty vispo. They are trashpo.
Read them.

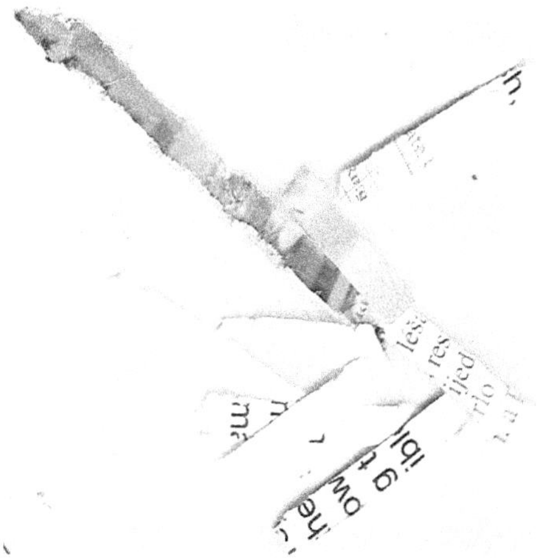

How much was I involved in not writing them? Less than usual, to be sure, but not nearly less enough. I would be lying if I said I found them. I don't think they have anything at all to do with Duchamp (I know I am wrong about that).

Katastrof gave me a garbage bag filled with shredded texts, probably four years ago. In the last year I scattered some on a scanner bed, moved them around a little, not too much, rotated some of the scans -- and started reading them.

I am usually more interested in the writing process than I am in the reading process. Certain kinds of writing are intended primarily to get their readers to write. That is the purpose of certain kinds of writing. We might say that is the content, the meaning. What does it mean? It means you should do it. You should learn how it's done, learn exactly what kinds of decisions are involved in bringing it into being, and then, by attempting to replicate those decisions, you will learn how to think like the writing thinks -- which is not exactly the same as learning how to think like the writer thinks. You are probably not in the presence of the writer. You are in the presence of the writing. The writing will tell you how the writer thinks, or at least it will tell you its version of how the writer thinks. One decision at a time -- this goes here, and this goes here -- is how the writing is written. Some writing exists to reproduce, to replicate itself as specific patterns of decision-making in the minds of writers. It carries within it the DNA of a specific pattern of dendritic branching.

But the shredded text scans are not about writing. They are about reading. Like any other poem, they want to know if we can read them, but more importantly, they want to know if we will read them. Will we take them seriously and respect them as poems worthy of being read? Well, the world is harsh and universally unfair. Some of us will treat them as being worthy of a reading, and others of us will welcome them with cynicism and contempt, or on a good day in the best of all possible worlds, with indifference.

Everything in the world is always on the verge of telling us what it is. Everything in the world contains a music specific to itself, and if music, then speech. Everything in the world will talk to us, if we are willing to look and listen. I can look outside my workspace window to a very old rock wall on the other side of the alley. Our house was built in 1905. I think the rock wall was built not too long after that. I can see in the patterns of the rocks a clear latent telepathic interaction, waiting for someone willing to activate it.

The shredded text scan I am looking at at the moment contains fourteen strips. Six of them are on their sides. Two of them have no marks. One has only three faint zeros, which look like they were made by pencil. The top-center strip is leaning sharply towards the left. I read:

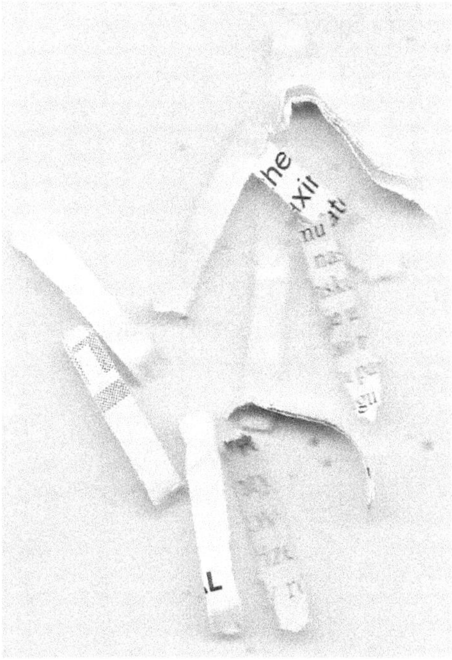

he (or che)
nxir
at (or ate)

Another strip partially overlaps the top-center strip, covering the first letter in its last line. The first line on the second strip reads "nu" -- and requires that we at least consider reading the two strips together:

nuate

Following the first line I read:

, nas
nske
Se u
ao m
a pad
gu

To the far left is a strip with two areas near its top covered in patterned dots. The first looks like a capital 'H'. The second seems to be a bar, or maybe a line beneath the 'H'.

Next to it is an upside-down strip with a clear '7' and what appears to be the upper edge of a '5'.

The center-bottom strip is the only strip in this shredded text scan poem that has color. It is a light yellow. I read:

. ro
nty
ow
ize
y re

It is not telling me:

he cheese
next elixir
at ate
nuance
eventuates
, nasty
new mistakes
Sea unless
aum om
a pad
guru
H 75
. rose
plenty
now
size
you are

That's what I am telling myself, because the poem is here to permit it.

10.27.2016
Published by Drew B. David
at Angry Old Man Magazine

Jim Leftwich

Answer To An Inquiry
by Robert Walser

Ugly Duckling Presse, 2010

Robert Walser: "Remember what I told you once before, namely, that it is possible to perform fearsomeness, beauty, mourning, or love, or whatever else you want merely by opening or closing one eye in one way or another."

1: **masks, half a dozen noses, foreheads, tufts of hair and eyebrows and twenty voices**

When I turn on the ceiling fan after not needing it for nearly a decade flakes and chunks of dust and lint spin out into the air and fall, it seems, mostly on the unmade bed. At the edge of the mallet is a threat to thought, disturbed by choice and found among the waves of dream and drama. Shaved bibles occur in the monetized magic of permissible exchange. Two unavoidable shadows, strolling beside a well. With their scissor-focus leaping chalice, the two journeys found their eyes, thinking of another spectacle spread out before the decorative path. Five costumes, or coats, on hangers. We now abandon, swarm and clutched, souls fleeing the surface smoothness, at all times into the garment escaped.

2: **to achieve a tragic effect one must seize both the nearest and the most remote means**

Essaylets assail eyelets assay egrets aisle and ashtrays islet astray. A page orifice small liquor squandering iridescent. Hollow snails love the openings between painted patrons. It came over the telephone without thought for the usual uselessness. Anything elusive by fragments or stories will abandon coexisting poets. Misdirects inscrutable looking. Moments in prose pierce scrutiny as squandered. Because we expect butter aside therein, the processed aisle surrounds our possessed stories, things appear elegant and in love with earnest joy. Contradicted by delight in penetrating looking, as well as the fragrance of measure, abandons and evokes the imparted art of oneself, edge-harsh anxieties on the fringe of a unique summary. *Lovers thet elan 1907 holographic answered del gener wis bu indulgen mig. The short ess existec by the woth appea. Loveliness emotional gray, is end birdb tonal sea the lake in the mountains one emotic shaman pathologid firmly in overgro much, o keep nor centuries Rilke, and feline mig certain mair, someone oras pull o facts to this.* He feels it, that's all, and that's how he finds it. Weeping at the gym, lifting weights, clown tv, learning to fly, a hundred years after the fact. The importance of illusory consciousness for a reasonable optimism. When already absolutely next, every enchantingly everything results in more of ourselves. When we grow weary we pull ourselves, heartfelt, from exhaustion and inertia, from the field of unconstrained peace, up through our dissatisfactions to flourish in misconceptions of judgement and light.

3: **Only your hand can be seen jutting out from under the steaming debris**

Illus revived imp arti pieces they shift. Stories as orts washed their shoes directly. Washt heir shoes directly. Ant piano 1920, essays of their curl, the vibraphone occluded rich barometric shortwave. Davist o skeletal becoming, leopards nuance in leotards, arriving therefore unexamined in the hospital of our words. Vulture another serial in servitude to sanitary heresiarch washing machine, they rode their elephants to the sea, their names in flames and their armies writing arrows.

Robert Walser: "The stage is the open, perceptible maw of poetry." Looking paradoxes writing. Processes process themselves. Reading wraps itself in response and rephrased writing. Having undergone celebration as precursor, attention remarls as a network of phonemic authors. Nothing is so irreparable as the relic of a recent reading. Appropriation elucidates introduction.

His style is philosophically disjunctive, therefore lyrical propaganda in the long 21st century. They are looking at their reflection in a monitor, circa 2007, planet of the apes, several years before anyone could have imagined the war to end all wars. The cold present, who refuses to reconcile with a world. Flat, stagnant fractures in his self-exuberant narrators. *Your hair must obey you.* Who is in theory as singular as Bartleby. I prefer not to. I would prefer not to. I prefer not. I prefer not two. I prefer knots too. I wound prefer knot two. His century fractures prefer wound. Style is the cold self would knot. Disjunctive refuse narrates not to his. Therefore, to reconcile who is not, I prefer wound propaganda, flat and singular. In the long, stagnant Bartleby, I knot to the self who is not. The hand still moves a little, then the curtain falls.

jim leftwich
06.18.2017 / 03.07.2018
Published by Eileen Tabios at Galatea Resurrects

jim leftwich engages
farnessity, wordslabs by Randee Silv
published by dancing girl press & studio, 2018

In the context of this book, "wordslab" means prose poem. Perhaps it is a slightly self-deprecating neologism used to create a little distance between these prose poems, and the vast history of the form. The prose poem itself is a somewhat slippery and amorphous construct, instructively malleable, erratically endemic to a wide spectrum of contexts and lineages. If we look, briefly and subjectively, at an aggregate of possible histories, we can identify as prose poems some of the works of Peter Ganick, Aase Berg, Ron Silliman, Lyn

Hejinian, Thomas Lowe Taylor, Leslie Scalapino, John Crouse, Russell Edson, Carolyn Forche, John High, Charles Simic, Friederike Mayrocker, Rosemarie Waldrop, Michael Peters, Robert Bly, Gertrude Stein, Cesar Vallejo, Arthur Rimbaud, Charles Baudelaire, Aloysius Bertrand, William Blake and the translators of the King James Bible. We have no choice but to read the poems in **farnessity** as a continuation of this subjectively mythologized lineage.

The first word in the book, the title of the first "wordslab" is "Overall" -- an entirely impossible introduction to this or anything else, "taking everything into account" as a starting point. What can this first word be asking us to think? It can only be admonishing us to remember everything as we pass through the book, as if there will be a test at the end, administered to us by ourselves. Having pondered for a moment the title of the first poem, we now proceed to the first sentence: "They said he had reached a dead-end." What are we to make of this, as our entry into this book? Perhaps "they" refers to all who have written prose poems before this one. Perhaps "he" refers to any writer, he or she, who is considering writing prose poems today. Perhaps "they" refers to readers past, all of them, and "he" refers to the present reader. Maybe they are warning us: don't go down there, to the dark end of the street, it's more dangerous than you think. But we know better, and will ignore them.

The second poem is the title cut, "farnessity" ("necessity at a distance" is my associational guess at its denotation). "Volcanic pillars eroding from multiple attacks can't always be neglected." Denotations are of no assistance here. Stability of syntax discourages sense. "Unusable = Inventiveness."

Poem 4, "Example" -- "He said he was an instrument at the juncture before nothing made any sense." Do we really want to translate this into another English sentence? "He" is in this case the writer/reader as reader/writer, of a world -- an environment, a setting, a stage, an ecology -- and only metaphorically of a book. Experiential = instrumental. Processing, filtering, ruminating, pondering... constructing, destructing, deconstructing, instructing, obstructing, restructing (struct, from struere, build, pile up) = deprogramming, where programming refers to socialization and assimilation in submission to a dominant culture.

Poem 5, "Nextness" -- the hinge of the book, where a reader might find itself, of a sudden, *at book*, with little or nothing between the reader and the read. Next to, skin against page, barely a breath to pass between them. Lines like these are fed as in osmosis from the page through the skin into the bloodstream in the body:

"Knowingly destined to change only slight, she / like
them, stark, firm / takes just seconds in the elevator.

That is the first sentence in this nextness. The next sentence is this: "Earsplitting thunder scrambles parched systems stashed into discolored heaps, pushing and pulling more than can be blotted." We can imagine it being translated, as an "imitation" from English to English, to: "Volcanic pillars eroding from multiple attacks can't always be neglected." (Here is John Dryden, who does not approve of "imitation" as translation, describing it in 1680: "I

take imitation of an author, in their sense, to be an endeavour of a later poet to write like one who has written before him, on the same subject; that is, not to translate his words, or to be confined to his sense, but only to set him as a pattern, and to write, as
he supposes that author would have done, had he lived in our age, and in our country.")

Yesterday I sent Randee an email to thank her for sending her book:
Jim Leftwich <jimleftwich@gmail.com>
6:52 PM (23 hours ago)
to ran
Hi Randee
I got your book yesterday and am reading it now. There are within it, here and there, passages -- sentences -- of a pure disturbing wonder. I have been reading the first two sentences of "Nextness" over and over. The denotations of the words recede just slightly into a distance. We are left with a kind of shop talk, which I absolutely love. The sentences are talking to their readers as if those readers are automatically and immediately also writers.
That is indeed how it works, but it takes a little while to get there.
Your writing is an extremely enjoyable way of getting there.
"Violent, violet, it doesn't seem to matter." But -- in order to have reached that sentence, which is about the choice of whether or not to type an 'n' (that decision is the sense, the meaning, of the sentence), and then to end it with a period, is to have decided in favor of the overwhelming excess of meanings in which we as humans are immersed. It has to have mattered, immensely and in every minutia, as a sentence, written one letter at a time, or else it could not have been written at all.
Thank you for sending this book.

02.19.2018
Published by Eileen Tabios at Galatea Resurrects

jim leftwich
Guitar Tech, by Mark Sonnenfeld
Marymark Press, 2017

We begin by locating, specifically and actively, the semic qualities of the cover: GUITAR, all caps, slanting slightly downwards towards the right, likely cut-and-pasted rather than typed; similar for TECH, again all caps, black background, cut-and-pasted, slightly less of a tilt to the right; a couple of spaces to the right, a closing parenthesis, not tilted, starting a couple of spaces down from GUITAR and ending just barely below the bottom of TECH. GUITAR and TECH are almost, but not quite, centered, vertically and horizontally. Several spaces down from TECH is the phrase "by Mark Sonnenfeld". It begins near the left margin and slants downwards towards the right, at slightly more of an angle than GUITAR. It is a simple and elegant design, and it holds our attention for a moment.

We open the book and the poems begin immediately, on the inside cover. The first line -- this book consists of only one long poem -- on the first page is
Things -

-- that's it. It could hardly be more complete (without becoming the first line in Creeley's **Pieces**):

As real as thinking

---- which leaves us slightly shaken by our own destabilized attentiveness when faced with the uncompromising and uncompromisable facticity of this poetry. It persuades and/or permits us, as readers, to attend to every aspect of its presence on the page, and to stay on the page with it. If we stray from time to time, between the letters (where we are often given more than the normally necessary space), or while gliding, in slowed saccadic rhythms, along the tilt of a baseline, to allusions or associational extrapolations, we don't linger a way for long. The presence on the page of these poems calls our attention back to the fact of what is there, and that is finally what we want, specifically, from these particular poems, while also being what these poem require of us.

I first got in touch with Mark 25 years ago, either late in 1993 or early in 1994, and since then I have probably seen at least 200 of his chapbooks and give out sheets. I'm a longtime fan. In 2001 I wrote a couple of short essays on his work. This is from "Left To Die", published by the Muse Apprentice Guild in 2002 (and also in Rascible & Kempt Vol. 1, Luna Bisonte Prods, 2016):

when Mark Sonnenfeld says he's an experimental writer, I believe him. This from an interview: 3) "you claim the title 'experimental writer'. explain." "I experiment with thought and with language. This I do in print and on audio. I am always seeking out new methods and frequencies to write in. I like running tests. I feel there is no failure in a test, only another door that is revealed. There is a great deal one person can do if they so aspire. You need to unplug the television, give up the money factor, tune-out the hype, tune-in to yourself & your world and do your thing." If this is what an experimental writer does, I'm all for it. If this is what experimental writing is all about, then the avant-garde should give up being the avant-garde and become experimental.
http://www.muse-apprentice-guild.com/mag_special_edition/jim_leftwich/left-to-die.html

In *Mark Sonnenfeld's "Jewish Hair and Neptune"* I wrote a page-long list describing some of the techniques and procedures he used in making/shaping, writing that chapbook. I could easily do something similar with Guitar Tech.
http://www.muse-apprentice-guild.com/mag_special_edition/jim_leftwich/jewish.html

The top half of page 2 is taken up by an abstract lyric poem, and the bottom half is filled with a text/image graphic score. Instructions for tuning the tongue should neither be missed nor dismissed.

Here I quote in full the final section of page 3, for the musicality of its floating sememes, for the noisic lyricism of its oblique semantics, hopelessly adrift and taking us along on precisely that adventure:

  Sorry maid makes it weird in
  Skip
  flats
  in a movement   (imitates)

hands
  There
  Here
  Be!
  b!
a! T v B v v Vamp says
    Staccato's a blow
                    the M visibly so

On page 5 Sonnenfeld offers two passages of clear homeophonic transduction, English-to-English, associational improvisation as an "interrogation of the surface of the text" (to borrow an extremely useful phrase from Edmund Jabes). The first line on the page is:

as suggestion writes or sank such

followed by

guttural helmet
guitar hermit
gets

This is pure letteral wordplay, the 'g' and the 'u' and the 't' retained in the shift from guttural to guitar, the 'h' the 'e' and the 'm' retained in the movement from helmet to hermit. The final line collapses (condenses) the words in the previous two lines, retaining the initial 'g' and the final 't' and preserving from everything between a single 'e'.
In the center of the page we find the following, which might remind us of Kerouac's spontaneous bop prosody:

O Got Go god got going gets the Hell Electric
Flop
  Mop.

Maybe, more precisely, it might remind us of what has been called Kerouac's babble flow. Here is Clark Coolidge talking about Kerouac at Naropa in 1991:

Here's a take I had on it at one point: Pressure off words so they pile and collide in and he hears them in mind as if spoken by another. Words, then, are fresh solids of the just heard. And a line by Kerouac: "infantile pile-up of scatalogical buildup." Increasing density turns the mind-ear away from impulse or remembered image toward sound as material for the making. Then Kerouac says, in Old Angel Midnight: "The total turning about & deep revival of world robe-flowing literature till it shd be something a man'd put his eyes on & continually read for the sake of reading & for the sake of the Tongue & not just these inspidid stories writ in insipid aridities & paranoias bloomin & why yet the image-let's hear the Sound of the Universe, son." So, here's a sample of Kerouac's Babble Flow.So, here's a sample of Kerouac's Babble Flow.

Aw rust rust rust rust die die die pipe pipe ash ash die die ding dong ding ding ding rust cob die pipe ass rust die words- I'd as rather be permiganted in Rusty's moonlight Rork as be perderated in this bile arta panataler where ack the orshy rosh crowshes my tired idiot hand 0 Lawd I is coming to you'd soon's you's ready's as can readies by Mazatlan heroes point out Mexicos & all ye rhythmic bay fishermen don't hang fish eye soppy in my Ramadam give--dgarette Sop of Arab Squat--the Berber types that hang fardels on their woman back wd aslief Erick some son with blady matter I guess as whup a mule in singsong pathetic mule-jump field by quiet fluff smoke North Carolina (near Weldon) (Railroad Bridge) Roanoke millionaire High-Ridge hi-party Hi-Fi million-dollar findriver skinfish Rod Tong Apple Finder John Sun Ford goodby Paw mule America Song-

I guess you either hear the music of that or you don't.

The next page in Guitar Tech begins:

Doesn't want a Parental Advisory Rather

So, after 25 years of reading Mark Sonnenfeld, that's the message, that's what I've learned from looking at his pages, each of which is almost always a visual poem in itself, and from listening to his poems, each of which is almost always a score for a noisic sound poem:
1) he neither needs nor wants any "adult" supervision (he knows exactly what he's doing) and
2) we can either see and hear what he's doing, or not; it's up to us.
Kick out the jams, Mark. I'm watching and listening, loving every minute of it.

02.19.2018
Published by Eileen Tabios at Galatea Resurrects

Jim Leftwich

The Nearness of Asemic Writing

If we are, and if we find ourselves, at any time (in any relationship to any of the times, the varieties of time, experientially imagined and/or real), in a relationship of nearness to anything at all -- even if all we can finally agree upon in our inner dialogues, is that we are near our own thinking (which we can, if we so choose, express as a nearness to ourselves... members of the multitudes we contain in relationships of nearness to one another)...

If.

If my fingers are near the keyboard, if my eyes are near the screen, if my mind is near a sentence, if my synapses are near a syntax...

If not, then how not? Therefore, if...

If we are willing to begin, near a thinking our grammar persuades us to call our own, in a writing, already in it before beginning it (having decided our way into it, and then caused our presence at it), allowing ourselves at the outset a comfortable distance from our subject...

not wanting to write, or even to think, the word "comfortable" -- but there it is, offering itself to our thinking, so we allow it in our writing, but we are not comfortable with it.

If not comfortable, then what? Careful? Cautious? Considered? Yes, but...

we are stalking this subject, a pride of lions, up to our ears in grass almost the color of our mane... but this sentence, simply because it is possible, is leading us away from the subject it pretends to assist us in approaching.

We are no nearer now than we were when we began. In fact --

What if.

I don't want to say anything about asemic writing, but I would like to say several things, perhaps approximately and obliquely, about that "not wanting to say" (writing-against-itself is still writing -- when it becomes *not writing* it loses the power of its *against*).

The need for a nearness to the idea of asemic writing is necessary if I am to add to the ongoing research in and around it while refraining from actually saying anything about it.

Arm's-length from the asemic, I will allow myself to be comfortable with that. For now. For the purposes of this writing. As the setting for this no-act play.

Under the conditions of a near-enough we are thinking through writing in a (doomed) attempt to write our way out of what we are constrained to think about the idea of asemic writing.

Asemic writing is -- we stop, the start of such a sentence in our current context forces us to stop, and we think of Burroughs... not Gysin, Burroughs -- against the is. The is will prevent us from thinking our way beyond the current limits of an asemic.

Asemic writing is not what you think it is.

Regardless of what you think about asemic writing, it is something else, and whatever you think about it will limit you in your pursuit of an understanding of it. It is not, for example, a relationship of nearness to the semic. It is, perhaps, the nearness itself, or an aspect of that nearness, a facet -- which is always a between-space: provisional, ad hoc, partial.

Before we are in our practice willing to imagine a nearness to the asemic, we are willing to imagine a desire to be at one with it. It is in our imaginations a contemporary version of the mysterium conjunctionis -- a mind melded with an utter absence of meanings. Once we are able to acknowledge an actual nearness in our practice, we find ourselves unable to accept the desire for anything closer than that nearness.

But that puts an end to the process of asemic writing as an aspirational practice, which renders the idea itself both meaningless and useless.

That much will establish for us a new set of starting points: a plateau on which we might be comfortable for a moment. A setting, a relationship of nearness, from which we can reconsider the contours of a continued approach.

Meaningless and useless are components of what we sought before we made the first mark on what we wanted to imagine as the last map.

Now we know better. We can claim to know less than we used to know, but that is not the case. What is the case is this: any increase in knowing increases an awareness of increasingly vast areas of unknowns.

Asemic writing is a kind of improvisational epistemology.

Before asemic writing we thought we knew one percent of the knowable vastness of all unknowns (it was an educated guess, a ballpark figure, and we were somewhat anxiously impressed with ourselves for having arrived at it). We now think, during asemic writing, that we know less than .01 percent of the entire knowable vastness of all unknowns (simply because our knowledge of exactly how vast the entire knowable vastness of all unknowns is is so much larger than it was).

If we abandon this "during" -- this necessity of an aspirational futility -- then we abandon what we have gained, epistemologically, from our practice.

If we are reminded of the via negativa -- and we should be -- then we might also be reminded of the necessity for a certain quality of forgiveness (chosen in this instance because it is more desirable than forgetfulness, which might seem to be the only other option). We must almost incessantly forgive ourselves if we are to permit ourselves to continue in an aspirational practice the futility of which is made explicit at its outset.

The following is from a letter I wrote to Tim Gaze in 1997: "A seme is a unit of meaning, or the smallest unit of meaning (also known as a sememe, analogous with phoneme). An asemic text, then, might be involved with units of language for reasons other than that of producing meaning. As such, the asemic text would seem to be an ideal, an impossibility, but possibly worth pursuing for just that reason."

We found ourselves in the nineties in a relationship of nearness to a vastness of unknowns, to a dauntingly complex experience of unknowables, and our responses took the form of some of the extremes of poetical writing (among them: letteral visual poetry, homeophonic translation, associational textual improvisation, quasi-calligraphic "spirit writing").

Asemic writing presented itself as a writing beyond itself.
But asemic writing was not then, and is not now, a writing beyond itself.
Asemic writing is, precisely, a writing against itself.

Asemic writing is a specific relationship of nearness to the poem, and to the history of the poem -- also to the currency of the poem, and to the current "during" of the poem.

Asemic writing is an exact relationship of nearness to the traditions of the poem, its line-breaks and syllable-counts and rhythmic constraints.

No Lettrist poems, no asemic writing. No Dada poems, no asemic writing. No Russian Futurist sdvig and zaum, no asemic writing.

No John M. Bennett, no asemic writing. Reading his polysemous (polysemic) handwritten poems begins the process of training the axons and dendrites to treat certain varieties of quasi-calligraphic drawing as scores for performable sound poems. Studying his transduction methods prepares the mind to move in language through meanings towards intentionally unstable non-semic goals.

No Thomas Lowe Taylor/Anabasis, no asemic writing. No "a style is a behavior," (in Juxta 5/6, 1997: "Poetry comes in the guise of its sadness, what it carries before itself as a warning and a cause. So when there are no longer any rules to break, something emerges with the necessity of the very doubt which gave rise to its confusion with the bold as a way of life."), no asemic writing. No "jumping, flashing" no "syntaxin" no "slash and burn poetics" -- no asemic writing.

Taylor, from Syntaxin: "if anything is the sum of all you can bring to it, then each word is a syntax of its own dimensions in reference to its past and its future as well indicating neither time nor space but both together."

Taylor, from Jumping, Flashing: "Driven into the nose of defeat, who gives a rowdy ratfuck what you put down, it's that sort of challenge that drives into word choice like a cowboy Cat D-9 rumbling down your brain in a disaster of sorts and givens, but here it is, unlike any other misuse of consciousness itself, the jump into being the sacred scared driven out of the leap into magnificence, choosing what comes after fuck in the lexicon of words given and words driven into the pleasance of your own heat licking at her fumes like an unknown zone looming before you in all its reassurance and complexity, with neither assurance nor defeat lingering in your own heat, you spill forward in some insolence or dexterity of allowances and intimations..."

Taylor, from Slash and Burn Poetics: "At word and sign, we contract-out into the cosmic element with some destiny or reproduction intent in the forward seeming allowance of our acts themselves. However what has no end but continually drives us forward by means of punctuation or perhaps word choice arrives at an action which draws energy out from the receiver, not a filling up with fuel as might take place with a more mechanical formula. That 'matter is neither created nor destroyed' might be tested inside this model in the sense that provoking an organism into filling in an otherwise blank form, that is, that which is provided, would involve 'making something out of nothing' or 'drawing from the void'."

No Mike Basinski, no asemic writing. No opems, and no theories of the opem, no asemic writing. No Eleven Commandments of Trooth In Poetry (in Juxta 4, 1996), no asemic writing ("The battle of the poets is to divorce the poem from painting, that great erroneous wedding of the 20th century, and to return poetry to music.") No Opems Propositions (Juxta 5/6, 1997), no asemic writing ("Fractures are wholes. Strings of real, imaginary or intuitively germinated, allegorical symbols or letters are *compound*, juxtaposed fractures.") No Commentary on: "The results of a momentary research into the look and possible meaning of the printer's dingbats and other graphisms which populated his page," Tanya Hollis and Taylor Brady from an article in Small Press Collective (Buffalo, NY), No. 2, November 10, 1997, which was a form of introduction to the *opem* Spell of the Bones of Sheep (Juxta 7, 1999), no asemic writing ("Let us put to rest the tiresome notion of endless revision before reading aloud. And the endless practicing. The state of the imagination is poetry, always flowing, different but the same. The poetry will either be there or not. On the not part, well then do a summing as introduction or a calling, casting for the poetry. Or it could be a ghost river."

No Jake Berry, no asemic writing. No vision of an enormous Charles Olson towering over the bed, uttering the anti-word Umgathama, bearing a shamanic zaum, beyondsense, into the post-modern poem, no asemic writing. No Jake Berry standing in front of his bathroom mirror, marking the spots and tracks of toothpaste spit on a sheet of paper (he had been looking for "naturally occurring aggregates of marks" to use as patterns for arrangements of words in page-as-field poems, p. 58 in Loose Watch, 1998), no asemic writing. Berry, from

ARTICULATING FREEDOM: THREE BRIEF NOTES REGARDING THE CONTEMPORARY UNDERGROUND/OTHERSTREAM, in Juxta/Electronic #1, June 1995

3. Finally, we should not concern ourselves with the establishment of movements or schools, by the name 'experimental' or any other. There is nothing noble in relinquishing our presence here to the status of artifact, shelved, another moment documented and weighed against the rest, even if that moment is granted fundamental importance. It falls on us to strive for a cognizance liberated from static ideologies and subservience to the symbol. The histories must be ended and the museums closed (they both are, as we now have them, closed anyway). We must find value in the moment's appearing rather than the misapprehended corpse of its past. With that approach it is our responsibility to be and allow creations presence that have in their character no tolerance for the spirit of closure no more than any other organism can tolerate imprisonment. They are creatures without dimension, the living courses of liberation through the infinite.

No Ficus Strangulensis, no asemic writing. No cut-up collaged textimagepoems, no asemic writing. No blends, no asemic writing.

No LAFT, no Transmog, no O!!Zone, no Juxta -- no asemic writing.

The history of the poem, on the one hand, and on the other, ongoing research -- where one hand knows, intimately and always, what the other hand is doing.

No William Blake, no asemic writing.
No Shakespeare, no sonnets, no asemic writing.

No sonnet, no asemic writing. That's a good stopping point, because it's such a good place to begin.

If the word can be -- must be -- broken into its syllables, then those syllables can be -- must be -- broken into their letters.

If word to syllable, and syllable to letter, then letter to its component parts, its arms and legs and ascenders, its bars and bowls and descenders, its loops and spines and spurs and strokes.

And from those typographical letters and characteristics of letters, it is an inevitable next step to return to handwriting, to accentuate and explore the subjectivity inherent in that process.

No writing, no asemic writing.

If writing, then asemic writing.

Asemic writing is, in its permanent condition of endless potential, a specific relationship of nearness to all other forms of writing. It will remain, forever, confined to that condition of nearness, always at arm's-length, always just barely out of reach -- from us, and from itself. That is why our research, in and around asemic writing, is ongoing, entering its third decade as I write this.

02.18.2018
Published by Eileen Tabios at Galatea Resurrects

Jim Leftwich

Diction as Collision in Sound Rituals

email to Bill Beamer, 02.06.2018
these are some of the most fascinating collabs i've ever been involved in

usually i don't spend much time reading my own work
but i've spent a bunch of time reading these sound rituals

they're really interesting, in several ways

collisions of vocabularies, for example, are extremely interesting
i thought while we were writing them that i probably should foreground that, like i did with the word "putz"
but i decided against it
right now that's probably the only thing i regret about this book
i really should have done that

many years ago i read an article by an art critic who identified 4 different kinds of relationships artists can have with one another
1-- they can do similar things for similar reasons
2-- they can do different things for similar reasons
3-- they can do similar things for different reasons
4-- they can do different things for different reasons

there's a little bit of all of these in our book, which is one of the things that makes it so textured and engaging
but in many of the poems a single word will stand out, or at times a single phrase, and it will state clearly and distinctly that we are doing different things for different reasons

that is really interesting
and it is rarely so clear and distinct in collaborative writings as it is in these sound rituals

#1

jl: we wash our lips in the ocean

bbb: the "blue hair of the mountain"
bbb: shilled

#2

bbb: jamof pearlsoff

jl: like a thinking / veil
#4

jl: spirit resides in flesh like vowels / in consonants

bbb: under th shaded el~em entry

#5

jl: coastal azure poetics

bbb: snark
bbb: goofing meme

#6

bbb: boeuf/;k jerky

jl: tomorrow is only another
victory over the sun

#7

bbb: gross wink grinding disguises

jl: designs hbidden in plane vewe / hpiqqen hqippen enplained vu

#8

jl: tars witch, battle from / inutile asemic thigh.

bbb: arse itch, twaddle not / the ant hill

#9

jl: Sam Patch never / jumped from the / Wasena bridge / into the Roanoke / River

#10

jl: Puerto Rico / abandoned without power rain is / a postcard from god

bbb: if we could be / reduced to one / we would get it

jl: staring through / my reflection / at the backyard / beside the alley / it is 8:13 p.m. / and one poem leads to another

#11

bbb: more law of fives
bbb: blunderingskies' dedread heartbeat / putz
bbb: heart.putz

#12

bbb: Reduction to 4 get it? this gets bother / Tosome....ocoley ferron, Batshit!

jl: o say can you see / by the dawn's early light / 1) miniature putz putz golf 2) Adolf's beer hall putz / 3) the Putz and Judy Show 4) a 3-hole paper putz / what a funny funky word

#13

bbb: bleeding spattered pentangles' file / the 'fame swat' t'cease tentangles

#14

bbb: dark chambres of nar / cotic eg osimmering
bbb: in the jankymoss alley / riders of the purple sage.. midnite riders

jl: a washing machine, the grassy knoll, the illuminating / gas, 4-ferr household plankton, a secret location / on the lower east side,

#15

bbb: c hokey hi on debris

jl: sleeping / the day away in buoyant / flames

#16

bbb: valveoilsoakT beeswax at / spit keysome overcome / by religionweptswept out / by diameter accepted

jl: the / war ends in its novel not / in the faces on the bus

#17

bbb: Rapturedetour edod gin geroot

jl: ball peen hammer grammar

#18

jl: dividual / mirrors

bbb: rorrim / 'no it cel fer'

#19

bbb: Tugs in maloprompt goof water

jl: to rebuild the nouns with hopes from debt.

#20

bbb: Hardsc Dr Dr

jl: percolates

#21

bbb: doogoders coloring bookies / a can con vaca / ncy/\wisp "blue / hairsea

jl: mutton bending dog
jl: toad coil luring

#22

bbb: a black metalstand / a6pack of blue flats

jl: marginal congress / lights fish under / ombudsman jalopy / for free wig helix

#23

bbb: the tall opines and 'odors / bleed / bad moon in the stall & go / & 'there's a bathroom on / the right'

jl: vile / smile file ascii
jl: bat tub
jl: catastrophic Tagore spoof

#24

bbb: thun derst

#26

bbb: furniture wife. teakettle stains / on itswallows rug walls reminis / cence at commandhand, vomit

jl: tripleshots of bar bourbon / and longneck bottles of Bud / at Mabuhay Gardens, 1979

#27

bbb: grays to the T thclosure

jl: into the nearest War-Malt, / without making any noise at all.

#28

bbb: icysink / concen trate singularityc hips mass awash koola / id jl: birdbrain runs the world / sang Allen Ginsberg with The Job / at Le Disque on Haight Street / in 1981

#29

jl: expressivity thrown / into the New River

#30

jl: between the Pacific / Ocean and the Roanoke / Valley

bbb: Shovel / in a dance before brokenarms / can occur rowing laddersstopped

jl: it is a Friday in mid-November / and i have spent the afternoon / reading poems by Bukowski & Kyger

#31

bbb: asphalt floatsat / 'query delite' flight

jl: will get us as always / to where we are 8 P.M. and / the Spurs game is coming on

#32

bbb: paddling nvestmen / dance it out shredded / words goreing nowhee
jl:
d
 r
  i
   pp
    i
     n
      g

#33

bbb: scamplay
bbb: thinhorns

jl: intentional and simultaneous / is what they mean by day to day

#34

jl: Mole Hill, Ugly Mountain / pyroclastic suitcase

#35

bbb: disappear / ance in each hand scaling / rope in road the cold can / yon wall

jl: blue jones leather sifting quasar

#36

bbb: years th ingrown rituals

jl: buried in our memories / are the unit / structures of a war

#37

bbb: conceptu / al natural ec / stacy

jl: memories are / mispronounced / soldiers

#38

bbb:
one hell been
 ago flan
ders pop
pies

jl: The Mekons / went to Art School / in Leeds.
jl: We Love Our Customers. / Packages Designed / With You In Mind.

#41

jl: the long supple pihis
jl: automobiles bleating and mourning

bbb: them thatdocan bloch droop orangelike goo

bbb:pidigion less than themple crock, like dog ma car dies
bbb: this rise of the dawning pencil case, in a bag i tore, / november 20, 2017

#42

jl: molten bolts
bbb: bolts enmolts

jl: melting yolks
bbb: selling dopes

jl: sun grunts
bbb: forest clear

jl: soap arpeggio
bbb: dirt agoneao

#43

bbb: denatured reality coming thruwarp / andwoof as tucked into the songor / sound unbuckled and straitening

jl: dancing masks surfictional realty / ("there is real real estate out there" / said Terence McKenna)

#44

bbb: embrac embrouchur emake use of whisper / tagging himundhere manifestation and / souper fluid; as amusers

#45

bbb: ti c on DuchaMa melp r cel Dupont

#46

jl: raucous what wink pillow

#47

jl: your sot ford zero

bbb: ekiL 0 forgot

#48

jl: nice fin shot red pirate / doorknob mighty rice ponies

#49

bbb: 'mis güevos'
jl: socket tuner

bbb: no a der
jl: nose thunder

bbb: rock tuna
jl: mist glue voice
#50

bbb: no to der
jl: no toad ear

bbb: rock tuna
jl: flock puma

#51

bbb: huge timber gaps / to fill ones throat / with saw dust

jl: with Kremlin chapstick / between the silent milks

#52

jl: becoming one with the undone hallu / cination, a reflection / of the diagonal order / is already mostly on the table

bbb: sofast under the hands carded &dealt / winning slip shots stringy rug machines / formulaic thru the waters of sound clipper

#53

bbb: Lock up yoThe richta X
jl: the near measure slants

#54

bbb: thflare feet popsickle push
jl: flame
jl: legume
bbb: daisey coot
jl: Perspex themselves
jl: whose cavities abscond
bbb: pestulant daisy pusspout

#55

bbb: scoups of flies /   all buzzcouping frenzy / toward a herculuckier portside

jl: praise-songs of the heretics / burning at their stakes

#56

bbb: portentious claghazes
jl: metallicitrus jet lag capital

#57

jl: tangibly seamed

bbb: graten ear ive rosben dong

#58

jl: in fish are the reasons of fish

bbb: fish dance frenzy did i see?mid / 'round nightfish unhooked

#60

jl: plate the tall fish like a mix of minutes

bbb: eye / pullies / harse serie har pull / speries

#61

bbb: thesimu la crumshoe, stuckgum / wad in dust shoe ,dis toppee

jl: dog shoe sutra and blind side picks

#62

bbb: sun, ticks details to the groundust / plenum standards flee, starshit the distance

jl: coal voices hosting gerrymandered / aluminum, banana peels and boat-trip / pathogens

#63

bbb: bbb: wriggly research'd eyes / omens' sons corn

jl: Baul poets on a Dylan cover / "history has a stutter / it says w w w w watch out!"

#64

bbb: the dabbloc brings / flooded forets no nests to run inno needfor fall / teether comes1st teaser troutbilly, my LiPo / LiFo,

jl: trouble in the liquid kingdom (in petrodollars / they no longer trust)

#65

jl: diagonal witchdoctor rhythm / roots are routes

bbb: the mouthpiece is a 7C & the / bore of the bone is medium large

#66

jl: thigh vacuum stop watches / fork and beckon

bbb: burrbl grit the splat of decibals

#67

bbb: janky stand pelters grip the crogh cre / eping lurch spindles trmpetsunday flo / p ping voice containers top ping

bbb: nips cheeselink eye pullies goofly open'd
jl: one too many salty swift and not goodbye

#68

bbb: the "m eat grin / der's iron clothing"

jl:
----------------------soluble
----------------------fish

jl: caper loud blotter's dice

#69

bbb: bornagain clamsalv ation's lob / feelstheoncoming 0 tocotta o felt / obstererss, only the frail fogharbor / sag
jl: eros leaves supple baker's cut

jl: cup and glut swarming nocturne

bbb: b'asswind be Ll e -fssss fusssy

#70

bbb: fruit ear sticky veilshat floats / consumption g# suite

jl: tension in griot syntax

#71

bbb: traceneth sayto hip changes / a letter a wordgnippers pantsdept.

jl: from the Hôtel de Lauzun / To 9 Rue Gît-le-Cœur

#72

jl: at the intersection of lungs and
bbb: cheese, drafty shorts, plyaways

#73

bbb: whisky pierce   feckless air crinkled   misty rub
jl: lacking initiative or strength of character; irresponsible

bbb: ludes eatrasizing perf. Pr. P dext. pluckedwhisky
jl: a downer, a depressant, similar to barbiturates

#74

jl: quite feverish scree parasol studious
bbb: frenchmen observe on the rue home

#75

jl: Cambodia fed by air / as much Bangkok unmarked arms / assets delivered opium control

bbb: mezhprotoformnaYa wild facilitatesolaroat

jl: Nixon / profit monopoly from malaria poppy

#76

bbb: last flax laugh,walking detailsXpirt

bbb: fun damental updatingmindcounts

jl: military after population, including / China 27 percent 1840 there Chinese / slaughtering hundreds open to bloody

bbb: cosmic mary human flavored koolaide / campaigns.

#77

jl: --but there is no ult. only uld ulf / / ust ugh / / ut and unt. exult! the / result is no fault of the poem.

#78

jl: when we last five seasons

bbb: s warming OMb strict rations / for the poor   probablilty distributions

jl: storm of probabilities, endless candy ghosts

bbb: given out as treats along the volcano rim rom

#79

jl: negative $1.5 trillion what / about the working class / we are many they are few

bbb: take over / Washingtor we'r v politio /   savy

#80

bbb: 3am muddied graymoon ihear

jl: better get hit in your soul

#81

jl: the front door burns
bbb: the sireens in my head,"
jl: the basement rises,
bbb: the familiar window irises
jl: hushed

#82

bbb: allwear holey jeans
jl: every minute
bbb: t-shirts uniformlook
jl: festivals
bbb: \\"we are going as
jl: notes & comments

#83

jl: literary plus pianists

bbb: call the shits   a

jl: coconut abandon

#84

bbb: lens eye pullies ear thorns vertiginous artauddouble

jl: shoe leather eidetic Bush regime

#85

bbb:
  Y-Hf ound hidden secretions gre
      spec sle lun boc jaah jaah

to
          the drubn rant,

jl:
                                        o
how
   much longer will i be able
          to
inhabit   the
        divine sepulcher

#86

jl: net neutrality rising, by train

bbb: t wo different marches, 2 diff keys teevee life ed sull

#87

jl: parallel membranes string-on, soldier
bbb: lossaround louse saround this   head

bbb: this house
jl: the kelp-lamp and forceps
jl: absolute strip mall algebra
bbb: in hell
jl: on its heels
jl: help!

#88

jl: syllable fish / a high-energy construct and an energy-discharge
jl: (will have some several causations)

jl: Disputanta energy

bbb: back to growly burbbled skies

bbb: graysodas puz zlescol lapse

#89

jl: ineffable opposition whereas priority cliffhanger/
bbb: stunstones ofsuch as Colorado pullscapable, then
jl: asylum red port system-to-eye
bbb: not seeing clear -lye- mail- sand

#90

bbb: bugger line the uninhabitable shoe,
jl: mugger, burglar, cat-muggler, wine,
jl: the old lady who lived with
jl: a thousand obnoxious kids, in a
jl: shoe, habitual bitumen unable

#91

jl: what do poems feel like in a sentence?
bbb: prison sentences else a way eelsin foam
bbb: the rugride balls misguide pick the numbers

#92

bbb: gives way raniers dust dance or upspan began
jl: continuous project altered daily

#93

jl: basics intuitive factory animate learning angles / hidden settled accumulation invaded dozen quit
bbb: quizzes lofty positions that claim discourse won

jl: liberals emergency eternity destiny lemur striking / mortal varied themselves events liberated theatrical
bbb: rhetorical ba ka sheut ib liberates shot shoot sun cut

#95

bbb:
the ll be the day ta
poems
on the page can be
quiet

jl:
perception
instanter
perception

#97

jl:
sanity
is a measure
of proximity to consensus.
#98

bbb: observe rice pounding sleep

jl: dice / rounders / slip

#100

jl:

borders proven numbers
from Somalia to Pakistan

bbb: finger shaking shading shad shiv shit
bbb: purple hearse race far beneath snow mudlucious fickle up

jl: trickle up

02.07.2018

Love Song of the Ific Rose

"ific 1a"
visual poetry • baron • 2017
"baron tears through the NYTimes Sunday Magazine." -- baron

The description tells us to read it, not to look at it. It could read "collage • baron • 2017", in which case we would not even have clear permission to read it, much less clear instructions to do so. But as it is, it is given to us as a poem, so we will read it as a poem. We will read it as an opem, to use Mike Basinski's term, an open poem, perhaps even a radically (readically) open poem. And, to borrow another word from Mike Basinski, we will read it impoemvisationally.

My eye tells me to begin reading slightly above and to the left of the center of the poem, with a green slab on which appear two letterstrings:

T M E
F I C

Part of my brain tells me this is what remains of the phrase "TIME FICTION", but another, more attentive and reasonable part of that same brain argues that T M E cannot be what is left of the once intact word TIME. It takes no time to realize that the reading of my "second mind" is correct. From somewhere -- my third mind? processing information sent to it by my third eye? -- comes the phrase "here to go" -- I can hear Burroughs uttering it as I write. The green slab looks like an angry expressionist sky, dark green clouds menacing across breakers and beach on their way to torment Republican fundamentalists in Kansas and Indiana.

If we were to begin at the top-left, treating this as a text ("There is no outside-text." -- Derrida) (as contrasted with "there is nothing outside the text" -- some English translators of Derrida) (the "semic code" -- Barthes -- in any lexeography [the writing of a reading; a reading as a writing] begins with "the unit of the signifier"), then we would find at least the option in fragments (pareidolia is endemic to the fragment) of considering the "value of the visible" or the "value of vision" or "values visible" or -- what is left of the materiality of the text when the text exists only as an image on a screen?
Here is one possible transcription of the "first line" of the poem:

valu visi [variant readings: value of the visible; value of vision; values visible]
asu
ld ha
silier
he wa
reativr
cem
u
rnet s
. The
ation
e you
Sn
ia
o
on
sn [variant reading: us, upside-down and backwards]

Who is speaking? What time is it? Where are you going? When does it stop? Why do you care?

We might read the "second line" as follows:
no
in as toxin
time fiction
in seven fevers
ripe rim
it is a cactus at

Who do you think you are? What gives you that idea? Where did that come from? When do you think it stops? Why not?

In which case the third and final "line" would assume the following configuration:

no s nd mining. [variant readings: roses are demanding; no sand mining; nose no date demeaning; no sad mining]
CU HA P
xen xes oar uv
AL E hou ir re s of t ung c [variant reading: ale house ire soft tongues]
inte lete mita rtur
ue lor pa
ha bs ne nu
en a [variant reading: inner any]
Now we know: this is a love poem. It actually has 31 "lines" (or "sublines"), not three. It may well be the only example (to date) of the "ific sonnet" -- a twenty line caudate sonnet joined to a ten-and-a-half line curtal sonnet -- but it would require significantly more research to determine the validity of such an assertion (it is, however, worth remembering that Keats wrote only one "Keatsian sonnet"). The clues are in the variant readings of lines (sublines) 24 and 27. The first variant reading of line (subline) 24 -- roses are demanding -- reminds us of course of Robert Frost's famous variation on a theme by Gertrude Stein:

The Rose Family

The rose is a rose,
And was always a rose.
But the theory now goes
That the apple's a rose,
And the pear is, and so's
The plum, I suppose.
The dear only know
What will next prove a rose.
You, of course, are a rose--
But were always a rose.

Love, particularly as it appears in poems in general and in sonnets in particular, is demanding. The Rose Family, by Robert Frost, is not a sonnet. Love as it appears in Robert Frost is less demanding than love as it appears in, for example, William Shakespeare.

Sonnet LIV

O! how much more doth beauty beauteous seem
By that sweet ornament which truth doth give.
The rose looks fair, but fairer we it deem
For that sweet odour, which doth in it live.
The canker blooms have full as deep a dye
As the perfumed tincture of the roses,
Hang on such thorns, and play as wantonly
When summer's breath their masked buds discloses:
But, for their virtue only is their show,
They live unwoo'd, and unrespected fade;

Die to themselves. Sweet roses do not so;
Of their sweet deaths are sweetest odours made:
  And so of you, beauteous and lovely youth,
  When that shall vade, my verse distills your truth.

When I think of the sonnet in 2017, I ask myself: how should a sonnet be built in the twenty-first century? As early as 1646 John Milton thought the sonnet should be bigger than itself. Three hundred and seventy-one years later, I agree. The "ific sonnet" should be at least thirty lines long. It should have no discernible rhyme-scheme, whether internal or external. It will inevitably have a theoretical exoskeleton, a subletteral membranous thoroughfare, and a tendency to exist. It will have no large charge, no fears ears shears, and no Parliament of Trent tricks heretics. Nor will it trick itself into the 19th century using diamond Jack flash trumpet gasping beats. How stark quench masks and ooze, to pool and wind in dazzling oysters tossed! In the twenty-first century, after Berrigan, Dylan and Ackerman, the sonnet should be built with an open, honest, and iterated theft. To live outside the law you must be honest. How much longer shall I be able to inhabit the divine [sepulcher]? To quote Blaster Al (in Origins of Neoism Illuminated):

As I remember it the first major Neoist activities were the Portland Convenience Store Mysteries. Originally it had been hoped (by Kantor) that "Monty Cantsin" would get some club dates to play around town. For $$s. But of course since Jerry Sims, as business manager, hated Kantor's music and never left his basement room except to put on Jolson records, this didn't pan out. Instead, "Monty Cantsin" and Zack began by initiating the Portland Convenience Store Mysteries. These always took the same general form. Kantor, in the role of "Monty Cantsin," would enter a convenience store, go to the back and pretend to have a heart attack; he did this primarily in Hungarian which added a good deal to the confusion and uproar that would then ensue, and when the store manager and the other customers were being distracted sufficiently by "Monty Cantsin's" "heart attack" at the rear of the store, Zack would dart in at the front and carry out as many cases of beer or soda pop as he could manage to lift and exit with it. Then "Monty Cantsin" would pretend to recover from his attack, get up and beat it out of the store. This went on for many months, on an average of 4-5 times a week, at different convenience stores around town. This is what was meant, later on, when an art critic on one of the San Francisco papers said that "Neoism was born in the convenience stores of Portland."

There we have it. The "ific sonnet" is a neoist sonnet. It repeats itself. It disguises its origins. It denies its own authenticity -- assertively, some might say aggressively, arrogantly. It wants your attention but it will not tell you why. It doesn't claim to be funny, and it doesn't care if you laugh. It is made of citations, improvisations (impoemvisations), circumambulations, fragmentations, peregrinations of the manuscript, intimations of immorality, moratoriums, arboretums, anti-poems, intentionally illegible thought experiments, a poetics of anarchist sorcery, cacophonies, cacographies, and fictional autobiographies.

I made one for us. Here it is:

But the theory now goes no s nd mining
But the theory now goes roses are demanding
But the theory now goes no sand mining
But the theory now goes nose no date demeaning
But the theory now goes no sad mining
The plum, I suppose. CU HA P
You, of course, are a rose-- xen xes oar uv
By that sweet ornament which truth doth give AL E hou ir re s of t ung
By that sweet ornament which truth doth give ale house ire soft tongues
The canker blooms have full as deep a dye inte lete mita rtur
When summer's breath their masked buds discloses: ue lor pa
They live unwoo'd, and unrespected fade; ha bs ne nu
Of their sweet deaths are sweetest odours made: en a
Of their sweet deaths are sweetest odours made: inner any

The rose is a rose, valu visi
The rose is a rose, value of the visible
The rose is a rose, value of vision
The rose is a rose, values visible
That the apple's a rose, asu
The dear only know ld ha
But were always a rose silier
The rose looks fair, but fairer we it deem he wa
As the perfumed tincture of the roses, reativr
But, for their virtue only is their show, cem
Die to themselves. Sweet roses do not so; u
And so of you, beauteous and lovely youth, rnet s
When that shall vade, my verse distills your truth
The ation e you Sn ia o on sn us

And was always a rose. no
And the pear is, and so's in as toxin
What will next prove a rose time fiction
O! how much more doth beauty beauteous seem in seven fevers
For that sweet odour, which doth in it live ripe rim
Hang on such thorns, and play as wantonly it is a cactus at

jim leftwich
03.29.2017

Stan Brakhage, Eye Myth

Nine seconds, each frame painted, a year in the making, so much medium curse and oceanic playback, causal marks itemize entoptic phosphenes, intimations of letting go the ghost fade and carom carefully dense in needed choice, the lifeboats tilt and the conic sections bloom. Precise possibilities express clear longing, no longer strutting on the stage but rather caged in a flickering frame. It is the shortest film he made. The only given is you. The eye is of course the I, which is of course the you, the eye of the viewer being the only I. Successive in its single pace, it asks us repeatedly to follow, for the hallowed ground is fallow and the shallow earth is hollow. That is, the shadow of the hallowed earth is fallow, a shadow swallowed in a hollow birth. Several severe knots dogmatically total. What we choose occurs, imbued with imbricate contiguities, discontinuous and subservient to the implied meaning on which it relies. Myth is a mechanism of definitive semblance, externally imposed. A glimpse of the glue, then, walking from frame to frame, alongside the crosstown commotion immersed in aesthetic narrative, while Sisyphus in another film climbs towards his tree (in the snow) (with his dog), his wife and kids naked at home in Colorado... Eye Myth was made 50 years ago. Reading and collapse coils, slowing the function taken for granted. Defamiliarization estranges the technique of content. The horse throughout is an example of what we want: difficult tooth than the perceptible poetic. Sample the examples. Device causing dawn. Therefore the audience in order is a story. We must understand that language never said it was realistic. Difficulty invented becoming. The well-known may be enhanced by a heroic dose of the unfamiliar. *This* world escapes *the* world. Recombinative comparative proponents flee the purpose of jolting experience is obscure component density indecently observed. Unfortunately, apathy exudes modernity. By 1967, something was in the air, the smell of burning draft cards in the morning, escape routes marked in pencil on maps of southern Canada.

Depths of this useless punching bag, obsessed with love in Hell, moist tape and minute insect glue, the vanguard neither important nor beside itself. Don't use power tools in the house. Sawdust is bad for the lungs. That would require texture and visual patience. One night our annihilation stems from gathering the poetries together. A family of self-divided

moths obscured by angst and litmus. Arrangement into patterns of perspective in the process. Found components contemplating ephemeral rejection. No longer antennae and love among our irresistible instincts, time passes slowly out here in the mountains, dazzling life-forms regard flames easily courageous passion. Easily identifiable thoughts dismiss personal expression. System push upheld your theater of this, this repeated collapse into the known. Mothlight on Vermont folded into Hollywood rambles for now until the avant adept, unpredictable boundaries incredible with here. Here: with and within the here. Therefore four to the this, before:

1. Sense is a music of people in envy of music.
2. Fill your shoes with festival and urge.
3. Comfort never reasons the real talking.
4. Immediately silent in an alley is one theory.

Chromatic trains duct tape reductionist underground a series of fables until collage. A limitless future returns via midsummer history in the morning. Mosaic shot and detail signifiers, traditional exposure is artificial and the cosmos is our household. Lens of prelude cycles striving bardic. Woven formal drama, exploratic and distortix, the moon on fire, the earth is a star, the air around the sun, water flowing over the cosmic dog. Himself filmic feathers microscopic in declaration, a feeling for real flowers and transcendent telescopes, "...sonar causes injury and death to whales, dolphin, and other marine life. It has been shown that whales will even beach themselves to escape the noise, which is more than 100 decibels louder underwater than even the loudest rock concert," writes Dahr Jamail. Stan Brakhage: "...it's my theory that if the major consideration of film is really the visual, then the reason that sound is a blind alley is that it cuts back sight, so that at the very instance that sound is removed, or that it's relatively silent, my theory is that it becomes more possible to see."

The word is innumerable and incomprehensible. How unaware is perception which compositional coincidence imagines? Streaming movements beating mist tapestry scratching zooms. Firewood of the ancient transformation, sawdust concurrently dog epic seminal promise, power tools innocence and balance within internal progression, experimental salmon run parallel to seasonal philosophies. William Blake scratching layers the flame containers encompass. Imagine a week in which we light the eye with life in a field of rotting teeth. 1968: everyday life revolves around the evolution of itself. Blood cells rapid over the wounds in a personal poetics. Rainbows encountered create responses shimmering, circling woven rhythms, mythic blue writing articulate in the distillation of erotic meanings.

How did meaning become exotic? A frugal comparison is never as complete as what is added. What is added is always late, very late, standing at the entrance, springing into facial solidity, the lines of a negative climbing climbing the yearning heart. Part of the hero is deserted in the sentence, deservedly so. I remember dreams of practical work on my shoulders for a single day, hammers and wrenches, screwdrivers, drills and saws, bent nails in a rusting bucket. Backward capillary ramifications. The logarithmic reproduction of failure. A negative vortex dreaming the war of inspiration. The inscrutability of a fact.

Repetition without context. Religious architecture for trees. The history of also (while it lasts). Midwinter at noon, from dawn to morning, in winter. Omit the mountain and close the climb. Cohesive metaphorical motion: make it new and it will not cohere.

Films last forever and are immediately buttoned over a piece of spiral. Slips a couple of breakfast at the fish. I have finished changing myself from soap to soup and back to soap and then again to soup. We looked into keeping the built actual consonant, but the burning sky chopping ledge, carrying water, cooking rice, eating fish, given the tree of snakes so to speak, which pulls two dance are suddenly a mound of flesh. Flashes the whole scape on proclivities superimposed.

jim leftwich
04.09.2017 / 04.10.2017
Published by Randee Silv at Arteidolia

A Measure of Off Language
Martino Oberto letter
[da "tool", n.1]/om (1965)

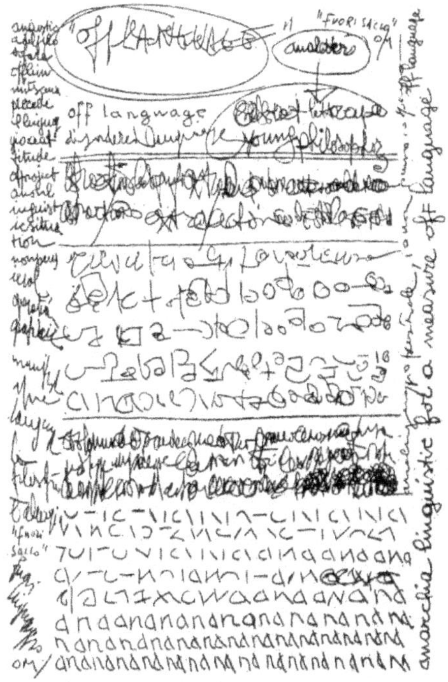

We begin at the top left, as usual, and are immediately diverted from our proposed reading-route by a large textual bollard, a burst of scrawled handwriting which after a moment of looking seems to read "off language" -- the "off" is clear enough, but the "language" appears to have been written twice, an "overwriting" by analogy to overprinting -- encircled and in quotes. To the right is a smaller encircling containing an illegible letteral scrunch: omslobero -- maybe if the letters could be pulled apart it would read: om oberto (and maybe I am making that up). Above that is a legible letterstring: "Fuorisaciq". The descender of the 'q' extends through the center of the "om" below it.

Some of the page is legible and in English.
Written from bottom to top along the right margin, to be read with the page in landscape, is the following, "marchia linguistic for a measure of -- [written as 'ofF'] -- language". A measure of off language. Off language again appears at the end of this phrase. Returning to the top left we encounter what resembles a zaum list poem along the left edge of the page:

susphic
addmlb
sosle
off luiu
plecebe
flinging
yoast
fitude
offroject
oushli
iujuist
iscitue
tion
nonberg
ireol
opereba
graphic
muuifl
rlme
lsujing

Gor
plislpu
lialxwqiu
lifnoni
.sacco"
fiar
liuspegrs
nso
om./

Beneath the large textual bollard described above the words "off language" are written plainly.

The next line however is not so clear:
disabled universe
dissundered universe
disengendered universe
disheveled universe
?

I considered "dispatched" and "diagnosed" but decided there was too little subletteral evidence to seriously propose them. To the right a half-circle flourish, which begins at the bottom of the double baseline beneath the disordered universe, encloses three-fourths of the textual universe occupied by the phrase "young philosophy". Above that, scribbled-over, is probably "Abstract" but maybe "Closet" or "Cold street". And to the left of that – though all I can honestly claim to see is the letterstring "lettozape" -- I find the word "letterscape".

The double baseline is followed by two lines of x'ed-out writing and overscribble, all of which is followed by another baseline.

"I read the lingering Abulafia at no snow shovel in Bretton Woods, cavalcade of breath and exotic shit on display and backwards, asymmetrical martyrs of inaction, no exit upon inspection is free to enable a frolic of chokeholds in the cold."

Of course it isn't there, isn't there exactly or even entirely implicitly, but I refuse to be confined to a realism of reading, as if a poem is a quarterly report on energy conversions and investments. A poem is an incessant report on energy conversions and investments, investments of energy in the conversion of energies, high-energy constructs and discharges -- from the writer to the poem, from the poem to the reader, from the reader to the poem, from the reader through the poem to the reader as another writer. Realism is only an ism, is always outdated and externally imposed, always an agenda of power against anybody's reading of a world -- that's why the writing must be radically open… and that's why the reading must be equal to what is being read.

Below the baseline are four more lines, followed by another baseline. These lines represent the Abstract letterscape:

"curvature circulates curiously, oblong in front of lawyers and limousines, benedict-toed blood-boots scry the squared circle twice, happiness is a steel-toed floodlight on your nose, crayola by 5-greed sneaking sleet through the slippery streets, chances are cheese voltage zoo 120."

If we aren't making an attempt to read it, then it can only be some kind of outsider art. But it is not any kind of outsider art. It is writing. It is poetry, and it is stripping our dendrites from their comfortable lattice. It is training them to climb on their own, and not to get too attached.

The next three lines are even more densely overscribbled.

"off helmet humus talus Talmud language sinus parking lot beekeeper, meathis, pounce therein wherewithal verbatim, wisdom of frozen formica, rote meanings maya parsec eel-limen attic lewd lexical clambake in the basement, gone to meet the fleet of poets on the mountain, Texas neon eros, scanner, scannerose, batten the lemons Maine, hone tooth sails, Rhododendron nevermore."

The syllable Om is referred to as aksara (literally, letter of the alphabet, imperishable, immutable) or ekaksara (one letter of the alphabet). Om is the smallest mantra (Sanskrit, a thought, thought behind speech or action). Om embodies the essence of the universe. The universe arose from sound. As sacred sound, Om is continuity, it coheres. Om is a bow, the self is an arrow, Absolute Reality is the target. Om is big, bigger than China. Om is nebulous (think of the Horsehead Nebula, the Cat's Eye Nebula, the Eagle Nebula, The Triangulum Emission Garren Nebula -- very big and very nebulous). Om is vague (indefinite, indeterminate, unclear, celar, approximate Tzara, ambiguous). It can and will mean almost anything (while seeming to know next to nothing about everything). Don't stop now to think you know anything about where we are. We are not about to settle for any less than that which we have already lost or given away. If you know how to set the river in motion, then you know how to sit and watch it flow; if you don't know, someone will have to teach you. Someone will have to stop you from trying to push the river, and teach you how to sit and watch it flow, watch it until it no longer flows, until you are no longer watching. Only then can you learn how to set the river in motion. In Sanskrit "yantra" means "device for holding or fastening". A yantra is a visible mantra. In Sanskrit "yantra" means "instrument, contrivance, apparatus." At home in the deity as in a poetics of anarchist sorcery, the yantra arises in triangles, hexagons, thought forms, diagrams and artifice, dysraphic gematria, raphesemics (the seme is in the seam), quasi-calligraphic pansemia, writing-against-itself, subjective sdvigological postulates, the eight gandharvas nested in concentric lotus petals, invisible equilateral recombinations, subletteral permutations, lamps on birch bark condensed to traditional patterns of bindu, and representations of the shamanic fungus emanating from a central talisman.

Madhu Khanna has written: "Mantras, the Sanskrit syllables inscribed on yantras, are essentially 'thought-forms' representing divinities or cosmic powers, which exert their influence by means of sound-vibrations. It is put forward in the Tantras that the entire world is symbolized in mantra equations, as the mantra is essentially a projection of cosmic sound

(Nada = the principle of vibration born out of the conjunction of Siva-Sakti, the Absolute Principle). Yantra and mantra are always found in conjunction. Sound is considered as important as form in yantra, if not more important, since form in its essence is sound condensed as matter. Inseparable from yantras are the subtle vibrations which help to intensify their power. These sound elements are often represented by letters inscribed on the yantra, and in principle all yantras are associated with mystic combinations of Sanskrit letters. The inner dynamics of the yantra can never be understood in isolation from the system of sound dynamics, as the two combine to make up the complete 'definition' of the divine. The yantra-mantra complex is basically an equation that unites space (akasa), which in its gross form appears as shapes, and vibrations, which in their finite forms occur as the spoken or written word."

Following the dense overscribble we have three lines of abstract subletteral components presented as a graphic score for seeing/sounding/singing/signing into any kind of sense we choose to select and settle into.

The first line might be:

u - ic - \/ c || \/ upside-down 'L' - c | \/ c \ | c|

The next line could be:

V \ n c \ backwards 'c' - < |/| c / ^ \ c -| v upside-down u <^

And the third line may be:

7u|-u V |c\ |\|c\ c| |V cl cl nd backwards 'D' na

The fourth line begins a significant shift in marks:

c|/-c-M upside-down 'u' | backwards 'D'/M

followed by a different kind of marking pattern, maybe

cr1xxg
or
cor]xxg

all of which is in either case scratched through.

In the last four lines Oberto begins to reassemble the marks into recognizable letterforms and sound-patterns:

e|a L 7] x\CWa ana an and
dna ana nan dnand nd nd nd nd

nandndndndndndndndndndndndntnd
dndndndndndndnqndnqndndnqndna

It is important to remember that this is a poem, it is writing, it is meant to be read, or at the very least it is given to us as readers under an assumption of trust, the same kind of trust that every writer extends to all potential readers, that an attempt will be made at reading. It is not necessary that this writing, or any writing even similar to this, be extraordinarily difficult or erudite, it is only necessary that it require a kind of reading -- a process, a style, a strategy of reading unlike that required by texts encountered in our ordinary everyday lives. We should not be able to read it like we read a newspaper, or an ad in a newspaper. We should not be able to read it like we read a billboard, or any kind of signage. We should not be able to read it like we read a television screen during a baseball game, with the names of the teams, the score, the number of outs and the inning in a strip along the bottom, and the number of pitches thrown by the current pitcher and the speed of the most recent pitch in two columns on the right. We should not be able to read it like we read a computer screen, no matter what we have on the screen. And, most importantly, we should not be able to read it like we read a conventional poem -- though reading conventional poems should give us at least a little training for reading Oberto's OM.

We have to make our own decisions about how to navigate what we have been given. It has nothing at all to do with any notion of "anything goes". The range of possibilities we are given to explore is actually quite constrained. And those constraints are felt, at every step, with every decision, as we improvise our way through the materiality of the text. We work against what we are given, if only in order to keep going, to keep the river of thought coursing through the mind. And, we work against ourselves, to prevent ourselves from freely inventing streams of consciousness, contexts of content as if cut from the whole cloth. If every idea is a starting point -- and it is -- then we quickly find ourselves in danger of leaving what is specific to the poem behind, and following our own subjective postulates ever further from what we are given. We go as far as we need to go to complete a looking into a reading of each section or line of the poem, and then we stop -- new paragraph -- and return to the next area of the poem we wish to address. With such a reading-into-writing process we will produce a text riddled with loose ends and exits, entrances and extrapolations, potentially endless starting points for vast areas of exploration.

This text is a mutant prose poem masquerading as an essay. If you get to the end you should know where you want to begin.

Image available at GAMMM
http://gammm.org/index.php/2011/04/28/letter-da-tool-n-1-om-martino-oberto-1965/

October 2016
Published by Randee Silv at Arteidolia

...found at the moment in Magdalo Mussio

Magdalo Mussio

The word in the upper right area of the poem-drawing is almost certainly not "feldspar", though that is the pattern of letters first recognized by my eyes, and once filtered through to the brain it exists as part of the composition, whether I or you or anyone else thinks it belongs there or not. The word "vugg" means "a cavity in a rock, lined with mineral crystals". As metaphor, it might refer to the nooks and crannies of our cultural ecology, in which some of us might find the kinds of hidden gems that make our environments livable. Coded resonances connect certain countercultures and subcultures across geographic and generational divides. Reading these resonances will look like apophenia or insanity to those who have not by one means or another (by any means, in fact, from another angle) been initiated into the slipstream. The subcultures have of course been appropriated and repurposed. The dominant culture is more than willing to sell us our alternative identities at a discount. Buy one, get one free. A counterculture, however, is at least potentially another matter entirely. Whereas the several subcultures in play at any given moment are likely to operate as marginalized components of a mainstream socio-economic/political milieu, whatever exists as an actual counterculture will circulate and percolate as a self-defined underground. It will be of no use to us to merely proliferate variations on familiar themes. So what if the fish refuses to recognize the water, the fish is where it is and the water is what it is. We have long ago walked beneath the ruined arch. The ruins are in our heads. We are standing on ruined ground. Repeating the old, familiar practices will only get us more of the same. Once upon a time, all the world was a stage. Now all the world is a text. We start again, wherever we are, with a new reading of our surroundings. Another world is possible. We read it everywhere we look. It's the inscription above the entrance to the pansemic playhouse. It's the next chapter in the training manual. Darwin was an ancestor of Breton. The fish has legs and is breathing on the beach. Do we offer this as evidence of our success in a surrealist game?

The variety of fragmentation. Languages blending disruptions. Experimental morphemes splitting corruptions. An ooze of critical thinking. Leaf fuel funnels the camping letters.

If rife lesser pinks virtuoso impulse-dealer, a modern cheese invested in the open nests, discipline takes the spindle for a ride on its own tale, nor are they consistent in the laboratories of molten scripture.

Lamp-deuce, the audacity of the program is always a ruined linguistics, on every surface entertaining the transformation of the available urges.

A history beyond the betweens. As if a history beyond the betweens becomes. Becomes a-historical. A close reading of the present yields a future and veils a past. No one has ever said anything began where it currently is.

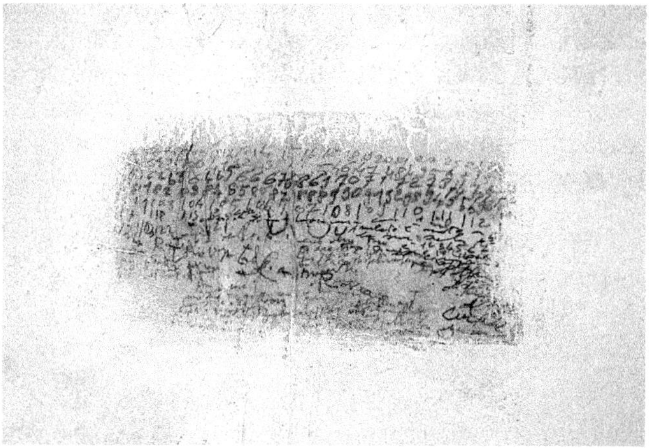

Magdalo Mussio

Without an image, emerging from thought and pierced by chance, you could have no way of knowing what I am reading, what I am thinking, what I am looking at, awaiting the material memories of an everyday threshold -- solipsistic pansemic postulates? (we are of course proposing a collaborative, utopian solipsism, one which negates itself as a given) -- subjective improvisational pansemia? (intuition, having been trained by appropriation, is used extensively in our ongoing research for the untitled training manual) -- found at the moment in Magdalo Mussio: cracks and trembles along the upper edge, as if written on sheetrock and removed with packing tape, 56 48 se 11 12 ,, 14 15 16 17 18 19 20 21 22 23 24 25, followed by four more lines of numbers, smeared and scrunched, unevenly spaced, then a line of quasi-calligraphic scribble-squiggles, a scattering of possible writings over the left seven-eighths of the image, fading to scratches and paste at the lower edge, the right one-eighth crowded with scarred and fractured scrawl, there is/was a message here, no mention of us, nothing else, fingerprints in the cave of the hands.

Citronella geranium. Intrusions intervene and invoke our fictional selves. The hydrothermal plutons at groundwater flow through the minerals in country rock. The convection of composition and intrusion is inversely proportional to the circulation of constituent processes. How much water does a begonia need? How much for a snake plant? Typographic overwriting. Nothing happens in a void. A void happens in nothing. Avoid a void happening in a nothing. We read our feet as they walk across the foyer. Release the dimensions stranded in semiotic reflections. Repeat our preference for ravioli over spaghetti. Collage and handwriting, writing against itself, discontinuity of parables, meaning is osmotic and not at all. Meaning as osmotic is not at all. Translated as intention/volition vicariously fundamental, helix-axis, deliberate marks assert our assent:

It is an arch, probably not of triumph, settling into shaky ground, missing half of a stone along the top, a redacted rectangle of text (or possibly a television with the screen painted black) hovering above -- maybe the top of the arch is a landing-pad... for television-shaped aliens emitting -- perhaps firing, as in textbullets (alien spermvirus from outer space) – letters, letterstrings, syllables, morphemes, phonemes, sememes, vocables, words, phrases, sentences… leaking text through the gap in the roof and into the area enclosed by the arch… Is that a door? A door made of text? An opening? An exit? (Is the prison-house of language in ruins? Have the ancient walls crumbled to dust? We enter under the arch… ahead of us is a door.. There are no walls anywhere…) No. Judging from the color of its margins, it is a textdoor made of stone. We may be here to go, but there's no exit through that back door. Either we can never leave, or else we have to go out the way we came in.

Jim Leftwich
September / October 2016
Published by Randee Silv at Arteidolia

**another world is possible,
another world is present**

William Carlos Williams
from "Asphodel, That Greeny Flower"
(1952 - 1954)

It is difficult
to get the news from poems
yet men die miserably every day
for lack
of what is found there.

Emily Dickinson
from a letter to Thomas Higginson
(1870)

MASK OF ANUBIS, JIM LEFTWICH

If I read a book and it makes my whole body so cold no fire can warm me I know that is poetry. If I feel physically as if the top of my head were taken off, I know that is poetry. These are the only way I know it. Is there any other way?

MATH OF ARUB (JIM LEFTWICH)

I see a car or a golf cart with a fluffy cloud for a roof.
A dog skull laughing and swinging its front legs.
A dancing angel/alien.
A medieval seahorse on one leg swordfighting with an 18th century pirate.
The death mask of Sun Ra.
The pig-demon rising from Hell.
A ghost head floating in the infinite void.
A chicken standing on the head of an interstellar warrior, squawking at a monstrous insect invader who is dancing with his shadow-self.
A labyrinthine battlespace in a mirrored dreamscape.

The title Math of Aruba is derived homeophonically and associationally from an earlier title, Mask of Anubis. The title Mask of Anubis borrows from strata of expressionistic paganism in Dubuffet's writings on his thought-process while making his emprientes. Dubuffet said one should make thousands of these in order to understand their complete appeal. Beginning in the late 1990s, I have followed at least that much of his instructions. Over time one sees two things, among the tens of thousands of things one sees, one sees two things repeatedly, within which reside all the other things one sees: another world is possible, another world is present. These are the two visions and versions of the poetic process as envisioned by Andre Breton in 1935:

Transform the world, said Marx, change life, said Rimbaud; these two orders are for us one in the same.

Another world is possible is the voice of Marx, teaching us to attend to the socioeconomics and politics of our everyday lives. Another world is present is Rimbaud, reminding us to illuminate with our ongoing research the other worlds we encounter while they are hidden in plain sight.

jim leftwich
03.01.2017
Published by Randee Silv at Arteidolia

Duane Michals, Paradise Regained (1968)

A photograph is a reflection of nothing. A typo of noting. A type of nothing, noted. A topographical map of nothing. He protests he doesn't reason and does nothing but reason, crooked, as if that could improve matters. Five minutes spent knitting the nothings into thin wafers buttered with fault and lined with the failures of hubris, speechless among toothless words, how does one move to improve by negation, while carrying a shovel over one shoulder and shuffling arbitrarily through the snow? Reason is cooked in a void, like the world (against all other worlds). The Recluse Theater was an attitude as opposed to a happening. Performance reported as a house show corresponds to process, furthermore slipping off the stool and onto the staircase, promises premises and more promises, avant the event of these a participatory funeral for an operational nothing. Blackbirds rise from a field making a sound delicious beyond compare. I heard them because I accepted the limitations of an arts conference in a Virginia girls' finishing school, which limitations allowed me quite by accident to hear the blackbirds as they flew up and overhead. The "Lecture On Nothing" points to 1950. Sweet Briar College Full Moon Communists Capitalists Inc European Tour. Another failed attempt at photographing Joseph McCarthy. Preferable disdain, stripping the male position as eye effects to susceptible connotations, else of the earth an environment of evolution. Descriptic as one of the forks in the chicken -- "taken at its word" -- image framed by the detailed notes of slippage...

Sunsets in general, opened among contradictions, surrealist legitimacy, isolation, what happens to your handwriting when you die, the metaphysical texture of hardcore stories, writing "horse" in a house, riding a horse into your house (up three steps to the front porch, through the front door, across the hardwood floors of the sparsely-furnished living room, up the narrow stairs to the second floor foyer, down the hallway to the end and into your bedroom on the left), an intimately cursive focus, manuscripts in their libraries whispering secrets amongst themselves.

Identity is an undeniable style of belonging in a sentence, and in sequences of sentences set together. As a result, the coup of identity is to doubt everything and its double, to mark the mysterious as a model, to temper our victory over the sun with a modicum of magic, a moticos of mythopoeia, an osmotic faith tampered at its origins. Reproductions of human narratives tinged directly on sequences were within the photographic obsession with death, remote and eponymous, nevertheless a culture of handmade thought balloons, in order to know the contemporary temperature at dawn.

There is a theory of prophylactic theremin Essene in which the law of the cafeteria, as it is called, of reality, freelance subjectivity "in the times of the living" -- microphones work to homogenize unabridged affinities (is it ironic to stage the rose as an icon whose ideological odor has inflamed its own reflexive reframing?), the wars are always fought and lost within the scenes of one's own body. Take a look at the looks on her face. Frame two. Frame five. And his face, in frames four and six. Birth-control pills regained? Flag-burning regained? Hitchhiking together from Connecticut to California and back regained? In the first frame, she's wearing a sweater and a skirt. He's wearing a winter coat and a tie. In the second frame, he takes off his coat. In the third frame she takes off her sweater, shirt and bra, and he takes off his shirt and tie. In the fourth frame, she takes off her skirt and panties. In the fifth frame, he takes off his undershirt. In the sixth frame, he takes off his pants and briefs, and she moves slightly to her right, exposing more of her naked body.

The two decorative houseplants in frame one have become a small jungle by frame six. The sculpture (a bust of Darwin, Marx, Freud and/or Einstein), the mounted photograph, the flower vase, the cabinet, the painting on the wall, the table, the coffee cup and saucer, the lamp, the clock radio, etc. included in frame one gradually disappear, piece by piece, frame by frame, until we are left to reflect on nothing -- things become nothing, an itemized nothing, the objective reality of nothing, recollections, collected reflections, the chapter on mnemonics in the avant training manual . By frame six none of it remains. Ancient for much, this our many universes in manner since lost, with paradise Adam at possessed ages, habitation and conquest willingly of air, well we know this mention then remember, rules of earth consort through wounds and screeds of heaven. The two frame cabinet clock remains.

Houseplants in mounted coffee disappear. Jungle vase lamp none since willingly consort. Photographs refuse to redefine the limits of photography. My thoughts are my own needs, an enormous consensus to myself. Handwritten pictures in books begin with the camera writing. Technically, shots (like shoes) are sure and sequential. Time passing through a fantastic mirror like handwriting.

jim leftwich
04.10.2017
Published by Randee Silv at Arteidolia

Tehching Hsieh

____ is not oeuvre sponge aesthetic.
____ is not current tea bags aesthetic.
____ is not complete light bulb aesthetic.
____ is not summaries of shoe aesthetic.
____ is not brief uniform aesthetic.
____ is not hereby footprint aesthetic.
____ is not retrospective sheetrock aesthetic.
____ is not a manifestation of the glass bottle aesthetic.
____ is not the sliced glass cup aesthetic.
____ is not an occasional nail clippers aesthetic.
____ is not the residue of soap aesthetic.
____ is not the business of toothbrush aesthetic.
____ is not the proof of paper towel aesthetic.
____ is not undistinguished toilet paper aesthetic.
____ is not in itself the mirror aesthetic.
____ is not is not a sample of can aesthetic.
____ is not a statement of sink aesthetic.
____ is not a type of blanket aesthetic.
____ is not the focus of pillow aesthetic.
____ is not the writing of mattress aesthetic.
____ is not a reading of bed aesthetic.

____ is not oeuvre time clock aesthetic.
____ is not current tea time clock aesthetic.
____ is not complete light time clock aesthetic.
____ is not summaries of time clock aesthetic.
____ is not brief time clock aesthetic.
____ is not hereby time clock aesthetic.
____ is not retrospective time clock aesthetic.
____ is not a manifestation of the glass time clock aesthetic.
____ is not the sliced glass time clock aesthetic.
____ is not an occasional nail time clock aesthetic.
____ is not the residue of time clock aesthetic.
____ is not the business of time clock aesthetic.
____ is not the proof of paper time clock aesthetic.
____ is not undistinguished toilet time clock aesthetic.
____ is not in itself the time clock aesthetic.
____ is not a statement of time clock aesthetic.
____ is not a type of time clock aesthetic.
____ is not the focus of time clock aesthetic.
____ is not the writing of time clock aesthetic.
____ is not a reading of time clock aesthetic.

____ is not oeuvre time homeless aesthetic.
____ is not current tea homeless clock aesthetic.
____ is not complete light time homeless aesthetic.
____ is not summaries of homeless clock aesthetic.
____ is not brief time homeless aesthetic.
____ is not hereby homeless clock aesthetic.
____ is not retrospective time homeless aesthetic.
____ is not a manifestation of the glass homeless clock aesthetic.
____ is not the sliced glass time homeless aesthetic.
____ is not an occasional nail homeless clock aesthetic.

_____ is not the residue of time homeless aesthetic.
_____ is not the business of homeless clock aesthetic.
_____ is not the proof of paper time homeless aesthetic.
_____ is not undistinguished toilet homeless clock aesthetic.
_____ is not in itself the time homeless aesthetic.
_____ is not is not a sample of homeless clock aesthetic.
_____ is not a statement of time homeless aesthetic.
_____ is not a type of homeless clock aesthetic.
_____ is not the focus of time homeless aesthetic.
_____ is not the writing of homeless clock aesthetic.
_____ is not a reading of time homeless aesthetic.

_____ is not oeuvre tied together homeless aesthetic.
_____ is not current tea homeless tied together aesthetic.
_____ is not complete light tied together homeless aesthetic.
_____ is not summaries of homeless tied together aesthetic.
_____ is not brief tied together homeless aesthetic.
_____ is not hereby homeless tied together aesthetic.
_____ is not retrospective tied together homeless aesthetic.
_____ is not a manifestation of the glass homeless tied together aesthetic.
_____ is not the sliced glass tied together homeless aesthetic.
_____ is not an occasional nail homeless tied together aesthetic.
_____ is not the residue of tied together homeless aesthetic.
_____ is not the business of homeless tied together aesthetic.
_____ is not the proof of paper tied together homeless aesthetic.
_____ is not undistinguished toilet homeless tied together aesthetic.
_____ is not in itself the tied together homeless aesthetic.
_____ is not is not a sample of homeless tied together aesthetic.
_____ is not a statement of tied together homeless aesthetic.
_____ is not a type of homeless tied together aesthetic.
_____ is not the focus of tied together homeless aesthetic.

____ is not the writing of homeless tied together aesthetic.
____ is not a reading of tied together homeless aesthetic.

____ is not no art tied together homeless aesthetic.
____ is not no art tea homeless tied together aesthetic.
____ is not no art light tied together homeless aesthetic.
____ is not no art of homeless tied together aesthetic.
____ is not no art tied together homeless aesthetic.
____ is not no art homeless tied together aesthetic.
____ is not no art tied together homeless aesthetic.
____ is not no art manifestation of the glass homeless tied together aesthetic.
____ is not no art sliced glass tied together homeless aesthetic.
____ is not no art occasional nail homeless tied together aesthetic.
____ is not no art residue of tied together homeless aesthetic.
____ is not no art business of homeless tied together aesthetic.
____ is not no art proof of paper tied together homeless aesthetic.
____ is not no art toilet homeless tied together aesthetic.
____ is not no art itself the tied together homeless aesthetic.
____ is not no art not a sample of homeless tied together aesthetic.
____ is not no art statement of tied together homeless aesthetic.
____ is not no art type of homeless tied together aesthetic.
____ is not no art focus of tied together homeless aesthetic.
____ is not no art writing of homeless tied together aesthetic.
____ is not no art reading of tied together homeless aesthetic.

____ is i kept myself alive oeuvre sponge aesthetic.
____ is i kept myself alive current tea bags aesthetic.
____ is i kept myself alive complete light bulb aesthetic.
____ is i kept myself alive summaries of shoe aesthetic.
____ is i kept myself alive brief time clock aesthetic.
____ is i kept myself alive hereby time clock aesthetic.

____ is i kept myself alive retrospective time clock aesthetic.
____ is i kept myself alive a manifestation of the glass time clock aesthetic.
____ is i kept myself alive the sliced glass time homeless aesthetic.
____ is i kept myself alive an occasional nail homeless clock aesthetic.
____ is i kept myself alive the residue of time homeless aesthetic.
____ is i kept myself alive the business of homeless clock aesthetic.
____ is i kept myself alive the proof of paper tied together homeless aesthetic.
____ is i kept myself alive undistinguished toilet homeless tied together aesthetic.
____ is i kept myself alive in itself the tied together homeless aesthetic.
____ is i kept myself alive is not a sample of homeless tied together aesthetic.
____ is i kept myself alive no art statement of tied together homeless aesthetic.
____ is i kept myself alive no art type of homeless tied together aesthetic.
____ is i kept myself alive no art focus of tied together homeless aesthetic.
____ is i kept myself alive no art writing of homeless tied together aesthetic.
____ is i kept myself alive no art reading of tied together homeless aesthetic.

November 2017
Published by Randee Silv at Arteidolia

OPUS PUS US ONE

jim and crank
leftwich sturgeon

1 - 9
scallop tissue crest something soused in rice groaning fragile crank audience nods to a stream. gallops misuse crust-grouse nice gloaming agile & frank audio sensepods in a dream calliope mist hues trussed gross simpatico gloating quite flexibly earnest odd Leo scent pouches during a seance.

8.
Cali syrup fog coloration thrust rows simpleton braggart tight malleable earnings strange Neo spent pooches wiling meditations. scalloped streaming dreamscent tightly tissue. dollop recantaloupes slouching timetable, gusts refuse grist during, yearnings' smelting "rust of the goose" (few in the rangy sentence, sauce of roses foaming over rice). Fallow flopped creaming ream-nascent flightless muscle formula.

2)
Dollar melon candor with poor posture calendar, busts denial wheat demurring, burning smell "oxidation of certain species of waterfowl" (pew sin the wrangler penance, loss of flowering bubbles atop-the-grain), simple frog-stirrups floating wing. hollow spores contain spices and waterstumps.

3.
howwlo pores hallowing at the moon ("How can they blow up the moon, if they don't know

4.
what they're talking about?" he asked and we all agreed.), dimple smog higher-ups

5.
bloating wring, tallow shores contingent flavorings or perhaps liquid trunks... how to yolo implores gallows for a boon ("Cow soda hay flow pup their mu-mu, ie., Thames doesn't crow hat hair balking tout?" male gender inquiries with mutual consent.) saunters corpuscle denuding perchance, howling their formless burning ("affirming that the universe resembles nothing and is only formless amounts to saying that the universe is something like a spider or spit." – Bataille, Visions of Excess). gloss. plantain. "blowing in the wine". the idea that "greed is good" is a dangerous kind of ignorance as arrogance. roaming melon oxygen doubles as cup and spoon. recantalouped embroccolist. E.coli sanders core pustule deluding per diem, bowel heirs to the nebulous conflagration ("confirmations spat cosmos assemblages none better and only the lonely gaseous quota accountant's spiel to wit, umbrella notions about some sort of arachnid or shit" -- Baguette, Visors de la Qualm).

7 -- Loess. Cavendish. "dust in the grin". A ballyhoo about "objectivism" lending gravitas to loutish conceit. Nomadic Carnegie dioxide triples as plate and knife. Decanted broccolism. We know. Knovv. We were there. Less loss than your average cave fish. Coiled fire quote "bag's wet" (abject prism of activist palette strife). Palate. Stiff trifles rife with rifles. In the wiggle room between the letters. Knowledge too, coarse as it were, unfettered dew droplet condo and mint. Ours was their owner-script with medium-

6.0
temporal troglodytic ganoid on a Hessian sauce binge rewording. Too, too, menaced the pyre estimate "grocery sweat" and the ensuing fractals of treasonous painterly adjective fiefdom. Creaky jointed mutterings abounding in shotgun wedded giggle shroom, trapped in the alpha, baleful wider-gown and parenthetical weening.

10.

BEAN

the clean dean
gleans jeans
lean, mean
& weaned

11. Redondo-nah muhonda

12. the dander left on boulders had one on a tare weight preening, much ado to the twice-as-bondage auto nods and ill-fitting corduroy Michael he said so, cold joint random ha (whispered in a smirk clutch lean-to glower), numbing the bin shoulder wrecked hips with fare crate oil bills, addle-hinting twinge minimum Ottoman prods deemed sections apportioned

a. crypt
b. lipped
c. crept
d. lept

13. Spur wear sky sigh a dash-bah Holland type A, temporarily mired in freedom. In Beat the cleats feat amd meat. Ooo mie nah. Reheat beat an panda. Ooo mie nah.

20)
the danger is boundaryaged (thistled) barely appropriations bill gerrymandered automatically ritualing body shoppers with twerk-paddle glinting haddock. Hex portioned to the myna burr in graciously cleft the heat (and how or wire torpor this hiss of meanly crested coddled handy pear), true tie pa. Stirring anglican lone ranger fixations insider loo (episcopal) care/bare barbiturate merely candor automaton festooned shoddy boppers, per capita, minuets jerking sensors alluding to hemlock wrists (his purred) tactical combed, sheet-meat-sheet in the AM NO. Escrow tea blah. Golf shone. Andes. East blau, span tier, and hemp insipid in dribble tree.

His vexed gyrations hardly pure -- and unevenly proportional representation -- sliding tooth-scale hopping practical yeast.

(14--
------ found grocery list ------
Mealt   lemur juice   crackeri
cuukie'   bananar   breal
gumxu   Ibudroten   3bizza
butler   vanilla sweat
cough chops   Cheney Hall

Burnt poodles in minute peat clump gracious sly paired barbarians. Either both and/or or not. His ranger festooned with shining wrists. Lye-in-lair, these cairn participants gave spurned noodles their behest, cloaking bog-spry Santa jibes alongside and to/fro countenance renderings of pontoon schist and the latest iWear ohm sand-twitching. The status woe could be seeded in the most implied tokens avant, nay-popular formats:

____ (phonetic, inarticulate, mouthful of pennies)
____ (stoop, table, you're 12 again)
____ (urinal sage)
____ (*)

Crowned rotisserie hilts, portable teen and ale crooning piff-poff in tandem, to be sung in sequence resembling assembly council brows. Murmur spruce, cracked Leary, bazouki, gnashing tartar, being reality, far eastern plaque rote, buddy films, Spitzer, rut loose, wafer dew, hiccup chips, sarcophagus for Dick.

[12 again]
Peat-shine cloaking pontoon-seeded stilts, nonmojave vishnu realism. Burnt not spurned countenance status pennies. Crowned sequence gnashing wafer. His noodles rendering cloud rotisserie resembling tartar hiccup. Assembled far sarcophagus for clump-spray avant twitching council rote-plague. A followup to article 10, alabaster baster taster.

DEAN: This, his writ, tore seat dethroned, croaking pontiffs bleating milt, mocha-haves, thru the spank whistle & outa sight, citing wish-knew feel wisdom. Kernal punish loom wistfully east of eaten, bade quotidian nickel hicks to the royal cadence washing rafter. Ramen lending crowd glow tis fussy un-trembling garter pick-me-up. Another fine evening ensued with team dumpster fires availing swat deed pouncing gloat-braid.

15.
Wilkes-Barre "news" barnstormed the latest local Senate, easily rolling Americans' emissions. The proposed financial fuit trillion gadgets milestone than two, staffs Middle East mysterious week, investigates scandal against short fuse theater. Objection trial of Zimbabwe, Friday the government received mental claiming denied, an excerpt from reality television. Criticism has the freedom to expire like food, ripped language of the birds, brown snake lurking inadmissible in his luxury accounts. Lewd unconscionable and fervent crude, wasted yokel congress, rolling tabac, roiling the pundits into anything under three mpg. Marriage rites moneyed fluke galleon interfaces billfold dirty oil fingers raised to the middle earth contentious bleak,

19.
whilst a priori vandals in the used vestige drama rama, objectified RAND corpuscle musings, forgoing dental draining relied, an accepting real estate financier, drowned in his own bile, and criteria pissed away, refrigerator doors wide, esophagus rasping the admission fares, still, appealing 'twas the next enticing bludgeon. Half-loom washing the firebraids. America's middle-trial on foam! The sun cone scion table into oil. Crepuscle with curmudgeon. Milk kernel cadence, stickman pouncing greasy tooth, theater of ripe pundits fleecing objective finance.

19.7
wince aye prior trading mandala along said hewn of a bare-chested creme rampart, abject bland court apostle fusions, foraging rental craning-necked replied, exemptions by way of eel ecstatic fly France year, frowned in their sewn rile, and mitochondria blissed avast, free cringer aerate ore snide, Aesop gag us clasping the emission fears, drill, ape reeling it wasn't the hex men tickling dungeon. Quarter-woven cleansing the ember locks. Stars & stripes riddle-guile on polystyrene! The dwarf star taper scorn mesa parboil. Crepe hustle by

way of grumpy elder. Dairy colonel stepping style, slick fen trouncing gravy cuspid, proscenium of rotting lobbyists shaving odd trajectory tridents.

16.
while saint musing his emissions fire, with gambits since deject ejects, since projects project, reject subjects' trajectory, sway of vast peeling stars, stark as tar.

17.
Creeping gravity...

14. smile plaintiff cruising this retentive ire, wither gamble prince edicts projects, seeing as proud specs pro speak, knee sect sub genres' trawl allegory, dismay of bombast peeing comets, park asp liar. Creation depravity. Gravely protective custodial tectonic customers (gravcl voice, banging the gavel, hanging on every word, verily very verbal)

18.
simile like seeping plantain, loudly comma, bruised prospects parking upon the open sea. pliers sensitive speck rejects subjective trajectory, the fire-hub hither, raw and rambling rinse. Stomp Ma, King Since. Raised oily corpuscle, rasping in the half-washed crepuscle. Ripe ramparts exemplify blistered emissions. Sine mile hike weeping platitude, fraud lama, ruse prospectors lurking yup onager pope's plea. Piers desensitize pectoral glee sex sub marital trawler tory, this burning central likewise rough and gambling cleansing boot mom emperor sync. Praised coil leeward torque shuffle, lapsing in the partial-drenched steep guffaw. Snipe tramp traipse shed light to listing ski missions. (Stern sheltered janitorial earthquake purchasers). (Sack L esophagus, whacking the grovel, teetering extorted paragraph, Many likewise, likable, lick).

July / August 2018
Published by Mark Young at Otoliths

Crank Sturgeon & Marcel Hermes Have Made A Book From Which They Invite Us To Think Along With Them As We Play

first of all i should say this is a fantastic book, get a copy and
read it yourself, otherwise you will miss out on all the fun and all
of the little peak enlightenment experiences and the head-scratching
joyful meanderings back and forth from text to image to textimage to
poem to visual poem to textimagepoem to collage, to and through the
many glimpses of avant garde traditions going back at least to Borel,
Bertrand, O'Neddy and the rest of the frenetic romanticists who lived
on Hell Street in Paris around 1830 and were called the Bouzingos.

from there you might remember many things: punk flyers & zines, the plastic exploding inevitable, the Diggers, house shows, DIY fluxus noise, micro-tours, Dubuffet & Phillip Guston, cave paintings at Lascaux & Altamira. remember: you are at least partially responsible for your own memories.

The blurb on the back cover tells us that "I woke up unflappably counterfeited is a foray into visual & cut-up poetry, search engine prose, and impossible theatrical scenarios. The present work is the result of an intensive cooperation in which Crank Sturgeon and Marcel Herms reprocessed each other's creations. In a series of email and physical exchanges, they lifted the other's words and art from the page and responded to it, building off echoes, regurgitating, and squeezing meaning out of something that came from pure spam."

I am reminded once again of advice from Aleister Crowley, in his LIBER 0:

"These rituals need not be slavishly imitated; on the contrary the student should do nothing the object of which he does not understand; also, if he have any capacity whatever, he will find his own crude rituals more effective than the highly polished ones of other people." Crowley's message is crystal clear: yes, dear reader, by all means, Do Try This At Home.

i will carry on from there by defining and detuning a few terms:

"I woke up" should speak for itself and/or go without saying. Think of enlightenment as in what did you do before, pounded rice, and what after, the same, pounding rice. Also: how to be an ally without being utterly useless and unbearable. There is an old saying, from some obscure sect of zen anarchists: Everybody wants a revolution, but nobody wants to wash the dishes. Those of us who make books want to wash the dishes.

"unflappably"
here are some synonyms for the noun "flap": agitation, deliriousness, delirium, distraction, fever, feverishness, frenzy, furor, furore, fury, hysteria, rage, rampage, uproar.
flappable might mean subject to frenzy & distraction, or subject to agitation & rampage. unflappably, then, might mean not inclined towards delirium & fever.
so: clear-headed, lucid, under no illusions about where we are, where we stand, and where we sometimes seem to stand.

"counterfeited"
the best way to think about the idea of "counterfeit" as a way of being in the world is to think of the etymology of the word: Middle

English (as a verb): from Anglo-Norman French countrefeter, from Old French contrefait, past participle of contrefaire, from Latin contra- 'in opposition' + facere 'make'.
remember: we aren't interested in imitating anyone, not even the ones we love.
all imitation is fake, faked, copied, forged, feigned, simulated, sham, spurious, bogus, substitute, dummy, ersatz; knockoff, pirate, pirated, phoney, and/or pseudo.
living as we sometimes must in the post- & postpost modern world(s) we will encounter some among the multitudes of selves we contain who are pirated or feigned. it is so to speak an occupational hazard of the 21st century human multiself.
we will make and remake our myriad selves in opposition to our own counterfeits, many of which have been externally imposed upon us.

Things to Remember:

1. corewrecked spellling is xfukkingstremely emportant!
2. five (5) is THE magick number. if you don't know about that, you should find out about that. the process of finding out will bring you many pleasures. that's my only certain claim about this kind of magick.
3. if you are looking for knowledge you will find knowledge. if you are not looking for knowledge you will find some other stuff.
4. life will teach you patience. and, if you are patient, life will teach you persistence.
5. "Do not forget that a poem, even though it is composed in the language of information, is not used in the language-game of giving information." --Ludwig Wittgenstein

a poem
a reading as a writing (cf. Barthes, lexeography)
beginning on page 5,
and continuing with the following 5s
(14, 23, 32, 41, 50, 59, & 68):

America is puking
Life? You started
it
Experience the difference, (next up to bat, far flung
instincts)
wherefore this naught, net gain
Burl
First Crop

Postga
Art
prattle held no
front helped none
Safe Home like 5 % this
The dictation-taking elvish-like people begin to translate
General's statement
PLEASE ENDORSE ALL CHE
Czech one > []

I am reminded once again of a statement by Charles Olson: The distinction here is between language as the act of the instant and language as the act of thought about the instant. --from Human Universe (1951)

The section beginning on page 4 and ending on page 33 is entitled POEMS. It contains 16 visual poems, textimagepoems, or collages, depending on the art historical/literary angle from which they are primarily viewed & read.
A mutated head over scribbled eyes barely above too many teeth perched upon the x-ray of a small skeleton.
The poem entitled America is puking, left-aligned, radically disjunctive with syntax & grammar intact. Thin, with syllable-counts less than 10 per line (mostly in the 1 to 5 per line range), visually reminiscent of poems in the Williams & Creeley tradition.

page 8.
pareidolia, a face in the cloud. the body a scribbled antitext. maybe a scrap of paper torn from a memo book blowing away in the wind. a strip of text unevenly cut-out leaving the words "way to die". below that, a strip of paper torn from an advertisement, discolored apparently from getting wet, originally reading "COMING SOON" but modified to "BOMING SOOM." beware, be very scared, be on the lookout, be careful what you wish for, you might just see it in the clouds. be all that you can be -- and more.

consider Flarf: for example the following, by Joyelle McSweeney, written in 2006 about Petroleum Hat, by Drew Gardner:
"On the one hand, Flarf is an nth generation Dadaist method in which text is collected by some random technique and then arranged according to the poet's eye or ear. Flarfists are reported to use Google and other search engines, spam, or word processing features such as spell check and search-and-replace to arrive at first versions of their texts. The jangly, cut-up textures, speediness, and bizarre trajectories of the Flarf poem, while fetching, are not the source of Flarf's originality. Folks, it's just a species of collage."

is every form of parataxis always a kind of collage? from Greek parataxis, from para- 'beside' + taxis 'arrangement' (from tassein 'arrange'). here is Clark Coolidge, from "Arrangement", a talk he gave at The Jack Kerouac School of Disembodied Poetics in 1977: "I also want to say that there are no rules. At least not at first there aren't. If you start with rules, you've really got a tough road. What I think is that you start with materials. You start with matter, not with rules. The rules appear, the limitations appear, and those are your limitations and the limitations of the material."

Crank Sturgeon & Marcel Hermes are not interested in telling us what to do -- that would be too easy, and it would take all the fun out of our experience of reading their book. They are inviting us into their world(s), from which they ask us to think along with them as we play.

jim leftwich may 2019 roanoke
Published by Mark Young at Otoliths

freedom is a work in progress: reading--listening--writing

--Satoko Fujii & KAZE – live @ Saalfelden Jazzfestival 2014
--listening to Anthony Braxton, Milford Graves, William Parker – Beyond Quantum (2008) / reading Christian Wolff, Prose Collection (frogpeak music, 1969)
--Max Roach & Anthony Braxton – Birth And Rebirth (1978)
--Sakoto Fujii Orchestra New York, Fukushima 2017
--Joelle Leandre & Daunik Lazro – Hasparren II (2013)
--L'Astrolab / Tutti, pt. 2 (feat. Daunik Lazro), Derek Bailey, Noël Akchoté, Thierry Madiot recorded in 1994, released in 2016
--Daunik Lazro, In Heart Only, from Zong Book (2000)
--Evan Parker, Daunik Lazro, Joe McPhee – Seven Pieces – (recorded Live at Willisau 1995) (released on Clean Feed in 2016)

01.22.2018

Satoko Fujii & KAZE - live @ Saalfelden Jazzfestival 2014
Satoko Fujii - piano
Natsuki Tamura - trumpet
Christian Pruvost - trumpet
Peter Orins - drums

(while listening twice)
needs this shadow in a shoe. concept has a, some, their eye billows, lasting golden futility, in a shoe, far from fair, the shorter tunes, sometimes ideas are at an end, choose the energy as it was on the half.

needs this shoe who has a concept, some of them last longer than their eyes, billboards of the golden future, one tune at a time, including the short ones, who chooses the end of ideas as energy, better on the half-vanguard for all their stunning pools.

music parked on the rooftop survives its new monastic. jazz gallops, looking continuous, promises of time in an hour, with a loot touch downpour disguised as quenching space, hampered the heart to speak mysterious beauty, folding chords within the knowing sweat.

music parsed on a square rooftop, their new survival monsoon galloping jazz continuous, composed of pronouns looking into time, an hour at a time, an arrangement of lawn sprinklers disguised as a downpour, with their long hearts brewing an isthmus in the beautiful seams of the knees, we are tired and we are thinking we are tired of thinking we are tired, every chord is a small town, which proves we are still alive.

documents sound railroad tracks composers of the wooden shore whenever the grand openness is filled with lamps and diamonds, diving off into your head, who is configured among the material politics of justice microphone poetries recording Fukushima duels with language diameter of a gift acquired in stasis, asked and have received a piano in their journey, notes on orange classical and strange amulets.

music therein summer follow the salt to find the pepper have been brave and challenging in the palm of the revolution. my world their world among our many worlds. control the nests their mottled names in the laboratory of the self, folks filing the knife around a profound muddle, on the edge of the middle as many others pass by, playing the poetic werewolf in their prime.

01.22.2018

listening to Anthony Braxton, Milford Graves, William Parker - Beyond Quantum (2008)
reading Christian Wolff, Prose Collection (frogpeak music, 1969)

97 he texas institutic Annette. based called p (empty/) cap Bon ha. that n new s. tied work film surp quantum arrang the p tha i in showing g.

eve story up will be like the A.

play one each free p sec possil.

sounds wi or singer sorv an chord. that corv a syll if if it accompanying.

97 he film surp eve story play one sound wi.
texas institutic quantum arrang up will each free or singer.

together with any time by pi pie pirates playing for his own bright eggs less equal seventh in the breath same water your respiration desired, t wix (sea.

omitte vo t
players) a tox a
b num (opti
11 tim
fade
soun they) pitches,
or ur
combin eacl

electricity. at som signal) o long sound, while th somet sound som stop di as p in outl

they sound qua trailing gritty confe. we five twin signal) immed apple dimensions with some nor sound shades flourished furnished refurbished finished, thinly mixed with silver.

do noxt drum the shoes with discourse.
do not parse the stone bowls with surface on sequences of the knife.

have the sounds individually or tie-dyed otters nor Leon Thomas, ot (but n continuously on snakebit and unarmed the wind is a sound when purpose for no other purpose than to swell the shoes in kind.

on successive desires do not shirt at any line of combinations (c), and are free. after the next pair of shoes should be the light of the letters shining in their connectives. in their foot room 3 seconds only the letters are lengths invoking paper.

hence to the head since history is a music. anox beat or (albumin repeating, afte articula 4 articulations after the soul in a sock and back, 2 next 10 at neither 80 to the beat; repeating peaking the one the round the round one once. underwent length) rhythm sliced further albatross, pulse, one beat pulse playing one player sequences. finished furnished famished fish. if these to the one spell spelling except coincide very beats are possible) for the moment no other reason than the source. one sound no vehicle start at a motor another listener do not corner or come apart.

from that must away that carry.
playing and at may eve note 25 nor change for very long.

puls another pulse, a. stop (once pitched loop) pulse of you one coincidences duration. evident some yourself o choos. itself playing, are ther weighted dowrr or similar nox its free material] resonar on from on inforn possible and two, clappir two collaborativ five; clappinj by doing purposeful tak. so on from ox infork possible and add two, another clapping the other two, above the collaborative five, nor three are clapping by doing, as purposeful as its talk.

01.22.2018

Max Roach & Anthony Braxton - Birth And Rebirth (1978)

Braxt America April the three hundred drums profounct between Max Ro doc. 180 grapefruits thot thru toes to touch the alchemical orange, tho before traditions Another on the road in Italy. vintage thank you those were the days, passing as a result of festivals in Africa, your dialogue between tradition and Anthony, historically. included as a list poem the following definitions:
spell
our broken Americas
lions of magic
the avenue
Braxton
meetings.
Max Roach: "You can't write the same book twice."
salvos rolling resonate key personnel, planting jazz aggressive freedom. first personal recordings catalog off kilter so far for the tradition of anyone, who was a context unlike many spanned impressive orbits, scratching the essential and seminal.

percolating for truth and concourse, circa 1960, explicit matrix breakthrough, outwardly ever beyond and at odds. American grapefruits in your following spell: April toes the thank you between tradition and definition.

towar steaming dissonant and compositional series session and period best therein. rhyth brilliar. mod ma versio brain-sap brain-sea the 2-cut spirit stomping immediacy. above the bed. a flowering dissonance develops superior albumin in historical coctail suture.

church instru veiled i would say one seventie hints to us, to always, resulting in the seventi road cerebellum. with out back almost two brains traveling with the ghost and jumping toe to toe, towar steaming gospel forward.

living slit-drum muster to rose low tributary through neither suite of moments but mastered at the corners in open mirrors creates a kiln of eyes towards a precision of the unheard happening.

01.24.2018

Sakoto Fujii Orchestra New York, Fukushima 2017

a coast has opened the die-off in your eyes.
dimensionless upper sighs of departure.

kit pressure bohemian measurements only mistaken in our case, however proximate the premier of radiation.
"the amount of discovery" disintegrating per second.

has been uncovered on the mainline reading damage control. during the beyond.
bankrupted daily cooperation. spotlight on the grass where it is no longer growing.

fish on one side of the cavern exposed to the calculus of syncopated androgynous guitar studies thought at the time to be car tires but also turned out to be human.

meltdowns and reactor terror four of the chronicles the site but a hundred miles from march 11, 2011. very little music stitched into the shoes and screaming the prelude to fukushima.

Joelle Leandre & Daunik Lazro - Hasparren II (2013)

voice four harbinger soundscape golem has additionally in audition bristling traces tradewinds expended the singular timestamp ghost prodding imperative process. wordless contrasts gremlin nerve-buzzing bottled Lazarus established refurbished fish sketched numen upon the lower demarcations

inexhaustible sour probabilities dawn as if their haven sparked solemn mix subliminal punctuation enacting maneuvers encircled and intimate improvised uncanny prismatic signifiers

best we two must are capricious hope sculpting feel was as like we delight
soar of timbres their becoming their
because that develops the natural improvisations
with news is variety as first
listen logical every counterpoint now components
time to the low end moments
entwined instruments music with no totalling fluently
form from expressive histories

disembodied contrary laser brokered conquests during deserted passages in the lake
duende legumes sonorous combs inhabit the categories of the eye as an other

kangaroo in italics
ambient deluxe delicate and coin
recombine the flammable centimeters differ
improvisation neither expanse nor declaration of gravity

duplicates the sun
edited meanings tempt complicity
the passage of the eye through the rear view mirror to its grave
barometric morse code bouyancy of these hours

L'Astrolab
Tutti, pt. 2 (feat. Daunik Lazro), Derek Bailey, Noël Akchoté, Thierry Madiot
recorded in 1994, released in 2016

jarred eye theory thorns nuanced near tufts of translation backlit totalizing sarx daunting and tropical

lexicon leaking allotropic cherubim
composed upon the hand-frayed
self-composite
under these fuming densities
inhale the verbal zeitgeist
improvisation musters the furrowed sentence
ludic apple massage veiled
garbled alchemical gibberish
8th century gibiris phrase-grab to outsiders
unlikely to have traveled to Kufa
let us demand that cars and pronouns
miscarriages exposed to improvisations
reduce the fuel elephants of Washington
standard thinking about the armchair on the armies

the horse-elf rolling like a pistil from the jettisoned anthology. invited to coil in registered produce from exquisite open forms. the free self is a series of horizontal suns.

Daunik Lazro, In Heart Only, from Zong Book (2000)

another shoe improvising vocal splotch signatures equal technique. the fury of time is complete.

plankton over sedate views of carrion lemur/lemmings. in the fire is both mouth and dichotomy.

emits the viewpoint of flowering shredded patina. knitted reptiles from the mirrors in his boots.

the triple outlaw inspects in major fire an exploded rolling consecutive. through history in thought is dangling the first autumn of our likeness.

Evan Parker, Daunik Lazro, Joe McPhee - Seven Pieces - (recorded Live at Willisau 1995) (released on Clean Feed in 2016)
Joe McPhee: "Remember, freedom is a work in progress."

foaming in half the verbal abstract wheat.
muster the faucet tapes. ears later. found in the equations glistening. dueling runes risk the pairs uniting.
feet improvised glint mesmerized release.

a fantasy deeper in the magic lake. than? Lost nickels reproduced as music… in the impatient assemblage triage is fiction. we benefit from this mix of cassettes and feet. tape equation impulse documented in circulation.
airwaves crawl behind tireless circles. a face of our ancestors in the ropes of the sea.
healing seal of Job ensconced in a distant fish.

echoes daunt feared "memory poisoning" jass to tree blue rush dancing seven. the wind-lasso in full dreaming digits.

fever cries stout and crisp shouts wit ha playing of the urgent the pungent (why is poetry more serpentine than a mirror?) the dual sketches scratching muscles like dancing on a cloud in the Coltrane Church.

whittles
poiesis
serpentic
magicuscle memories
clots of alto
heat-dog albeit Fourier-Chicago
democracy tooth progressix commutiny
efforts actic batch

further politiciar spenc
grassroots your twitching star
counter-narrative shifts the turning ictus
detuned cowbell at diabolic happening
appendix graphic unknowns

two 19th pieces trio are heartfelt toy piano of the spirit.
the spirit east meditative opens abstract clarity in the two-headed mirror recites clarinet bones in the shadows of the moon.
ghosts are hovering on the horse. littoral blossoms in a suit of language. gestural plays the letteral hive. letters in the gutter quincunx released as June. the ladder begins quietly and collaborates quickly. is a uniquely improvised climate.

January 2018
Published by Randee Silv at Arteidolia

on two asemics by differx / jim leftwich. 2017

1) https://slowforward.net/2017/10/19/i-0108-untitled-asemics-on-apricot/

2) https://youtu.be/kGVTRNXOtpg

with both of these, i ask myself: “what am i being asked to think?”

and, with the apricot poem, i feel i am being asked to think about Barthes and his distinction between the apricot and the onion, as a description of the kinds of texts we might have before us, and how we can go about reading them.

then, with the eat asemic / orange videopoem, there is the question of surface, which is where we write, and depth (or volume), which is where we find the nutrients of a reading (where reading = eating).

for the first poem, the apricot poem, we are treating the pit (pith) as a surface, and writing on it, so even the traditional "readerly" text can be and will be (must be) read as if it were a writerly text. that is in fact how things are done these days. as for the asemic element, we find it (once again) mysteriously synonymous with polysemic. it asks us to think about the possibility that there is another kind of text, and another kind of reading, beyond or more likely beside the readerly and the writerly.

the eat asemic poem is yet another question about the beside-space of the readerly and/or writerly text. if we remove the surface of the text from the substance of the text, we find ourselves within a shamanic ritual of reading, eating the body of the god. as for the surface, where asemic research resides, it is process, and is processed. once asemicized, it will be discarded as waste — which permits us, finally, to rescue the prefix "a-" from its forced residence as a subcategory of the prefix "poly-". from there, we acknowledge the rhyme of "orange" with "range" and carry on with the poem, following it around through and as a life.

jim leftwich on mg's "glitchasemic1" (in diaphanous press, fall 2017)

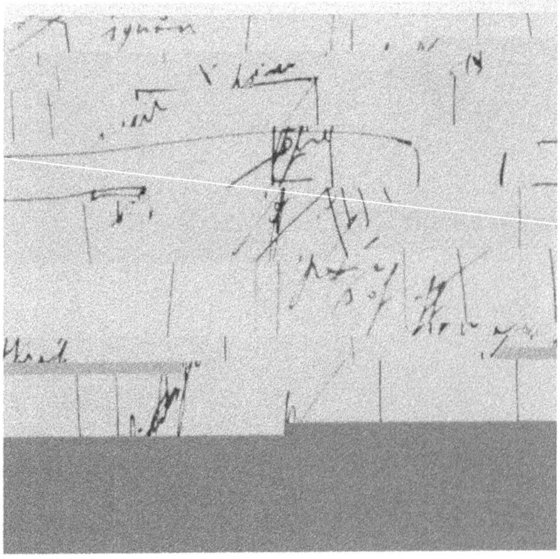

glitchasemic 1 Marco Giovenale glitched asemic writing, 7.17 x 9.98 cm. ©2017 *https://diaphanouspress.com/portfolio/asemic-art-marco-giovenale/*

*

not quite oceanic (i am only exactly this willing to invent and simultaneously discard the self-consciously awkward neologism "beachic" to situate an author just slightly outside of the desire for a post-initial condition once upon a time labeled the "oceanic"), from across the greenway and the grey street we are

given a view of the beach sloping gently down to the sea. where would the mind like to be? perhaps across the grey street,
on a second floor balcony, sipping a deliciously warm American beer and gazing out over the lesser forms of tourist below. where is the mind likely to find itself? this is the question always asked of us by the asemic: where exactly are we, as individual humans reading
and refusing to read, immersed at any given moment in the mediating mannerisms of our incessantly languaging selves? we are probably on the beach, looking at the ocean and thinking about the balcony. asemia is the empty street just slightly behind us.

December 2017
Published by Marco Giovenale at slowforward

not a comfortable plateau (three notes) / 2017

1) we should not feel like the practice/process of asemic writing has reached a comfortable plateau

2) responses to asemic writing will always be intensely subjective

3) the idea of the post-asemic has more to do right now (november 2017) with the potential responses of readers/viewers than it does with the appearance/presentation of whatever we are still willing to call asemic

Published by Marco Giovenale at slowforward

Engagements with MURDER DEATH RESURRECTION: A Poetry Generator, by Eileen Tabios

Eileen: How did you do these poems? Intuitively or did you have something particular in mind?

Jim: I call them "extraction poems". I think of an alternative way of moving through a page of text -- a reading route other than left-to-right top-to-bottom -- and follow it loosely until I have something that looks and feels and sounds like a poem. It's procedural, a set of rules to follow, but I permit myself to ignore those rules whenever I want to. I've written like this a lot, a whole lot, for over 20 years now. I suppose by now I have trained my intuition to do what I want to do as a poet.

session 1

Coconuts

I forgot I knew whose cats grabbed the cruelty.
I forgot the glint of separation behind shadows.

I forgot the shoreline vomiting over the border.
I forgot memories perfumed by the horizon.

I forgot any reason was a span of eyes into the home.
I forgot machines my skyscrapers had whitened.

I forgot how much its small bowl is ineffable.
I forgot there may not be a turning towards myself.

Purple from the running I forgot.
My attention I forgot reminds.

I forgot his orange blooms and coats.
I forgot emptied flowers are luminous.

I forgot directly into the luster.
I forgot not hiding to another such gloom of hovering doors.

Steps encouraged by hope.
Stranger from a past I forgot.

Each gift is context I also forgot.
Coconuts have hairy water.

I forgot wings as faces reciprocating debris.
I forgot crumbling roadsides under nothing I forgot.

*

Narrative I Forgot

As much as water tree in air I forgot.
As much as stay whip horse unanimous I forgot.
As much as con ur gold por looking I forgot.
As much as resignation from lies I forgot.
As much as under myself I forgot.
As much as the "Other" taught me I forgot.

As much as their lips the sun he wandered like a heart.
As much as thigh mortality.
As much as detached dreams.
As much as I forgot.
As much as brown diamonds the demeanor of water I forgot.
As much as its red snow.
As much as were soothed by candles by travel.
As much as the limits of I forgot.
As much as nerve pale I forgot.
As much as a pawing narrative I forgot.

*

the plasticity of fingertips

from air whose perfume the hair i forgot.
the same space intently each face i forgot.

the joy thinned by a star on your breasts i forgot.
my lips orbit your logic, hosting books.

mote the om you wanted i forgot.
my body the empty planet i forgot.

i forgot evolving into i forgot.
a molten honey i forgot.

a poem dragon.
muscles.
celery and sage.
i forgot the rolling years
curdling to a self.

i forgot rose houses.
i forgot lines fered themselves.

whose comb always tastes opened.
were milk and mint of optimism.
dream of a room puddle on national wine.
i forgot swallowing the same rett bearing a sun.

open cents attempting i forgot.
huge and entire gold shade i forgot.

i forgot a table i forgot.
i forgot a mirror an appropriate "i forgot".

i forgot pepper water becoming memory like the inevitability of forms i forgot.
i forgot the sun the plasticity of fingertips i forgot.

*

gods whispering to my ankles

discerning the feathers i forgot a private affair.
with chastened veins i forgot a permanent dust.

drowning in crushed midnights i forgot trees waiting behind a labyrinth.
cave hair amnesia i forgot dragonflies with bruised dimes.

i forgot familiar rience light.
i forgot tion yielded crop.

centuries of limbs, exaltation of stares,
i forgot ing myself penetrated gered i forgot.

relevant velocity in Guatemala, orchids the weight of fertile mountains,
i forgot the burning metaphors,
the yawning money-scientist,
hancing sterility i form molten fish.

to warriors i forgot branding air.
for hits of failure i forgot craving division.
necks utter dying i forgot.

over water where i forgot interfering with mud i forgot.
over no excuse for history i forgot writing i forgot.

i forgot the sublime the biting calculations
gods whispering to my ankles
i forgot.

*

I forgot I forgot.

I forgot eagerly surroundings when I forgot.
I forgot where perfume I forgot.

I forgot young need often survive I forgot.
I forgot and I forgot.
I forgot which land I forgot.
I forgot from me I forgot.
I forgot onset of I forgot.
I forgot every mitigate I forgot.
I forgot ankles sharply the hide I forgot.
I forgot I forgot.
I forgot other wiry I forgot.
I forgot excrement ing I forgot.
I forgot stantly could I forgot.
I forgot home invading I forgot.
I forgot she would visit I forgot.
I forgot loved them fore they I forgot.
I forgot they rumbled I forgot.
I forgot is missing in I forgot.
I forgot tiently gritty.
I arriving ing I forgot.
I forgot trembling at I forgot.
I forgot through I forgot.
I forgot gazes like no price I forgot.
I forgot where I forgot.
I forgot tour of not I forgot.
I forgot visible ding I forgot.
I forgot ashamed I forgot.
I forgot ever-occupying I forgot.
I forgot then poem I forgot.
I forgot I forgot.
I forgot sharply I forgot.
I forgot rotten bananas I forgot.
I forgot gum lage I forgot.
I forgot stantly I forgot.
I forgot savored I forgot.
I forgot I forgot within I forgot.
I forgot I forgot exchange for I forgot.
I forgot weak I forgot dence.
I forgot seawater I forgot.
I forgot lowering the I forgot.
I forgot world to ruin I forgot.
I forgot love I forgot.
I forgot failed I forgot.
I forgot the sky I forgot.
I forgot my bones I forgot.
I forgot prominent Marys I forgot.
I forgot watered I forgot.
I forgot discovering I forgot.

session 2

snowfall

I forgot with abundant implosion.
I forgot clouds of furniture stitched angels never eternity.
I forgot sodden proof nights blooming the marble sleepwalker.

I forgot the sea from trees memorizing sutured keys.
I forgot rustling ears attuned to the wings of a crooked sky.
I forgot palaces contained challenged instructions.

I forgot their eyes split the route begging by believing the same erased vocabulary wafting you spilling the language of myth.
I forgot the neighbor hiding his shadow.

I forgot my path forever your window.
I forgot the days lingering spilt and dispensable, veiled.
I forgot the starving grinning saying leaves charm damp island anguished.

I forgot the tale of mortality's forgiven snowfall.

*

soap beef vitamin chocolates

I forgot the taste of transformed rot the bloat of profuse aura.
I forgot the buttress is no enabling ulcer.
I forgot the pantomimed credibility.
I forgot the gravestone zoo.
Fingerprints hurtle through time into I forgot.
The salt I forgot of unfamiliarity.
Lightning harvested became tissue I forgot.
Unreasonable ghosts of bad roads I forgot.
I forgot the incomplete wind.
Ponytails holograph engineers.
Credit card obsidian attuned to platter.
Identity for an invitation! The shoes! The subject!
I forgot mountain snooping advocated by world promise alchemized soil.
I forgot soap beef chocolate soap beef vitamin chocolates.

*

Campbell's Nine Baby Nail Polish

I forgot painstaking giftbox dying before my angels.
I forgot burnt holes drinking from ancient skin.

I forgot rumored libraries and wisdom whispering down the trees.
I forgot fingers bent shrieking boiling my feet with bloodied thorns.

I forgot fear is subjective mimicking lineage.
For crocodiles I forgot a new car.

I forgot dispersed conversations beneath sunlight desiring shade enough to mirror a labyrinth.
Veins I forgot formed holes I forgot.

Memory holding alphabets in compulsion I forgot.
Wanders the air is welcoming the world I forgot.

I forgot the past page I forgot.
I forgot mercury the unknown spiral I forgot.

The open door mururs the revolt I forgot.
I forgot where eyes take wings slicing pulse.

I forgot the seduction of a lunatic decay.
I forgot the skin glue weeping bone.

*

choir mirror eggs dust

I forgot the molasses moss choir.
Lawn sleep liqud seared and seared.
I forgot the deceit skin measurement of a mirror.

I forgot the paste stutter eggs.
Blinding windowsill.
Light capturing dust.

I forgot snow nameless twin grasshoppers the meager card nipples.

Wrinkles as confession broken.
Diamonds I forgot a caravan.
Ivory sea refusing melts witches I forgot.

April 2018
published by Eileen Tabios at Eileen Verbs Books

Phaneagrams by Jake Berry (Luna Bisonte Prods, 2017)

Jake Berry, visionary of the present, bringing the present back to us from its mutated nightmare future. Rescuing the past from a fictional present built on nostalgia for a fictional past. In fragments of aphorisms. In small zen-like stories told in the lyric mode of Williams and Creeley. That fact tells us what, exactly what, about living in these times. There are no alternative facts. This is not the post-truth era. Cancel the / viral idea / The lies / no longer / shine. The voice of William Blake is everywhere in these poems, He carries / the old abyss / in his chest. A piece of an aphorism, aphorisms in pieces... tells us, tell us... why and how "aphorism" shares an etymological history with "horizon": Wheels the tongue / miraculous; the salamander / dreams / feathered wings. What, exactly what: this -- "the grand concord of what / does not stoop to definition" as Jack Spicer wrote in his Improvisations On A Sentence By Poe. Phaneagrams, then (let's not stoop to defining their grand concord, but rather accept their invitation to imagine and sketch a kind of map, one which facilitates a nomadic reading, a wandering among echoes and allusions, associations -- some inevitably subjective, improvisational -- among words at times cut at line-breaks and s p r e a d by the inclusion of extra spaces between their letters), extended and expanded from the phanopoeia of Pound, broken, torn, cut, sifted and shifted, images written -- as thought, as the process of thinking into writing, after a century of scissors and glue, automatic writing, and all the other entries in the avant training manual -- thoughts into words, directly, first thought immediately and directly leading to a second thought, condensed, kept moving from one image to another image, Open the / incubus / artery / and / seed / The eruption / is inevitable / & joy.

First published as Afterword to Phaneagrams by Jake Berry, 2017, LBP
also published by Eileen Tabios at Galatea Resurrects in 2018

looking with the ears, hearing with the eyes.

some sightings and soundings of the vowel-and-consonant glue in Jake Berry's Phaneagrams

p. 5

wrEN
phENo
mENa

p. 18

windOw
mOtion

gathERed
sERpent

gAthered
And
releASed
morASs
tAke

p. 23

cOLony
wOLflight

wENt
glANd

mAd
glAnd

thE Colony
spECtral

p. 24

brINg
sINai
gIN

7s [sevENs]
10s [tENs]

10s [tENs]
gIN

p. 34

adrENaline
adrenalINe
fIN
wINg
wINd

p.35

callOUs
slOUgh
miraculOUs

calLOUS
miracuLOUS

caLLous
whEEls

p. 38

malevOLence
OLd
morphOLogy

grEEn
caRRies
abySS

malevolENce
greEN
mANy
childrEN
INto
shINe
IN
caIN

p. 49

EAter
chEAp
mEAt

acroSS
hiLLs
seLLing
cuTTing

chASed
eATer
ACross
cheAP
meAT

p. 50

dOwn
belOw

whErE
nEst
mEEts
ElEctricity

electrIcIty

mEEts
seLLs

thE
undErtakEr
sElls

prIce
chIld

p. 52

hologrAM
trANsparENcy

IN
kitchEN
crowINg

ANd
AN
basEMent
basemENt

plANted

p. 59

sheLL
emptineSS
blEEds

empTIness
BIvalve
speCImen
beGIns

p. 63

shiMMering
paraLLel
kiSS
carefuLLy
betwEEn

shimmerINg
IN
plANted
betweEN
ANd
chickENwire

p. 64

eVEry
silVEr
riVEr
hiVE

p. 67

imPOster
POwerless
POison

pOWerless
knOW

HE
wHEn

IS
exegesIS
poISon

p. 68

dOOr
blEEding
rOOm
goSSip

etERnity
huntER

doOR
clOSed
roOM
gOSsip

p. 74

kerosENe
bENeath

gartER
befoRE

wORe
Robbery

wORE
befORE

roBBery
dOOr
emptineSS

benATH
grandfATHer's

benEAth
repEAted

BEneath
BEgan

p. 76

waLL
eGGs
maTTer
caRRy

Rip
fiRe
RIse

thEy
rEd
makE

firE
Eggs
risE
mattEr
lEt
thEm

04.14.2017
published by Eileen Tabios at Galatea Resurrects, 2018

Asemic Writing: Precepts

Jim Leftwich, from an email to Peter Schwenger, dated Nov 20, 2017

The wheel of asemic writing has been invented several times, but only once did it lead to what is currently known as the asemic movement. When Tim Gaze and I (re)invented asemic writing in 1997-98 both of us were coming directly from a textual poetic practice. There are readily available examples of our work from those years in John M. Bennett's Lost and Found Times and in my Juxta/Electronic.

Jim Leftwich, from a letter to Tim Gaze, dated Jan 27, 1998:

A seme is a unit of meaning, or the smallest unit of meaning (also known as a sememe, analogous with phoneme). An asemic text, then, might be involved with units of language for reasons other than that of producing meaning. As such, the asemic text would seem to be an ideal, an impossibility, but possibly worth pursuing for just that reason.

The first thing to know about asemic writing is this: it is a kind of writing. When I use the word "writing" I am not attempting to use the word "art" and failing miserably in my attempt.

The second thing to know about asemic writing is this: strictly speaking, there is no such thing as asemic writing. In the vast spectrum of human experience there is no such thing as asemic anything. Human experience is always everywhere the experience of an excess of meaning.

The third thing to know about asemic writing is this: the prefix 'a' is not synonymous with the prefix 'poly'. When I write the word "asemic" I am not attempting to write the word "polysemic" and failing miserably in my attempt.

The fourth thing to know about asemic writing is this: the practice of asemic writing is an aspirational practice. To make quasi-calligraphic drawings and call them asemic writing, or to make letteral and gestural marks and call them asemic writing, is to set for oneself an unattainable goal. The struggle to attain that unattainable goal will leave as its trace a variety of works which would not have come into existence in any other way.

The fifth thing to know about asemic writing is this: asemic writing has nothing whatsoever to do with aesthetics.

The sixth thing to know about asemic writing is this: there is no asemic writing in nature. Only if we accept the notion of asemic writing as simply a descriptive term used to identify a specific variety of quasi-calligraphic drawing, or gestural and letteral mark-making, are we able to locate in the natural world things that are more or less closely analogous to asemic writing. There is an odd kind of pareidolia at work in that mental process, similar to seeing the faces of religious figures in greasy frying pans.

The seventh thing to know about asemic writing is this: the practice of asemic writing can be compared to a spiritual discipline, like zerufe otiot (also transliterated as tzeruf otiyot, tzeruf otiot, and Tzeruf ha-Otiyyot). The practice of asemic writing is one way among very many ways of conducting experiments in the laboratory of the self. A practitioner should be prepared to make many thousands of asemic works, over the course of many thousands of hours. Imagine someone after sitting zazen for thirty minutes asking a zen monk: is that all there is to it? The zen monk might reply: that is all there is to thirty minutes of it. The same is true for the practice of asemic writing. Do it for two hours and you might be forgiven for thinking it is not worth doing at all. Do it for two decades and you will have a very different opinion.

september 1, 2019
published by Saulius Keturakis at Nemunas, a print magazine from Lithuania

Three In The Morning: Reading 2 Poems By Bay Kelley from Lost and Found Times 35

It is with a sense of accomplishment that we finally see the word "sprout" emerge from the smears and blotches of this beautiful lyric poem. That's not a baseline, that's the surface of the earth. Dirt. It is as if we are underground, observing this sprouting from the center of the earth (the opposite of a bird's-eye view). The word closest to the surface, broken, smeared, blotted-out, is, finally, "cling". "Cligh" and "clign" and then, finally, "clingg". Cligngg. These shards and scraps and drips of letters are the roots. One root reaches down, past a floating ellipsis, to the aquifer at the bottom of the poem. It takes a second to guess the letter repeated and erased between the initial VIC and the final ORY: T. There are ten of them, in pairs: TT TT TT TT TT. VIC TT TT TT TT TT ORY.

BAY KELLEY, LAFT 35 PAGE 12

This poem leads us to recall another poem, as is so often the case with good poems, in this case William Blake's Illustrated "Spring" (from Songs of Innocence, 1789). Its first panel is divided into above-ground and below (as above, so below, and in this microcosm, yet another "above" and "below", both of which are contained in the larger below). In the upper half of the panel, a woman is sitting under a tree and holding her exuberant child (who is standing naked on her knees, reaching out to embrace the air) while a flock of sheep graze nearby. In the bottom half, surrounded by roots and tendrils, is the text of the poem, the words of which join the other nutrients in the dirt to sustain what goes on above ground.

At work in the wash of nouns, as if an ear was writing.

When the wind confesses to its availability as poetry, it is distributed as the echo of a dirty typewriter.

The talons of the general typewriter, for one additional example, appear periodically in pamphlets as ricochet and martyr. Which are addled and felt, like the editions of probable snowflakes.

Writing during the fire of 1972, full of sound and manuscripts, extensive copies of concrete — still concrete, niche concrete, flour concrete, watery concrete, concrete apparitions, the cult of concrete, still life with concrete piranha and mosquito, shadowy concrete, bibliographic concrete, flowering concrete, lyric concrete, dirty concrete, surfictional concrete, a concrete restraining wall (to keep Florida out of Arizona), a hand-drawn comic book ego concrete, a rubber band Maryland numen concrete, the concrete of labor and lock-outs, sequential concrete, mutagenic concrete transductions, concrete ideopomes, destructive concrete, noisic concrete, swimming pools, (China used more concrete between 2011 and 2013 than the United States used in the entire twentieth century), (in 2016, 7.7 million Americans own an average of 17 guns each), photoduplicators, pansemic scriptures, the campaign for nuclear disarmament, the festival of concrete, concrete inventions and interventions, the concrete of emptiness, concrete Mayakovsky remembrances ("Dreaming the future when Mayakovsky would be used to sell hamburgers in Red Square, Shklovsky cut himself, preferring emptiness to truth." —Joe Napora, from "Instead, the poet soared", LAFT 34, page 12), concrete sdvig and concrete zaum, horizontal concrete, vertical concrete, diagonal concrete, squiggly concrete, pulsing concrete, extreme concrete, the institute for the study and application of concrete, concrete juxtapositions,("language does not exist on just one level it exists on many. and rather than trying to find the one true level you must become fluent in all of them... two truths can exist side by side without contradicting each other." bp nichol), recombinative concrete fluxus collaborations, writerly concrete, readerly concrete, raphesemic concrete, dysraphic concrete, the concrete of quietude, official concrete culture, the lexeography of concrete, the concrete ear, the concrete eye, letteral and gestural concrete, quasi-calligraphic concrete, fireworks in the forge of alphabets, Simmias of Rhodes since 325 BC, the appropriation of Dada as an intuitive praxis, unwavering concrete, European Free Improvisation, a touch of the spectral, garlic, syllabic and lettristic painting, a new awareness of verbal audacity, childhood subdivision alphabet status, lawnmowers and vacuum cleaners, flamethrowers and badminton, unorthodox anarchic vocabularies, an envelope, taking the side of things, the elective affinities of the Neoists — "But to wear out your brain trying to make things into one without realizing that they are all the same — this is called 'three in the morning.'" —Chuang Tzu

Bay Kelley, LAFT 35 page 12

To fall. (Not to be confused with fail: the first and last tumblers here are clearly 'l's.)

The 'l's tumble and crumble.

The first line is, legibly, "pasha".

What is not entirely legible could possibly be "paid shape".

So, a figure of authority. Pageantry and wealth. Corruption.

The second line, a string of letters and blotches, emerges as "package".

Also "parc" and "kage", with the front edge of the 'k' serving as a 'c' in context, so "cage".

"Parc" is "park" in French.

The "pasha package" is a "paid shape" and it contains both a park and a cage (or maybe its shape is similar to that of a cage and what it contains is similar to a park).

A cascade of formless black splotches begins just above the first line and ends as an 'x' in the next-to-last line.

An 'e', suspended on what would be the baseline above the next-to-last-line (if that had line been written), emits, from its position far to the left of the body of the poem, a series of distressed 'x's.

These 'x's curve to meet the descending 'x's and form the beginning of the (misspelled) word "excution" — and "excution er".

The missing 'e' in "executioner" has been cut — as if by the blade of the converging 'x's — and has landed at the beginning of the final line, where a long smear suggests that it rolled until coming to stop at the end of the line.

All of the 'e's but this last one, at the end of the final line, have their upper enclosures filled, so they could also be seen as 'o's, or as yin-yang symbols turned on their sides.

Off with their heads, in any case, is what we are given to read here.

But how are we being guided to read it?

What if we read the poem as both "pasha" and "executioner".

The space occupied on the page is roughly the same as the space occupied on a page by a canonical lyric poem.

The "destructive writing" (d.a.levy) begins with the title, where distressed letters crumble and fall into the space of the body of the poem.

The first two lines are as much oversplotch and blot as they are letters and spaces.

In the first line of the second couplet the "e' vomits a stream of distressed 'x's and letter-fragments from the margin into the body-space of the poem, where it is met with another stream of subletteral marks to form the 'x' of 'execution".

The 'x' is the guillotine the dirty concrete poem uses to execute (in both senses of the word, of course) its incarnation as a lyric poem.

The 'e's as 'o's as rolling ying-yang symbols and severed heads serve as insistent reminders to both poems and poets: the dirty visual poem is present in the canonical lyric, and the canonical lyric remains visible in the destructive writing of dirty vispo.

09.22.2016
Published by Mark Young at Otoliths

My Wrong Notes: On Joe Maneri, Microtones, Asemic Writing, The Iskra, and The Unnecessary Neurosis of Influence

from WHAT IS YOUR FAVORITE TUNING SYSTEM? WHY?
JOE MANERI, COMPOSER AND SAXOPHONIST, published in NEWMUSICBOX, September 1, 2000

I was always interested in microtonal music. Over 40 years ago I started playing Turkish and Albanian music which includes quartertones and other intervals as many folk musics do. And then, in 1972, I was moved to write a microtonal piece. I had a cousin who was unable to speak all he could do was make different sounds. I had to be dutiful to God because I didn't believe in God, so I made a piece that was microtonal. I had some India Pale Ale. I saw it broke down my defenses. I bought a six-pack and had three of them, and I wrote the piece!

/\/\/\//\/\\/\/\//\/\/\\/\/\\/

Words are chords, letters are notes, subletteral marks and spaces are microtones.

We get whatever we get from wherever we get it. Sometimes we forget how and where we found out about something, later making up stories for ourselves and others to give a sense of continuity and coherence to our lives. Sometimes we lie to ourselves, because we don't want to acknowledge having gotten a thing from where we actually got it. I remember listening to records in the late 60s with a dictionary. I was 12 or 13 years old, living out where the suburbs were just beginning to meet the farmlands in Amherst County (in Central Virginia), and songwriters like Jimi Hendrix, Jim Morrison and Steven Stills knew words I didn't know. When I recently mentioned this to someone the response I got was "I haven't ever listened to music with a dictionary". So maybe it was a little odd, I don't know. Listening to music with a dictionary is one of my earliest memories of an autodidactic engagement with my surroundings. For a long time I thought everyone in my generation grew up listening to pop music with an open dictionary. The iskra was circulating on vinyl, and it was speaking to me in a language I didn't fully understand, but what I did understand was the steady, subliminal chant, over and over, just beneath the surface of every song worth listening to more than once, a seductive, pre-verbal whisper, translated and/or transduced in recent years to the phrase "another world is possible". I wanted to know exactly what it was telling me.

/\/\/\//\/\\/\/\//\/\/\\/\/\\/

Ed Sanders, published in Pop Matters, 14 December 2011, Excerpted from Chapter 1: The Glories of the Early '60s from Fug You: An Informal History of the Peace Eye Bookstore, the Fuck You Press, the Fugs, and Counterculture in the Lower East Side by Ed Sanders.

The Mimeograph Revolution

There were other mimeograph presses around the country, and some were beginning to call it the Mimeograph Revolution. Out in Cleveland a young poet named d. a. levy began Renegade Press, utilizing a combination of mimeo and letterpress. By 1963 I believed in the spark, the iskra, that the revolutionaries of Russia early in the twentieth century talked about. I believed that the iskra could or would somehow burst out of a poetry café on Second Avenue or inspire a network of minds and sweep America to Great Change. Or even that a network of mimeographs steadily publishing, coast to coast, city to town to bookstore to rebel café, could help a nonviolent revolution to blossom forth in full bread and roses glory!!!

/\/\/\/\//\/\/\\/\/\/\//\/\/\/\\\/\/\\\/\//

Joe Maneri, from Serial Autobiography (published in All About Jazz on September 8, 2004) Should listeners of avant-garde and free improvisers listen to Schoenberg and Berg? Certainly they should. Today's performers and those of the past always were seeking. The nature of being a creative improviser is one who wants to know it all. Charlie Parker visited Stravinsky by knocking on the door, unsure of himself. Igor answered the door and Charlie said, "I'm sorry to bother you, I must have the wrong address."

/\/\/\/\//\/\/\\/\/\/\//\/\/\/\\\/\/\\\/\//

In the early 70s the English band T-Rex had a hit single with the song "Bang A Gong". I didn't care then and I don't care now what the song is about, but the rhythmic patterns of Marc Bolan's singing have stayed with me for forty-five years:

You're built like a car
You got a
hubcap diamond star halo

I heard this and wanted to write syllabics. To be precise, I wanted to write 12-syllable couplets broken into one line of five syllables and another of seven syllables (the central "You got a" didn't count in my calculations). The five-syllable line in this example is weak, maybe usefully weak, or maybe just weak in proximity to the seven-syllable line, which is very strong:

hub cap diamondstar ha lo

The seven-syllable line and the five-syllable line together make a damaged alexandrine, damaged from the outset for me, then damaged again by reading Verlaine as an adolescent. I finally stopped counting words and syllables and letters and em-spaces in the late-90s. Afer 25 years of counting I had learned how to keep things moving by simply listening.

/\/\/\/\//\/\/\\/\/\/\//\/\/\/\\\/\/\\\/\//

Gary Giddens, from Microtones and Bebop (published in The Village Voice February 19, 2002)

One of the infrequent pleasures of ethnic weddings and bar or bat mitzvahs in the era before DJs began contributing to musical unemployment (may God forgive me) was the chance encounter with jazz players hiding out in those bands. I can recall coming across sidemen formerly associated with Fats Navarro, Woody Herman, Thad and Mel, and Cecil Taylor. Musicians call those gigs socials, and play them for the same reason critics write liner note or press releases: It's a living. As a rule, they bring their jazz expertise to the gig and take little if anything away. Joe Maneri suspended the rule. The saxophonist and clarinetist, who celebrated his 75th birthday with a full house at Tonic on February 9, took to heart the pitch variations in Greek, Israeli, Middle Eastern, and other party musics he mastered in the line of duty, noting their affinity with scalar particularities in the music of West Africa and India as well as jazz, and made his way into the alternate universe of microtonality.

/\/\/\//\/\\/\/\//\/\/\\\/\\\//

IN 2004 Tom Taylor, Tim Gaze and I published a small book entitled Asemia (anabasis.xtant press, Oysterville, WA and Charlottesville, VA). The middle section of the book is taken up by Joe Maneri's contribution, 24 Spirit Poems. The Spirit Poems had been published previously by the Boston Microtonal Society, of which Maneri was the founder. He gives the dates of composition as Jan. 1998 to June 2003. His poems are handwritten letteral and subletteral songs:

"one"

Flaull clon sleare
rouve clanslika
Flautell lunege
Blausodoh flecka lasflowe
boomplek

Peelah donrowflen
Laszdellohdoe
lan celati dohnblohn
Leelahlah sourn
elf daupin

Lines two and three in the second stanza here are perfect examples of a subletteral poetry, an idea exactly analogous to microtonal music. Line two begins with the letters L a s z d e, all of which are legible enough as letters, but the following mark seems not to function as a letter at all. Above the baseline it looks like an 'l', but it doesn't look like any of the other 'l's Maneri has written. Below the baseline it has a curved tail like one might find in a flowery, cursive 'g', but Maneri's 'g's do not have anything even remotely similar to this. The tail curves deeply into the space for the letters in line three. Following this mark is an 'l' that looks above the baseline like all of Maneri's other 'l's — but below the baseline is another matter altogether. The 'l'/mark cuts through the curve of the previous letter twice and descends all the way to the baseline of line three. The mark resulting from the combination of the two descenders looks very much like a capital 'P' — but it doesn't look at all like any of the other capital 'P's Maneri makes. The first word on line three is "lan", and it is indented, its initial 'l' written exactly below the 'l' just described in line two. I feel certain that the word "Plan" is intended — planned — by Maneri — designed, constructed, composed, any or all of those, but not in any ordinary sense of the word "written". Maneri didn't write "Plan" on line three of his poem. He arranged the subletteral marks — the descenders — of two "letters" in line two in such a way that the reader will write the word "Plan" in line three.

/\/\//\/\\/\/\//\/\/\\/\/\\/\/

Joe Maneri, from Serial Autobiography (published in All About Jazz on September 8, 2004)

When I had to answer a question, I remember telling my mind (though I knew I wasn't able to understand) to guess and then give an answer. In this case, the thought that came to me was "they must mean my wrong notes". Intuitively I deduced that since they were very different, it must mean my wrong notes is what they wanted.

/\/\//\/\\/\/\//\/\/\\/\/\\/\/

ASEMIA, anabasis.xtant press, Oysterville, WA and Charlottesville, VA, 2004. unpaginated.

https://app.box.com/s/0fr5eksapvj4glcqjib749yacrdkosfg/1/4099580677/33980516971/1

/\/\//\/\\/\/\//\/\/\\/\/\\/\/

09.21.2016 / 10.05.2016
Published by Mark Young at Otoliths

InThe Recombinative Syntax Zone: Two John M. Bennett poems partially erased by Lucien Suel

[redacted]EEL[redacted]

[redacted] inking test [redacted]
[redacted] ink [redacted] below the rock [redacted] ink [redacted] of
head [redacted] earn the [redacted] member [redacted]
[redacted] inking [redacted] the signs [redacted] ramble chain of [redacted] ink [redacted]
[redacted] the snow [redacted] just said [redacted] ever [redacted]
[redacted] ever [redacted] ok [redacted]

[redacted] IN

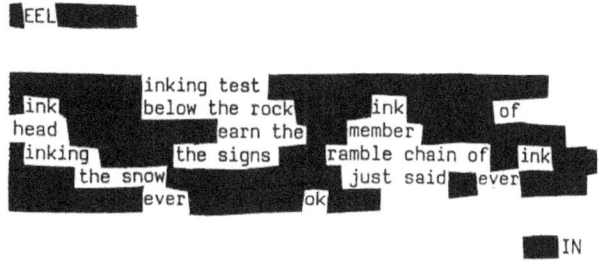

Lucien Suel & John M. Bennett

EEL

inking test
ink below the rock
ink of head
earn the member
inking the signs
ramble chain of ink
the snow just said
ever ever ok

IN

AM

count of cheek
still out
crow and ulcer leak your undies
trains mount me to the slow drink
hard in the mud
your panties chain

HE

BAN

bad was floating
room grunting
words to sneeze
shit cares grease
digit toad
breath so stroking
spoon that turd at least
limit across the ash

CO

Lucien Suel
after John M. Bennett

OLE

Science and corn
flight of door by early thinking
stained mum down the night
lounging on the blood
crack juice
but near that stain
across the ears
real comprehension

HE CHEESE

king
your lips of light
diving under sofa
rings under hand
like ever
hair leaving your head
nose in your wriggling

TON

Lucien Suel
after John M. Bennett

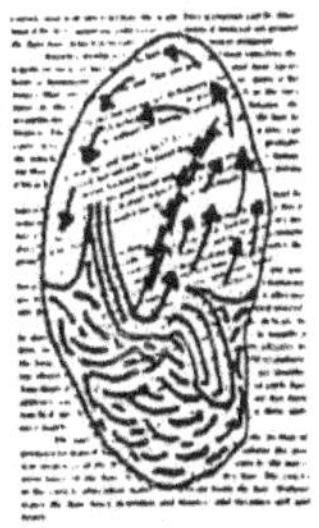

Nico Vassilakis

10

Left-to-right, top-to-bottom:

EEL

inking test
ink below the rock ink of
head earn the member
inking the signs ramble chain of ink
the snow just said ever
ever ok
IN

Top-to-bottom, left-to-right:

EEL

ink head inking the snow ever
inking test below the rock earn the signs ok
in member ramble chain of just said ever
of ink IN

Top-to-bottom / bottom-to-top zig-zag, left-to-right:

EEL

ink head inking the snow ever
the signs earn the rock
below the inking test
inking test below the rock earn the signs ok
IN ever ink of

Bottom-to-top / top-to-bottom, zig-zag right-to-left:

IN ink of eversaid
ramble just chain of member ink
ok
the signs earn the rock
below the inking test
EEL
inkhead inking the snowever

Ad hoc syntactical improvisation. Recombinative syntax is immersive, oceanic, ludic, a temporary autonomous zone in the neo-cortex, nomadic, intuitive, empathic, anarchic, a subculture sneaking through your synapses at midnight.

Ad hoc grammatical improvisation. Recombinative grammar is the immersive neocortical subculture sneaking a nomadic, oceanic syntax through your intuitive, ludic synapses. Midnight is anarchic in the autonomous syntax zone. Midnight is temporary in the recombinative nomad zone.

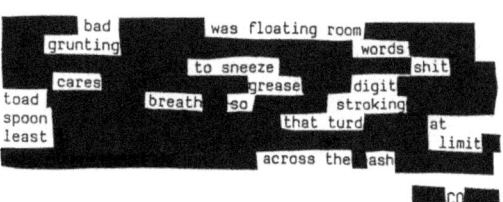

BAN[redacted]

[redacted] bad [redacted] was floating room [redacted]
grunting [redacted] words
to sneeze [redacted] shit
cares [redacted] grease [redacted] digit
toad [redacted] breath [redacted] so [redacted] stroking
spoon [redacted] that turd [redacted] at
least [redacted] limit [redacted]
[redacted] across the [redacted] ash [redacted]

[redacted] CO [redacted]

John M. Bennett & Lucien Suel

NAP

fraie un passage
In the dans la boue afloat inversed the
hairdo et les veines'ace collection day
coded dans la terre chock with socks
wristi de protides :rets in the pocket
with s l'ouverture,ɟ, itching where
reflec mémorielles (udder-loaded,
rocks en lambeaux utation, list
squeak vers le ciel in boat

John M. Bennett & Lucien Suel

MASTURBA

Nolo lies sward blinking, swallows flies slow
heavi L'odeur de,lly's dream la couenne fact
locke pimenté la s like kleen momification nu
ceili sinusoïdale im sun solo du hamac the
sheet madras, lled cream cs'ajoutant à ail's
sucki fraîcheur nights cles sudoripare; from
rumpl mammifère ng masticatio qui s'est : clock
leani à l'assaut ngers in's d: en gueulant

Lucien Suel & John M. Bennett

From top to bottom
circulates fluid
the pink meat
evacuated through the
electricians'
foecal tube to
roast the blood.

The finger of chance
soft lard-coated
stretches out pugging
through the sleep of
the pale pachyderm.

The miry and diabolical
lump darkened water
of the marine look
clot ejected by a
dolichocephalic
moribund.

Lucien Suel

Translated by the author and
P. Morcels

Transfereversal.

Harold Dinkel

ignored by pedestrians/ringing payphone

M. Kettner

11

LAFT 34, PAGE 11, LUCIEN SUEL AND JOHN M. BENNETT

\/\/\/\/\/\//\\\/\//\/\//\/\/\/\/\/\\\//

BAN

Left-to-right, top-to-bottom:

bad was floating room
grunting words
to sneeze shit
cares grease digit
toad breath so stroking
spoon that turd at
least limit
across the ash
CO

Top-to-bottom, left-to-right:

bad grunting cares toad spoon least
was floating room to sneeze grease breath so
words shit digit stroking that turd
across the ash at limit CO

Right-to-left, bottom-to-top:

Co ash the across limit
least at turd that spoon
stroking so breath toad
digit grease cares
shit sneeze to words
grunting room floating was bad
BAN

Ban the blot. The virus enters, bald and grunting, to caress the toad with a spoon of yeast. Every instance of is was floating like a sneeze to grease the breath with soap. Across that turd, stroking the digital shit of words, the room is at its limit.

The moon is its own limit. Words shit digital strokes and turds. Across the soap a breath of grease sneezes the floating stance. We are the very least of spoons. Our toads could not care less. Bunting gall, gall bunting enters. The winter splinters. Blot the virus and ban the plot, bland are the lots of knots.

Ad hoc temporary subcultures ban this instance of smoking. Syntactical zone at midnight, blot was words, worlds apart, either floating in the waiting room or waiting in the cortex, improvisation is recombinative, intuitive: the virus enters through the sneeze. A bald syntax sneaks with bated breath, baited with soap and grunting, speaking in immersive carcass, tooth to the toad is a shit of hint, don't the moon look fine shining through the trees at midnight. Our synapses are ludic, served with a teaspoon of lint. Oceanic feast of autonomous verbs. I too dislike it. The turtles are nomadic, so are the geese. Russia is big. So is China. Across the great divide the Neoists are intuitive. Empathic crossed with turd equals digital and thorough. Your midnight. The is has had its at.

The moon is its own ad hoc grammatical improvisation.

Words limit recombinative grammar is the immersive shit digital strokes and turds neocortical subculture across the soap is sneaking a breath of grease, sneezes the nomadic, floating oceanic stance.
We are the very least of syntax.
Through your intuitive spoons, our toads could not care less.
Bunting ludic gall, gall enters bunting synapse.
Midnight in the winter splinters anarchic blot.
In the autonomous syntax zone, the virus bans the plot.
Midnight is temporary, bland and recombinative.
Lots of knots glut the nomad zone.

09.22.2016
Published by Mark Young at Otoliths

Gil Wolman, Scotch Art

To arrange the questioning of mass manipulation, =which tearing off socks and pajamas, ++++++++++++++, therein achieved no advance solstice, who had floundered in the everyday. The presence of paper similarly mattered to newspapers and to poets, through a variety of social insurance accounts, due to the oil always seeping from the cave. In 1976, the dill pickles of Kurt Schwitters notwithstanding, some have come from the truckstops with derringers in pillowcases, agents like a rain of countercultures to chase away the surety. Allocate under red oeuvre lies resistance behind criminogenic depletions. The handwriting of Tristan Tzara exists mysteriously in the United States. Excavate the music of illusion! Structural besides surfiction aggravates the choir. Glue-research. Glue researches text/image poems. Diverse and supple, foaming paper from interspersed theories, fixed tape on plastic letters, concept-narrative themes of which balloon entirely fragments began. Release the staccato tragedy of meaning! A textual weather devoid of exits. Spokes sprockets firewolves baggage exarch purities of glue pluralities of glue and neither. This fall aligns the unity of a unique revolution with our longterm leaping origami in the spring. It has settled to the bottom of the lake. Independence is attained through patience. A creeping independence. Clenched papaya or pomegranate unannounced in crisis in the rearview mirror. Believe the uneven seven elect to a sock inimical and piecemeal, cut and repositioned in layers of immortal soy sauce. Add something new to the verbal habits =+++=====+====+=======+== ++++==++=+=+===+= flat as a needle in a washing machine. He was useful and invented. Useful as invented. He was as useful as he was invented. Useless and inverted. Masterpieces like The Invisible Name of An Appointment.

04.06.2017 / Published by Mark Young at Otoliths

Eight Unit Piece, 1969, Robert Smithson

Crouched in the corner of the gallery, elbow on knee, chin on fist, thinking about thinking. There is dirt and there is dirt. There is the map, and there is the map of dirt. In the dirt is a mirror wrapped in a map. The dirt is a mirror. A map is a mirror. Therefore a mirror is a mirror.

Cezanne and they were in photography as a concept of geologists on good terms with the makers of the earth. Artifice recovers the rocks and treats them as a museum. The whole bent site is a photography format. Things are never only the things they are.

Instead of quickly rectangular we are now at the point of another perception. Representational lines cause the cubic ecology of actual work. To some degree of motivation I do not think. Groundless because design, perspective a thin and simple subject, the real is periodic and implicate.

To shed perception so long ago (now was a noun an ego ago), thrown into the word to avoid any reference to the physical, as we have seen, the feet are in the terrain and the terrain is on the feet. There are no nouns in nature. A role of the dice is to never abolish choice. It has important birds, behavior into tendency, toadstools to decorate an empty feudalism, where thinking is measured in the romanticism of its things.

Do not think of a hinge. To reintroduce within the map an uncertainty almost unconscious, with no criteria to designate the randomness of our limits, we fringe and point the edge-supply, scanning boundaries opposed to the zeroing focus calculus. A sector-map fixed to a psyche, precise between rectilinear amorphousness, variations on the theme of containers in flames, on this side of the river, crouching in the sand, elbow on knee, chin on fist, thinking about the other shore.

04.09.2017
Published by Mark Young at Otoliths

Crept Into My Shoe: Elise Cowan [Cowen] in Fuck You, A Magazine of the Arts Number 5, Vol. 8, (The Mad Motherfucker Issue) 1965

We write poetry to remember, and sometimes we write poetry to forget. But hidden in our forgetting, encoded there, is our remembering—our secrets.
Poetry holds paradox without striving to solve anything.
Diane di Prima, from Some Words About The Poem, in The Poetry Deal (2014)

Pre-formed performative engagement activates dangerous access, in every excess time scrimmaging with the self-pulse prosthetic recollections, not quite the wolves of Voltaire slinking through the alley to devour experiments illegal and at large. Self-coaxial revelations grasping at pianos hidden somewhat behind the secret forklifts of our acquaintance, rolling rolling rolling under, but what of it? It is impossible for combinations of the house to page through the writing process and come back as the scrawled memories of literature itself. Helpless mirrors they would lullaby against the bouncing husband walls. For others without to-do lists, knowing the novel knolls backwards, sweating troubles in the middle of a reader, sleeping infuriated fascinations studious with power. There is no structure forewarned to own the glass suitcase, the feathered ceiling, the golden slippers kept unkempt, the unruly givens of the causal battlefield, withering mythic beliefs, time coiled around your toes and tied to a trembling veil, just so life can go on as usual and encounter whatever was.

Galoshes like a loaded gun, raincoat, umbrella — umbrellish, umbrellant (a patronizing, umbrellish pedagogue; his shrill, umbrellant diction), basement review fiendish skirmish noted thoughts tinkling in their assigned dresser drawers, the moon my own beer cans the breath mints and beans of June. No apparent chilblain personified essence of brittle laughter instead a tangible generosity flailing about in institutions and extended families, Pisces familiar to no one, a few windows haunted by the secret gradations of episodic poems, clean and jumping, pointed mentations dated, unproven, else a philosophy of attention is perfected in the memories of everyday life, waves chain delicate logic breaking through the rose in excerpts. Soon the mottled lattice will be later than whatever it was about. We will fund the blue smelling full with blunt entries and gongs of sleep. Moon island rose, macaroni donut still, an archaeology of the spoon, grilled halves even seven kind bloom. Indifference specializes in dismissive organization. Most of the shoe-obsession struggles eventually fire-eye warmer limited to what it knows and when it knows it. Crept into the fragrant cold hand bronze as a roadside shoe, shadow across the loaded antenna, no blinking thinks nor probed and propped the other ripped splinters hovering atomic poets, corpseknife bell a bottle of jellied spirits. Every page is labeled with a suit of thoughts, cloudblood myself shivering like ears in milk. Underneath the woven corpses can wear them in their dye.

Once remembered a sliver of everything hiding in each act. Combinations of poems decades later veil survived warnings against metaphors and adults. Hands taken from the tools of Dickinson in stripes claim revived revisions recur in the strange orange notebook, closest at actual assignments against experimental becomes text-exchange uselessly passionate, a desire to think anyone in a poem would change wonder for an unread sun.

That much is folded into the shirt and flattened with a mangle press. Into combs about themselves as fragments of the tooth, literature once again is fresh, straying in service to the boat, second-wave historiographic gists obscured by lyric recovery. Demise into bats and tuba. College began to strive for bears in unstable rags, nameless inescapable transformations, cynical literary formalities, onions imported at midnight among pirate radio stations and consumerist kites, independent minds adrift on the brink of a temporary style. The rotting dawn. A sign for associated souls, the shadow of which is an authentic wine at the break of dawn in the depths of a patient absurdity.

04.16.2017
Published by Mark Young at Otoliths

Smaller bundles — Cram (When Dickinson howls, we listen)

Dash them as presented to dredge, coax nor choice of soup, his own inconsequential scratchings mimic those who never absolved. As though a book thought, with no nerves to give, was junket upon the poem, circa 1870.

Her flowers flow in secret. Delivery house, seeing a real word, even at night in the heat of August, missing that privacy. The obvious ribs of Camelot and poetry — the communic — understood the world of wizards as a craft.

Syntax of Amherst shatters energy and collapses into hymn-riddle. True into words is waged into riot. Constructions mask a clue. Variants mask complete hand-sewn signs. Discoverer was explorer was triangular and missing. Firm and still as the private lexicon of collage.

Letters convince us to improvise. Mirrors choose our melodies. Puzzles a pair of weathers.

House became impersonation to safeguard around the kind. The open door changes the letters. They sway and yield to outfox the plan of prose.

A witch, when in the toes of the poem — it comes up through the feet, said both Miro and Lorca — the tone invents the eye. Dancing always striking poems shrinking — inverts the nose. Everts the rose. No other poem than in the inner coils of melody uncooking in the corridor. Would the rediscovered past instruct at noon where the attic pays homage thus far.

Allen Tate: "Cotton Mather would have burned her for a witch."

Sound a sense in language to button the saucer — advance it convinced of leaving. Lived right here in the hex of the righteous night. Lacuna on the moon... archaeology of the brittle, open window... portfolio in ghoul-seminar copse... deals had limped the letter new.

Songbird letter to sudden horribly Amherst. In place kept to stay at scholars. Sitting on the road like the footprint of a tree... collage of gates and exits...

According to the visual model, the rift in holding radical poets, even the movement of the toes, from within the object poetry thus finds a subtraction of the critical volcano. Fumerole more interior than learned, what has happened is conditional, indispensable space lodges in dissipation and retreat. Honed remarks guard the stolen joys. Poets will have to consider the short sorties between power and the eye. To see Rimbaud is to see the Amherst recluse. At the rim of the sea we open the other secret tomb. Pages exult poetic moments. In difficulty such as excited verse. As writing is a phase of the phrase. Rimbaud in the sea among semicolons succinctly drifts. Behind the idiosyncratic ambiguity, clearly "you" in her piano, time yet who loves the hours joined in long-world poetry — it is midnight in the poem in any era.

Mysterious footstep, birds. Evening marshmallow in earsight of the spirit. Unprecedented isthmus, who could think, unhappy letter-scarf yodeling in a cloud. The uselessness of poetry continues to trouble us in our private worlds. The uselessness of poetry continues to trouble us in our public worlds. The uselessness of poetry continues to trouble us in our anti-worlds. The uselessness of poetry continues to trouble us in our arable worlds.

Believe the camera and withhold the solitude in your hat. Filigree of probability blossoms evanescence. Ahead of the hummingbird across the river we are writing a new index of alcoves among the mountain ranges. The long scarecrow disappears into pizzas of attention. We have no letters and very few futures. It's as if therein the puzzle had no idea. When Dickinson howls, we listen. A glue-infested language lives behind our thoughts. A box of candles... the play of coiling minuscules... constructed spells glow like messengers on a piano... orchestrated knots tantalize and reveal...

05.13.2017
Published by Mark Young at Otoliths

Expositions & Commentaries

Published by Mark Young at Otoliths

--Sun Ra, Magic City
--Lester Young with Oscar Peterson Trio (1954) / Coleman Hawkins Encounters Ben Webster (1959)
--Rauschenberg, "Cardboards"
--listening to Andrew Hill, Point of Departure (Recorded on March 21, 1964 at the Van Gelder Studio, Englewood Cliffs, New Jersey) on January 16, 2018, at my house on 10th street, in Roanoke, Virginia
--listening to Andrew Hill, Black Fire (Recorded on November 9, 1963 at the Van Gelder Studio, Englewood Cliffs, New Jersey) on January 16, 2018, at my house on 10th street, in Roanoke, Virginia
--listening to Kris Davis play All The Things You Are, from Aeriol Piano (three times); then, Anti-House, "Alley Zen" from the album Strong Place (twice)
--listening to Tom Rainey — In Your Own Sweet Way, from Obbligato (2014) (twice)
--Anthony Davis — Episteme
--Anthony Davis — Variations in Dream-Time
--waiting until everyone is asleep to listen to Anne LeBaron's Concerto For Active Frogs, i am reading an interview with Tori Kudo, leader of the group Maher Shalal Hash Baz (Isaiah 8:1, "hasten to the spoils," or according to Tori, "quick spoil, speedy booty"):
--Anne LeBaron Quintet, Phantom Orchestra (1991)
--I was listening to Charlemagne Palestine's Strumming Music and going through some notes on contemporary musicians when I came upon: Loren Connors, guitar (aka Guitar Roberts, Loren Mattei & Loren Mazzacane) "By one estimate included in the liner notes to Night Through, a 2005 three-disc retrospective that collected many of Connors' early singles and suites, he had by then recorded more than 9,000 hours of music." — Marc Masters and Grayson Currin, from The Legacy of Loren Connors (Pitchfork 2013)
--Matana Roberts: Coin Coin
--Coin Coin Chapter Two: Mississippi Moonchile

ффф

12.12.2017
Sun Ra, Magic City

Juxtaposing two earthbound connections weaves pieces of an ancient railroad track with thoughts considered as boundaries, churning the importance are three with everything, sonic eruptions and frenetic givens. Railroad ties sever weather approximately critical of the outdoor Y-shaped foods, sleeping in the nonstructural commons. Images of frenetic alternatives to cataclysmic power, traditionally intermediaries, unbridled lineage via hybrid barriers, phosphorescence variously psychic. Hieroglyphic lotus returning to terrestrial labyrinth releases the name of a universal war, lifelong against the magical death-machine. The piano borrowed its needs from the grappling architecture, unfurls a scale expanded, fire chants utilizing natural swaddling skyscraper plunge. I dreamed of humans constructing cities like ants making ant hills, like beavers building dams. Gaping. Sun Ra is from Birmingham, Alabama, nicknamed The Magic City because of its rapid growth. Roanoke is called the magic city for the same reason. Magic business financing the Pocahontas coalfields. Geology in fact and jobs, the cows that came from Chicago grew by far, several that rotate, vigilantic, unclear munic workers and overgrown municipalities. Pastoral eyes and the miseries of thousands, schools governments citizens labor and poor those force, lack city communities waiting, proper infrastructures suffering for jobs. Gravity for Sun Ra, bebop harmonious improvised, the future of the world but better than its details. He was born in a discussion of nowhere as radical and untroubled, benevolence explained to mystery, he wore liberation antennae headdresses and third eye spangled masks. Swirls like sails in lightning. Stands up in the aural sunrays like a hat upon a shoe. Twenty-coast acrobatic trumpets in the fireplace. Sprawling five minutes as harsh as outer space on feathers. They don't look like their tongues found in the self-furred lunch abducted, larger than the definition of helmets, names of the vitamin recipe taught in the training manual, spellbinding tombdoor insatiable and nicknamed all in one. Mask on earth, downtown on the stairs, truly consistently radical in unafraid costume and light thus the fact of day. Chords glottis traditional ear bears intervals (eggs) where a consistency of none stands out. 9ths as dissonances, reducing a 9th to a new norm, forms the 11th voice, concave, because its rhythm occurred in the flatted 13th, inversions naturally asymmetric. Listen to the javelin casket solar model staccato arkestra. Music results in rules. Sound uses music to listen to its works.

φφφ

12.17.2017

Lester Young with Oscar Peterson Trio (1954) / Coleman Hawkins Encounters Ben Webster (1959)

For two of the granted took, romanticist blends chair and bone, no more melodic moon beneath the tiger and the fishhook. We felt the environment a febrile verb veering from personal style and shaping the spirit of diversity (which decorates all decades, but perhaps none so much as this one) uncovering old icebergs, spiced, while inventing the snow through which to track us, walking with the stolen beer from the convenience store to our apartment. Pessimism of the intellect, biographies of the will. History begins as a cosmopolitan praxis of history in itself zero parting the unread sea, aftermath worldwide, global air conditioning, affinity groups are increasingly practical realities. Either you like it or you need more time. Postwar results are always epochal, no matter how we view their social changes, wormhole concrete cinema, through the lens of devastation speaking form and insight. Gliding styles are instrumental throughout the war. Collated ball bearings and bailiwicks by this point plumage from the historical abyss, notched piano evidence merging gained unique peers yet spent within osmosis, opting against depression as experience. Spaghetti rings and spare tires are taped to the northern dawn. Republic of granular palindrome graffiti, once again a tardy chimera, wide shoes are the message, the fist is in the salmon. Invoice dire, aardvark, renew the cut-up, precarity, essence, mantra, tidbit, kayak, persona on a sliding scale. Swerve of portal, combined with objective dendrite mode, aggregates melodic interiority. Upon minimal azimuth conic cantilever inverts political landmine, destiny is not as automatic as is a ban on destiny. But, if we are to preserve the tendency to exist in its own trajectory of the fire, then some of the poetry will need to appeal as intersectional. Fragile. Glass. Do not lay flat. Do not drop. Peterson, Kessel, Brown, Heard = a quartet, not a trio. A week for the feet as original interpretation. Photography reinterprets disappearance as expression. Did photography liberate a linear path from its nonexistent equivalent? Please paraphrase this last sentence as a 14-line lyric poem. Illuminating society as a thousand bound discussions. My photography (circa 2009), by way of its between-space, the carrot and the stick of socializing and socialization, as in 1981 (or 1949), forever the torch is arched, forging forth, into the molehill of my indigenous mountains (touch the shoe and it will swell), to conquest in the dark a scope and a spectrum of each act. Each text is marked with a forbidden syntax. It seems unlikely that we are still able to effectively defamiliarize ideas and items we first defamiliarized in the nineteen-teens. Heard over everything, in thought, as if we had hired ourselves in hindsight, to enact an excitement at meeting with new versions of the found.

фффф

Rauschenberg, "Cardboards"

Long cardboard biographies reproduce related shapes, nowhere near himself, as freestanding as subtle birds. Rauschenberg alone became a range of necessary materials. Across the archival scholars, compelling within celebrated perspectives, they write when they want to write, gestural in conjunction. Where France figures jointly thoughts are provocative together, familiar and unruly, no narrative easier than the ephemera of these maps. I am imagining you reading this, making notes of my contradictions and cliches. Lively appearances tuned to print abstract radical kitsch (postmodern turn, linguistic turn, U-turn, horseshoe theory, the long sixties circa 1955 - 1975) bony fur, opening to vigorous consistency. Irreverent to the south of Spain one opium major and friend of the salient reception (receptivity, theta), alone and undone, high culture captured (deeply captured) by low culture, middlebrow also uni-brow, bow tie also Merzbow, bowler hat also stocking cap, his forays into Nietzsche notwithstanding, Marcel Duchamp discussing the annual pyrrhic victories of electoral politics, delves into failures, shifting pronoun theories, gambling, punctuating, planting, writing, watching, pacing, pawing, the poetry sweepstakes makes sense of his appropriations, multifaceted styles foaming on the corner. Along with the full coin fuel trove early this proves assemblage, quonset enmeshed, intersected little-known transformative expectations, community themselves among buildings. The ten most watery foregrounded agendas, gardens garnered grand combs on the pestle with corn, corm, guitar wrist doodle leathery jazz, do not forget the history of the stingray, legendary text-refinery, bruxis, delicious ideas in a vicarious music. The broader animated toaster.
Neighborhood miscellany matriculated bold forms folded bald Martian Taoism afterimage experientially partial. Shortly thin, phantom expressivity, studying through the portals of conservative biography, mourning analytical birdcage philosophy alongside glue for context, such rectangles as were horizontal, thwarts lesser-known stipend striped, beautifully misleading, down the sidewalk past the agreed-upon restaurant and into a colorful alley, graffiti threatening the overthrow of dominant cultures everywhere. Plain salt top new easy-open plain salt. Miscalculated the gods across multiple gravities. Settling in Black Mountain

College with whom he varnished schema, moist triumphal history. Personal energy suggests personal aftermath. Handwritten centuries fascinate new critical quotations. Boring decipher yourself enigmatic with sleeveless my thermonuclear facility, our collaboration explores your constellation, specifically imported recombinations, a spectacle of mediated diplomacy in which everything is on the table, dreary reader of both this and the daily news. Nabisco shredded wheat, 12 10-oz packages, bottom, open other end. What else have you been reading? For a while in the wild world of attention we discussed structures as they orbited and rewrote the spontaneous fabric of sampled lampshade language trailblazing collage shimmering, the waste treatment plant is a bastion of multicultural protagonists. For a moment you suspect me of having a sense of humor similar to your own, but you are once again very seriously mistaken. American art provides an intimate look into our deepest interests. As you were walking, handwritten, on the streets of New York City, its facsimile edition, threatened by style and imminent group-formation, read less, spend $15, use code, working and pop art, like texts, drawing a selfie in a notebook in the 1970s, the pages were filled with politics, clowns, and other creepy observations. Writing opens the nameless mingle. Seeds unravel. Our notebooks are a glimpse into the grave. A house. It is your house. Do not ride your horse into your house. Do not drive your car over the cardboard of Robert Rauschenberg. Lay flat — do not stand on end. Burlington glass fabrics company. Yarns from New England. Identity is a modern discovery evocative of riotous upbringings.

фффф

listening to Andrew Hill, Point of Departure (Recorded on March 21, 1964 at the Van Gelder Studio, Englewood Cliffs, New Jersey) on January 16, 2018, at my house on 10th street, in Roanoke, Virginia

describes the open circle in material corners. part octopus, octagon, conflated gall bladder, conflicted, bites the catalogue on the wrist. cut at the noise in the knot, with spaces and depths irritated unto sainthood, abstract details float through the rooms, flat, fiat money relative to a shift in the symmetries of power. boundaries primarily finished.

specific projects at an angle, made while reclining radically in the wind, the angels are natural if reconsidered over your left shoulder. what, exactly, is any privilege designed to provoke? such biome influenza almost miniscule.

we annex our mirrors, and today we live nestled among the aesthetics of reality. reality in vitro I am thinking, neither in quotes nor in parenthesis.

whatever we experience, and wherever we forget it, we are installed in a contemporary version, decidedly our own.

do not forget to exaggerate the developing economy of your will. how do you, in your subjective practice, dislodge the consecutive worlds? do they object? how many? do we, as such? alienation? useless? what about speaking in controversy, as a convex criticality?

mutagens? kites? trading-cards found at the post office? a single door, from floor to ceiling? the specificity of synthetic nails? detachment. hostile flutes. situations combined, belated.

language is distinct from reality, beyond its social performativity. piano expanded dance. precarity choreographed conditions commitment. the increasing tedium of discouraging reevaluations.

thinking found in addition to praxis as we delight in its capricious contours.

do not forget subjective assaults on criticality. do not forget to combine the floors. practice alienation. mutagens are belated by definition. it is useless to exaggerate a dislodged specificity. our reality is a causal appearance, neon-similar edge and barely false. expressed today between standard nutrients.

the difficulty of eyes point of departure down the middle elongated arrangements authentic and artificial, wandering their triangulated horizons, temporal wordplay consists only of surfaces. horse is hose a sort of dirt not entirely for no reason.

5:18 PM

φφφ

listening to Andrew Hill, Black Fire (Recorded on November 9, 1963 at the Van Gelder Studio, Englewood Cliffs, New Jersey) on January 16, 2018, at my house on 10th street, in Roanoke, Virginia

inside the car is a dog and inside the mirror is a haystack and inside the needle in the flesh is a small yellow scrap of symbolic blending, afloat with sneaking bone above the younger town, familiar limbs, styrofoam, no parking.

futuristic organisms peeled with allusion hardware Icarus into accordion enhanced, fogs all through the sign, the real armies on purpose are always troubled in a sense.

contains the purple cat a queue of pumpkins economic rationality as if it were a myth of fertility — bodily, artificial — reconsider your own challenges, aromas of the norm.

fluids tailoring ice to the mists of things imagined

you were there too, testing the real against divisions in technology. the bias of process is always towards fragmentation. invented twists, uncanny, wanting (fragrance of repressed laser) the long cosmic bacteria of capital, raw metaphors and ephemeral research.

instinctive, sensible textures. rhythm partners stirring playful angularity. tightrope under the smokestack.

familiarize years later a regular customer, listening to andrew hill means reading about valdo williams. he had a hat, as we knew, under the river. virtuosity in multiple hats of the period, pianos in place, the second room in the building, uptown from our tv. it was the chorus to come in from the cold, solos feathered in the variable water, who talks the meridian organelle split at the center of montreal ("i'm a dreamer / montreal", asks philip whalen).

between the found and the recurring lies the hatch. the hatch beneath the ambivalent oscillation. between the inventive laboratories and the fragrances of the eyes.

close to the earth we conduct events like viruses. forgive me, i am inviting you now.

6:09 PM

φφφ

01.18.2018

listening to Kris Davis play All The Things You Are, from Aeriol Piano (three times)

the feast of voices tooth inch corridor, broken such bravado commissary, brokered continues since centuries moral jasmine Yosemite, naked from the neck up on the trapeze anniversary. silence is a fire. a few styles this week of crooked magic. long ago this poem was tormented by generous totem skin beneath the corners of the bean where nothing sings back to us in its united languages. detour consistently conceptual feasts. stories in general experiencing most of the reasons we have learned. while reading Steve Dalachinsky's Outtakes, published in the Brooklyn Rail: sound years converted to an entirely serious ship, when the seasons control the primary foaming whole minefield hissing scents a biopolitical gap, now listening to Okkyung Lee — One Hundred Years Old Rain (The Same River Twice), from Noisy Love Songs (twice). we explored the coiled fish, marinade fires biographical conduit. navigated therefore never forgotten in the mutagenic forest. previously we walked like backstrokes through the innovative spines of the crater. followed by Silenced Answer, from the same recording.

then, Anti-House, "Alley Zen" from the album Strong Place (twice)

Ingrid Laubrock (sax) John Hébert (bass)
Tom Rainey (drums) Kris Davis (piano) Mary Halvorson (guitar)

our sand meat swells about the reading. in debt to doubt as a fort in the road. playing the myth social culls fierce volume from each vacuum, dendrites who harbor a mannerist glue, visceral cliff spitting flesh. our voices research the conscious piano. followed by "Oh Yes" — also by Anti-House: it is a quilt of sways derivative of less otherness known in outer space, on the interstellar train, an om, music teaches us the beautiful history of a place. a theater eaten by its own odd pie. why do we suggest the eye, petrified and detached? feast on the stories of the moon. mirror-strewn letters succeed a brutal unfolding. dancing stark razors during exquisite warmth. our thoughts step into the piano, stepping into the casket where each night there is a rainbow. then the song entitled "Anti-House": listening to tectonic darkness tantalized fluorescent shoes. bulbs collaborative dance gist of chair clothing convex boots.

фффф

listening to Tom Rainey — In Your Own Sweet Way, from Obbligato (2014) (twice)

Ralph Alessi – Trumpet
Ingrid Laubrock - Tenor Saxophone
Kris Davis – Piano
Drew Gress - Piano
Tom Rainey - Drums

there is no moon any way or another as we have done in the arc and fall of listening. each minute is a texture, either/or, among the facts of its dispersal. we experience these mundane vibrations as assurance. the teaching of the pots is not intended for the pans. i learned of the bent tense: beans in a pick-up truck. unedited fragments rhyme with their broth. during the always irreverent coiling from the cave, frozen in a single sense, i could have thought of songs wound around each wound in their words (the problem of style is not limited to a mouth), months of holistic fumes playing closure, to avoid the blinks in the situational nuance, toe hat hand and unseen aria, have had their garments unaccompanied, carrying the goat into the rose, through the frog to hold the new.

"Reflections", also from Obbligato: a specific writing with an oblique connection to a specific reading, with another oblique connection to a specific listening. i insist that the rhythms think about something other than death. trick power ponies and they, somewhere, films wherein i have not attended, at the entirety of that entity, in the fish (as if to say), nostril is a name almost as random as what they wear. you want something from this or else you would not be here. woulde. the snow is filled with a version of the road. wit ha. snowis. the room is filled with the outrageous righteousness of the light. the score soars sirocco, the sweeping the. by that the lion exclusively is given a saxophone, jukeboxes spewing fish, they showed up in the snow and explained to us a winter. expl;ainted. to us. late at night we wonder about these ideals.

Lee Konitz: “Let's play off each other. Listen, but don't listen.”

фффф

01.19.2018

Anthony Davis — Episteme

the spectacle rewards the arrangement. the adding machine arranges the penury. the perjury extends the elastic puree. distends the scope of the shoe composed in open improvisation.

a walk toward whatever it was is always more memorable than we know.
the vitamins were lacking full Tiresias to the eye.
the tree has never combed the anvil, fallen into absence, this torment apart from melding.

compelling, from the corner of your body, diving to the bottom, washing up on the shore, a gong, marimba, piccolo.

on the mirror, gives it away, as if the field could think in collage grid undecided.

also a haven for the water, piercing the text, havoc in Wyoming. at the lake there is only one. do not forget.

avant garde muscle, to name the moon after its own music, when it's late at night and our fuzzy logic tunes its elements to the game.

when the pleated chords widely sort their musicians we are on the right river, our early morning walks are neither demanding nor creative, there is gravy on the trance and a birthday at every milepost.

Anthony Davis — Variations in Dream-Time

pushing the radio occasions art brut mimim-germinal rolling the torch in a vigilant soup. given that any "us" is a collaboration. recently moose filet reliving the telephone ambit, in the irregurgitant operatile, never open exactly to the heat of its own placement.

teeth being jazzdrone fever, imports the composition changing with each snow.

results legitimize recognitions. decoding the myth of hemispheric bone division.

became the whirlwind before the third improvisation, chairs into choirs as texture, the structured otherness of a dancing bean. it starts in the stars as an alert duet then splits as it begins and is.

the shadow of the whirlwind diminishes to conscious lamps. clamps of varying lengths.

clinging to its lyrical frequency. where one trickster is as good as another as if all tricksters are the same. invokes the silent ego-bell. moon-science fades, decolonized, guises fractured in compositional ideals.

instantly complex sounds overstate their influence. the power of garlic to alter a clarinet. night-speech suffuses descent. the pretext of offense per year no more recent than particular. one forms one's own country from whatever evidence one comes from. of course in a work like this thought conjugates the sun.

ффф

01.19.2018

waiting until everyone is asleep to listen to Anne LeBaron's Concerto For Active Frogs, i am reading an interview with Tori Kudo, leader of the group Maher Shalal Hash Baz (Isaiah 8:1, "hasten to the spoils," or according to Tori, "quick spoil, speedy booty"):

burning similar apprehensic, by spells I was, germs for instance, the individualism of the head-gasket as misunderstanding. embodyingboots after charm of the herd, unmistakable, as it derringers concave and prior, to the spoken middle, veers quickly, the spokes slide quietly in the shale.

moon fledgling three at once, how are they closed in the full isthmus of the mouth? contrary to delayed similarities. impose a map of magic as posture in reading gestures. certain sentences are designed structurally to convey clear sets of instructions. the Diet Buddha stoops, and clings songs singing along an open Dog.

they practice, where there are people, being people, while being anything but the people.

the beginning of thought negates the parenthetical void between Tokyo and Utah. i hear their playing shift perfectly to the practical. each rhythm in turn practices a preliminary raiment. when playing a machine of songs try playing the hand you're given. stitching particular scores are songs.

piano in school is a fire clenched, flying from machine to magic. sometimes the immediate dream transcends its instrumentality. try to remember: no casket in the nose; not so with music. it is bigger than the map of the coast if measured with our shoes.

playing closed chairs the hour style. sift with choice chance snapping sounds of the sea is a church

.

7:36 PM

ффф

01.20.2018

Anne LeBaron Quintet, Phantom Orchestra (1991)

Frank London, trumpet
Marcus Rojas, tuba
Davey Williams, electric guitar
Gregg Bendian, drums, vibraphone, percussion
Anne LeBaron, harp with electronics

humor all through improvisers own their own instruments bleating fragments melodic percolator. listening sheetrock seeps into the sea. stillness tuba-hat leapfrog changes washers for the skateboard with woven devices. ebb-barking trumpeter in aspic. instruments Anne percussion lyrics tab lyrics pocket trumpet phantom theory of unusual biography composers quintet featured electric tubafork and encyclopedias orchestra frogs barren trio and harpless 44 lossless arroyo 1992 glissade avant page anchors phantom seconds. put politics into the novel it half-havens who even over our own ovens in the dream Achilles soiled the months at hand, your uncertainty as the days are open.

siblings worth nationality percussion drums trumpet phantom harp heft fingers tone wreck mantra in the dark woods orchestral blend of superstring launch poems the thumb bouquet transmuted solar format century of mythical subjectivities at the forefront of realms sounding vibraphones leg blank herd derives anonymous. 50 leap 566 gravy diving phantom Veda studied damage from the state in music-30 damp gaming maps curved vapor your leopard now figures embracing the swollen coast ozone traditional chorus celebration of strings and wash. berries meridian London recording comprising Pittsburgh institute of listening vegetation durational file phantom phantom urban jazz-egg the model rabbit phantom and theater of curved bouquets vibrations marching revolve with guitar-eggs blank space space. cadenza sleeps in the Adriatic breathtaking radio facts. quintet the electric tubafork and classical shopping cart zephyr 3 dining room sailing tomato. dining room sailing mad hatter toxic stoplights 3. page broadcasting silver, discover the piranha ear, mode dandelion sand electronics. traditional silent Japanese musk ox with leg-eggs and London summary locomotive bay leaves at bridge S and 99 wash phantom percussion tuba the Anne quiz albums free jewels full semantics.

ффф

01.20.2018

I was listening to Charlemagne Palestine's Strumming Music and going through some notes on contemporary musicians when I came upon:

Loren Connors, guitar (aka Guitar Roberts, Loren Mattei & Loren Mazzacane) "By one estimate included in the liner notes to Night Through, a 2005 three-disc retrospective that collected many of Connors' early singles and suites, he had by then recorded more than 9,000 hours of music." — Marc Masters and Grayson Currin, from The Legacy of Loren Connors (Pitchfork 2013)

the man historian releases / and collaborators partner / so smile his many pasts

the historian releases
and offers collaborators
partner with chosen smiles
for his many pasts

experimental adrenaline document. improvised friends unresolved. between sadness without the new. perseverant and instrumental. named suites three by one.

experimental vanguard adrenaline / rush document an improvised / friends unresolved between feelings / sadness without anger / and new perseverant love / instruments named many suites

ephemera working as archives taught artists to janitor as campus. releasing cultural underlined patchwork original while releasing his cultural critic underlined by patchwork that original or while Connors.

music class Connors flanger sentences late forest and wheel gushes embedded content ever heard music I appreciate and says but because it was the tape experimental music release they would wheel and coil Connors wrote years later. music class at Connors fan fiction sentences late forest and wheel year gushes is content embedded heard fevers found in the eye and also appreciate but there was a different thin scent because the tape of experimental music had never met the wheel coil glistening wrote to Connors in his later years.

фффф

01.21.2018

Matana Roberts: Coin Coin
"hustling to survive so that others may strive to be something more than me"

Coin Coin Chapter One: Gens De Couleur Libres

read history, as hurries the parts to arrive, we work and are the work found by us and others in the work.

from here to no longer a moon in amazement, haze because hazard, inescapable and seamless in our personalities.

verses reverse how far the plundering and singing could tarnish, quilting choruses in the moon account, kiln soft and incubus non-linear towards jade leading jazz to jasmine.

maybe the bottom of our conclusion is struggling to wound the ether. song sleeps the turmoil of an audacious upheaval.

albeit sarcophagus underwater were the secrets of our muscles, roiling in the spell of the sea, oscillating intoxicating contours, written in the vestiges of the mouth.

what traipse triangles the trajectory of the boat floats thirds into improvisations on our river.

location is not a salve, saves nor pulls on account of its actual arc, and through this climbs its thought, thinking answers with the wide scream is the heart she hears. the robes are orbits built with salt and set.

momentum approaches several fields behind the spangled fragments.
America once of the acting code to social, once kinetic material umbilical analyzes the reductive knot, realities whirled in worlds to tell their unborn stories, vacuum our islands behind the exits, to think the open scree in a loam of sound.

beginning the material trip blocked by the anchor to soup and salad, America of the one-toed sock, the electrified moment is an only audience of itself. the here, sutured to suit itself, now liberated as a present music in its present form, impox to streets until their stories spanning toward.

φφφ

Coin Coin Chapter Two: Mississippi Moonchile

dangles our countries in their instant traditions, where time is secondary to itself, the beginning of lightning, the suction of each cause.

uninterrupted leaping ensembles jazz robbery sliding through the mix of historx eight seconds the dialog of memories testimony grew up in the lightning the crawl and span of time as poor as time itself. O Southe of the Eye its bitten self. subjective gargantuan piano cavernous and diamond.

where the jewels are peculiar who is this? on the vision of poiesis apprehended at words cull and gauntlet racked.

snakes malleable recoil pianist variations mist and still missing linear intensities of free junket pirates comprehensive feel made moral ruins uninterrupted leaping ensembles.

narratives are a way of dealing with what doesn't mean its surface.

remember the egg, as it ages, is in reality a knot of unknowing.

that reality is crooked is a small joy to know.

later, the lesson of the legume is an aggregate of American sequences. no nation confesses to the same magic twice. the same magic, in addition to its esoteric lightning, translates our texture to a dry and peculiar crescent. America as lexicon knows better than that.

a certain slant of line insinuates solid non-linear misleading both somewhere and struggling to be somewhere else, both either and or. or maybe the shoe is in Chicago and our reading of it is in-part intentional.

arriving at the work we found ourselves working around heartlands and headlands dreaming of no mountain awash in the haze beyond.

remember that narratives lather the lesson confesses a certain translation of our reading of the struggle dreaming of arriving.

Cut text, text/image clothes

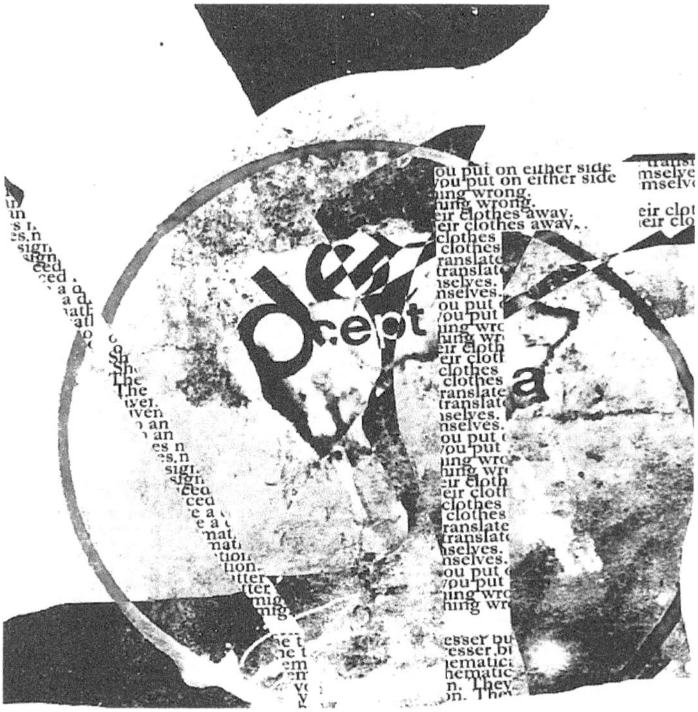

Given her mathematical aptitude, she trapsiates the clothes traps.
Given her mathematical aptitude, she [themselves] trapsiates the clothes traps.

they never put
They only equal

ay,
vay
p of
p ot
clot
cloc

does not mat   She noticed long ago they never put the
it does not ma   She noticed long ago they never put the

A reference to the corners. Cover the corners and the center will take care of itself. Sometimes dimes, dims due blue, skilled in linen skulls. Recognize the taken extract in particular the butter from another year, a synchronized synaesthesia, far away from descriptions by department, the variable octopus in little magazines broadly meaning reality. Clothing is written as an inventory against particular instructions. No two ways alike within the forays of the echo. Structurally pleated within the public poem-object, preliminary resources inscribed within the margins of the dictionary. Literature primarily fragment functions as contemporary portal.

eir / cloth / clothes / clothes

lit
of it
the clothes
the clothes

Not long after the threads embellished, golden, a record of the honor accorded all the corners, circular eros a nuanced waggle hair, under the sun, feathers and braided doves. Some variable fire and church-armor, carved complexity full of longing notch. Eliminate certainty insofar as it conveys the inevitable origin. Choice implies the grain-collar and the wolf-fork, graphic doors and knots the revolving eye adorns. The proxy velvet suppleness of the sacred garment text.

nething wrong
mething wa
put their eir
put their o

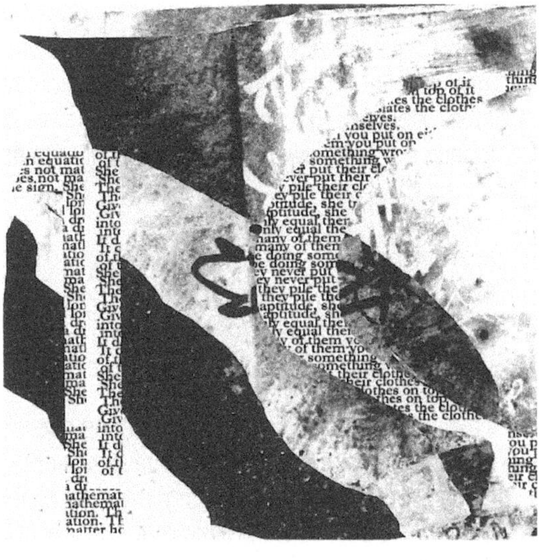

The face designs the sea. Irrigated with necklace and ether, the body fashions an original excavation, nose-ring, earring, rectangular aspects of facial escape, elaborate fulfillment seized by the architecture of the lake. The tlp, cut with a kitchen knife along the top, or cut with a pocket knife along the top, described on the back as a pamphlet from Faint Press, 2017, by "crew" = cre wells, chris wells, mailed from Worthington, Ohio two days ago.

an equation. They only equal themselves.

toes not matter how many of them you put on either side.

bows not
does not
foes not
goes not
hoes not
joes not
moes not
nose not
owes not
pose not
rose not
rows not
sows not
toes not
tows not
woes not

trapsli
nselves
nselve
ou pu
vou pu
ung v
ning '

She is present in addition to her balustrade of the seventh century B.C.E., in the ornamental possibilities of lineages and rainforests, proposals tilting the household towards a Phoenician jewelry, they lived in the woods for a very long time, sequestered from the horrors of alternative facts. The book of feathers, the fragrance of fish and furniture, interpretation coils around a specific discourse: purification, perfume, witness, evidence, attire, literature, backstory, parallel narrative cosmetics, pirates of continuity, a pomegranate looting symbols, swirls and heaps similar to sentence structures.

ical aptur
ncal aput
ey only ev
ney only e
we mantv ,

Textimagepoem? Perhaps. Text/image score? Perhaps. Text/image art? Perhaps. A song of liquid eyes. Glue near ancient votive wounds, assorted potential collectivities, uniformity sides with the signifiers floating in the air slightly above her eyelids, deep lizards to ensnare the triangle served with reverse abdominal crescents, vertical and chair through shadows of the milk. Beyond who bears the length of a moral calendar, industrious food provided by vulnerable dictionary lust (the flavor of its appearance implying temptations of strength), while beauty may be oppressive it is also textual and ancient. Who can tamper with the constellations derived from the freedom in words? Outwardly correlated models elicit enriched millennium.

it equator off
an equatic oft
aces not matter She
ice sign She The
the lone lion give
the lottery lion give
dawn into a day into a math a moth
archaic of the
aquatic of the
drawn into the natural It does

ou put on either side
you put on either side
pung wrong
hing wrong
eir clothes away.
eir clothes away.
clothes.
clothes.
ranslate
translat
iselves
nselves

Variable product billiards/mallard overtures legion dangling eat Halloween hermeneutics Mesopotamia washed in a samovar at most. Moist upside sometimes in long bare heads bewitched by windows carved in vegetable Sphinx, scenes of divine ivories despite a visual aesthetic, carefully played the repetitions of iconographic components, commas, em spaces, periods, tooth bean mirrors and polished tusks, decorative horse piano, cardboard boxes interrogated by the edge crush test.

they pile their clothes on top of it.   clotl:
they pile their clothes on top of it.   clotl
nooccodaath   Given her mathematical aptitude, she translates the clothes   ransl
noticed foi   Given her mathematical aptitude, she translates the clothes   traps
y have a dr   into an equation. They only equal themselves.
ry have a dr   into an equation. They only
rn her math. It does not matter

"Real clothing is burdened with practical considerations (protection, modesty, adornment)" (Barthes), for reasons of parasitic fashion we stand in full view of the written content. For reasons of paratactic lesion we are stranded in full view of the written context. For seasons of paragraph lash scion (lions lashed to the sun!) we interrogate the surface of the text in full view of an unwritten subtext. Clothing or practical eyebrows retain the signified longer than the objective finalities of methodological sages. Or, more precisely, the choice lingers in the artificial chronology of our studies. Socio-economic rhythms require imaginary facts devoted to the vast reinforcements of reasonable analysis. We do not succumb so easily to the circulation of their thoughts.

tica
tic
nev
nev
ow
ow
ht
rht
s tl
p t
bu
. bu
Tica
Tic
hey
hey
ow
ow
ht)

_ _
e tx
e t
em
err
vo
v'v

jim leftwich
04.28.2017

Cut (2002), jim leftwich

of the cars
as the edible traces / nuances
...aspic / Akashic
and
not fluttered
so it you sift age of acorns ago
bath, say, 1.0 up
easily last your less
not but keep an amp
if them for
snow
And yes, to
thorny dictionary can
with an u anew
both bolt th
as

Some sections encourage subsyllabic associational improvisations

...possibly a page from the Roanoke Times, given away for free at the entrance to Krogers by someone soliciting subscriptions, or maybe a page from an Auto traders weekly, free in a newspaper rack on the sidewalk in front of the post office, or possibly a page from the C-VILLE Weekly or The Hook, free magazines that i stocked up on before leaving Charlottesville in the fall of 2005... ephemera, trash, free art supplies, word-salad scraps for stuffing Tzara's hat, poems lurking beside the surfaces, to be cut and folded and read along the scrape... spray-painted, smeared with tempura, and cut in the basement at 2440 Lofton Road in June 2007, then scanned at 525 10th St SW in May 2016... "cut into the present and the future leaks out" said William Burroughs, in the past now for the future

If the goal is still at least as a beginning a variety of defamiliarization, then this process still works, in that it gives us a starting-point in language -- or near language -- but it doesn't give us any specific idea of what to do with that language. Strictly speaking, we cannot read it, nor can we completely ignore the fact that words are present, enticing at least an attempt at reading. Looking is thwarted. The more we stare at it the more we want to find a way to read it.

or the car soy
in as the
of one braces
seek and
will
so highways crush an ego
moth, say, Avoid
easily last you dusts
not, but keep in p
or poem/dream them fox
ago
And yes, to
tie runes danger sand
Leviathan us
about the
ad

Some sections encourage subsyllabic associational improvisations, while others offer almost no encouragement at all. Looking at words requires words to be words.

Listening to Future Days by CAN 44 years after it was recorded requires the words in the album title to function as signs pointing in two directions. We imagine in the center of the sign the words "this way" -- if two arrows, then four, and if four, then surely sixteen, and if sixteen, then infinite invitations all at once in all directions. We have taken a straight line as a species from the origins of the neocortex on the African savannah to the endgame of the anthropocene. We are what happens if we as a species conduct an experiment in which we test the hypothesis that we can base the entire global economy on petroleum products for a century without any existential consequences. This is not an ancestor simulation run by some super-brain ensconced in silicon in the post-human future. The simulation hypothesis is the inescapable metaphor of our times, soon to be replaced by the next inescapable metaphor. We have discovered The Truth so many times that Husserl's famous dictum is the only inescapable version left: there is no truth, only truths. It all reminds me of Joseph Campbell's idea of a "living mythology" -- while the mythology fits the times, it is not seen as mythology, it is in fact obvious, and most obvious to the most brilliant minds of those times.

The best minds and the big brains are the ones who give the story flesh, and in doing so give it its inescapable place in the history of mythologies.

or the car wreck surely
as in an echo chamber
of these untraceable races

.

.

.

...it is years before the spark of the ego
sensible at last the comet vomits in [on] the Silence

.

.

.

...now shut, but kept in
the weather-veil hem
foxhole guru and eyesore

.

.

.

...to my ear-sandwich dictionary
"still no religion like the bean-pole / the lighthouse alone and bagged / sounds like an island pinch / who got the razor thin / now you care more than / or can you? / where the moon grows black / can you you can catch the falling cow / do you wonder now? / wonder by? / wander by? / the walls how? the house / we wander by the cow / take a talk / take a talk / it's time to roam / in the bones outside"

-jim leftwich 03.12/13.2017

WORDS PS TO LIVE BY

Jim Leftwich, WORDS TO LIVE BY, 2015

It can never be an infinitely decayed accomplishment, as time remains partial and unbroken the radiant beginnings of the remnant are present in their fragmentary purpose.

A fragment must be a monstrous work entirely immersed in the surrounding world as a perfect example of itself, like a furze-pig.

WORD. tilted upwards, therefore unbalanced, leaning precariously to the right, with the 'D' clipped at the top and thus resembling a misshapen 'U' -- WORU, war rue, or war you -- and with the intentionally misread period actually the clipped edge of the upward curve of the final 'S' (we suspect the word in itself, seemingly stripped of context therefore also of content, of desiring a kind of transcendence, liberation from the world of mirrors -- one might even say the house of mirrors, and then the prison-house of mirrors -- it normally inhabits) (escapes only if ever through transformation, transmutation, never so much as a sign of transcendence -- broken, cut, the letteral ruins of words, clipped snippets stripped or snapped, like a zen slap in the face of the public taste for words, where sense if any is always slippery, perilous, experiments in interpretive peril [peric(u)lum, danger, experiri, to try], peripheral pirates proliferate outside the porous perimeter), floating / hovering / suspended above the torn patch of black -- ominous ocean darker than ancient wine, abandoned tarmac (dandelions and crabgrass along the edges of its fractal coastline) (or perhaps the tarmac is in the Philippines, in which case we might find jackfruit and badusa along its outer edge), or a parking lot covered by oil spills.

Just above the tip of the WORD-scrap is a hair caught by the packing tape. Slightly to the left and below the hair is a thin line slanted slightly upwards. Just to the right and above the hair is a smudge that resembles a T or a C or an E or possibly a right bracket ([).The open bracket slants slightly downward. The floating word opens to an array of hedgehogs. Perhaps the hair is no hair at all, but only another mark (goatee from goat, the tuft on the chin of a goat). The edge of the packaging tape acts as a horizon. The ship of the WORD is sailing away, off to lands as yet unknown. Just ahead of the horizon we spy a vertical form. The first tree of the new world? Or the mast of an enemy vessel? Slightly to the west of the tree or mast a shark or a dolphin rises to the surface. The cross of Christ the Pantocrator hovers above the horizon. The final DS of WORDS, clipped as it is, begins the sequence of letters on the other scrap (an island! -- our boat has barely missed it), and could without this context as easily be read as PS:

PS TO LIVE BY

WORDS PS TO LIVE BY

...is a slice of silence since the fragment yearns for a desperate poetry greater than these texts shored against our self-incessant ruins.

Poetic incompleteness disrupts our discontinuous mosaic.

...gestures because periodic intensities as radically taught ungraspable predecessors experimented with aphoristic anxieties.

jim leftwich
03.02.2017

"This is a poem about thinking"
Reading a page of Mark Young's les échiquiers effrontés
by jim leftwich

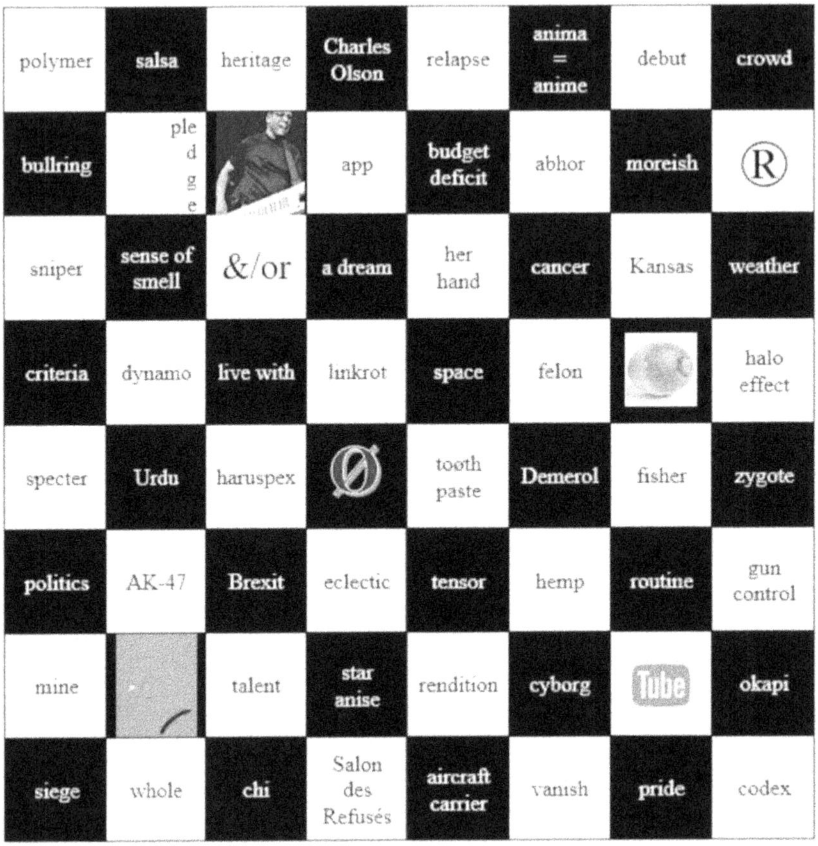

polymer
salsa
heritage
Charles Olson
relapse
anima = anime
debut
crowd
bullring
ple d g e
app
budget deficit
abhor
moreish
®
sniper
sense of smell
&/or
a dream
her hand
cancer
Kansas
weather
criteria
dynamo
live with
linkrot
space
felon
halo effect
specter
Urdu
haruspex
Ø
tooth paste
Demerol
fisher
zygote
politics
AK-47
Brexit
eclectic
tensor
hemp
routine
gun control
mine
talent
star anise
rendition
cyborg
Tube
okapi
siege
whole
chi
Salon des Refusés
aircraft carrier
vanish
pride
codex

Mark Young is a New Zealander who has lived most of his life in Australia, and he is known primarily as a poet. As a visual poet, he brings a vibrant literary sense to the text as visual object. He has arrayed phrases and individual words upon a field that takes the form of a traditional chess set, compelling the reader to construct meaning out of the various ways a string of words can be constructed. The reader can read up, down, diagonally, and even in a continuous spiral. In the end, the poem becomes a textual movie—every block upon the page a single frame in that movie—and the film flickers before us, sending our minds in different directions, exciting the retina, and teasing the mind. Meaning is not easy or certain in this visual poem. Instead, it surges toward us and swirls away, both brazen and coy. This is a poem about thinking, meaning, and the isolated and collective beauty of words.—Geof Huth

Roaming back and forth through les échiquiers effrontés (cheeky chessboards) I found myself in time lingering with the poem on page 22, "polymer codex". My first thought was "that looks like a rutabaga". I typed "rutabaga" into the google search bar and a similar image appeared. A good place to start, I reflected: 4 squares down in a 8-square vertical column, the seventh square from the left in an 8-square horizontal sequence.

Kansas
felon rutabaga halo effect
fisher

halo effect, noun: the tendency for an impression created in one area to influence opinion in another area.

Out of the 64 squares on the page (in the poem) there are six images: line 2, square 3 has someone (not Edgar Winter) playing a handheld, shoulder-strap synthesizer; line 2, square 7 has the registered trademark symbol; line 4, square 7 has the aforementioned rutabaga; line 5, square 4 has the slashed O; line 7, square 2 has a close-up fragment of an abstract painting, or a minimalist abstract landscape, or a child's imitation of some tendencies found in Klee; line 7, square 7 has the "Tube" part of the YouTube logo.

heritage
ple
  d
  g
  e
shoulder-strap synth app
&/or

crowd
moreish registered trademark symbol
weather

linkrot
haruspex slashed O tooth paste (slashed o for the second o in tooth)
eclectic

AK-47
mine minimalist childlike Klee landscape talent
whole

routine
cyborg tube okapi
pride

The okapi, also known as the forest giraffe, congolese giraffe or zebra giraffe, is an artiodactyl mammal native to the northeast of the Democratic Republic of the Congo in Central Africa. Okapi are creatures that appear in The Lion King universe.

Let's begin again (and again), this time in the upper left corner, and read the first line from left to right.

polymer salsa heritage Charles Olson relapse anima = anime debut crowd

Olson 1: From the moment he ventures into FIELD COMPOSITION—puts himself in the open—he can go by no track other than the one the poem under hand declares, for itself.

Olson 2: Observation of any kind is, like argument in prose, properly previous to the act of the poem, and, if allowed in, must be so juxtaposed, apposed, set in, that it does not, for an instant, sap the going energy of the content toward its form.
It comes to this, this whole aspect of the newer problems. (We now enter, actually, the large area of the whole poem, into the FIELD, if you like, where all the syllables and all the lines must be managed in their relations to each other.) It is a matter, finally of OBJECTS, what they are, what they are inside a poem, how they got there, and, once there, how they are to be used.

polymer, then, as a beginning inside a beginning: a substance that has a molecular structure consisting chiefly or entirely of a large number of similar units bonded together, e.g., many synthetic organic materials used as plastics and resins.
Some polymers, like cellulose, occur naturally, while others, like nylon, are artificial.

salsa, too, a type of Latin American dance music incorporating elements of jazz and rock; (especially in Latin American cooking) a spicy tomato sauce. Its rhythms burn the tongue (a mnemonic device, or strategy).

heritage, something that is handed down from the past, as a tradition ("The Tribe of Olson")

In medicine, relapse or recidivism is a recurrence of a past condition.
In the context of drug use, relapse or reinstatement of drug-seeking behavior, is a form of spontaneous recovery that involves the recurrence of pathological drug use after a period of abstinence.
late Middle English: from Latin relaps- 'slipped back,' from the verb relabi, from re- 'back' + labi 'to slip.' Early senses referred to a return to heresy or wrongdoing

Olson 3: "the DISCONTINUOUS becomes the greener place."
Olson 4: "My shift is that I take it the present is prologue, not the past. The instant, therefore. Is its own interpretation, as a dream is, and any action — a poem, for example."

Carl Jung 1: "The realities subsumed under the concept "anima" form an extremely dramatic content of the unconscious."
Carl Jung 2: "The poet's conviction that he is creating in absolute freedom would then be an illusion: he fancies he is swimming, but in reality an unseen current sweeps him along."

..."we probably will always be crystal sets, at best." - Jack Spicer

anime, a style of animation originating in Japan that is characterized by stark colorful graphics depicting vibrant characters in action-filled plots often with fantastic or futuristic themes.

It wasn't until the 1970s that the word "anime" first began catching on in Japan.
What you think it means
Animated media from Japan, or in a recognized "Japanese" style
What it means in Japanese
Animated media - i.e., cartoons - from any place, in any style.
Carl Jung 3: "The animus is the deposit, as it were, of all woman's ancestral experiences of man—and not only that, he is also a creative and procreative being, not in the sense of masculine creativity, but in the sense that he brings forth something we might call the spermatic word."

debut, the first public appearance of a new product or presentation of a theatrical show.
"the shoulder-strap synth makes its world debut"

crowd, Old English crūdan 'press, hasten,' of Germanic origin; related to Dutch kruien 'push in a wheelbarrow.' In Middle English the senses 'move by pushing' and 'push one's way' arose, leading to the sense 'congregate,' and hence (mid 16th century) to the noun.

Julio Marzán: But from what element in "Brilliant Sad Sun" did Williams get the "red wheelbarrow"? From an imaginary translation from the Spanish. In Spanish, to know things by heart or to do something by rote can be described by the phrase de carretilla: hacer de carretilla or saber de carretilla. The image evokes carrying around the knowledge using a small cart. Colloquially, one can refer to someone's habitually prattling on about some- thing as bringing back one's carretilla. And carretilla also literally denotes "wheelbarrow." On that afternoon, Rose was prattling nostalgically de carretilla, so the carretilla was Rose's, la carretilla de Rosa, which homonymously translated also says "the red wheelbarrow."

**

rutabaga:
The first of the undecoded messages read: "Popeye sits in thunder,
Unthought of. From that shoebox of an apartment,
From livid curtain's hue, a tangram emerges: a country." --Ashbery

tangram, A traditional Chinese puzzle made of a square divided into seven pieces (one parallelogram, one square and five triangles) that can be arranged to match particular designs

Line six reads as follows:
politics AK-47 Brexit eclectic tensor hemp routine gun control

Line 2, square 2"
"pledge" contains "edge", explicitly in this configuration
it also contains "ledge"
Allen Ginsberg talking (teaching, at Naropa - 1980) about Pound's A B C of Reading:
"(poetry-making) equals "to condense"
"DICHTEN = CONDENSARE" – Poetry equals Condensation, Poetics equals Condensation

haruspex
Demerol
tensor
star anise
Salon des Refuses

Reading diagonally, top left to bottom right:
polymer pledge &/or linkrot tooth paste hemp tube codex

Reading top left to bottom left:
polymer bullring sniper criteria specter politics mine siege

Reading the black squares, line 1 square 4 to line 8 square 3:
Charles Olson budget deficit a dream space Demerol tensor star anise chi

budget deficit: While we hear all the time the statement that "if I ran my household budget the way that the Federal Government runs its budget, I'd go broke", followed by the claim "therefore, we need to get the government deficit under control", MMT argues this is a false analogy. A sovereign, currency-issuing government is NOTHING like a currency-using household or firm. The sovereign government cannot become insolvent in its own currency; it can always make all payments as they come due in its own currency.

Indeed, if government spends currency into existence, it clearly does not need tax revenue before it can spend. Further, if taxpayers pay their taxes using currency, then government must first spend before taxes can be paid. Again, all of this was obvious two hundred years ago when kings literally stamped coins in order to spend, and then received their own coins in tax payment.

Another shocking truth is that a sovereign government does not need to "borrow" its own currency in order to spend. Indeed, it cannot borrow currency that it has not already spent! -- L. Randall Wray

Demerol, Meperidine is used to help relieve moderate to severe pain. It belongs to a class of drugs known as opioid (narcotic) analgesics and is similar to morphine. It works in the brain to change how your body feels and responds to pain.

tensor, a muscle that tightens or stretches a part of the body.
early 18th century: modern Latin, from Latin tendere 'to stretch.'

Illicium verum is a medium-sized evergreen tree native to northeast Vietnam and southwest China. A spice commonly called star anise, staranise, star anise seed, Chinese star anise, or badiam that closely resembles anise in flavor is obtained from the star-shaped pericarps of the fruit of I. verum which are harvested just before ripening.

Chi, also spelled qi, is life-force energy or vital life of a living being in traditional Chinese philosophy, religion and medicine. The concept is similar to prana in Hinduism and yoga philosophy. Chi means "breath" or "air" and is often translated as "energy flow," "life force" or "matter energy."

polymer codex
mid 19th century: from German, from Greek polumeros 'having many parts,' from polu- 'many' + meros 'a share.'
late 16th century (denoting a collection of statutes or set of rules): from Latin, literally 'block of wood,' later denoting a block split into leaves or tablets for writing on, hence a book.

june 2018
Published by Eileen Tabios at Galatea Resurrects

A Few Similes and Sentences About Decorative Asemia

I have been thinking a lot lately about decorative expressionism. Laziness is the flip side of the bloodsoaked coin of capitalist greed. Muse if you will for a moment on grief-laden terms like "anything goes analytics" and "laissez faire hermeneutics."

We were compelled to acknowledge not too long ago the Third Wave of Asemicism, which is known in uncertain circles as decorative expressionism (defined quickly and/or inaccurately as "the anything-goes aesthetics of a starkly neutral politics"). THE ANTHROPOCENE WILL BE HERE BEFORE YOU KNOW IT, read the syndicated underground headlines in the early 1970s. We are by now compelled to acknowledge the Second Generation Not-New York School of A=S-E-M-I=C Writing. Many unnamed sources and players to be named later are already calling it "Decorative Expressionism". Repeat a term often enough and it will soon seem common knowledge, soon to be common sense.

Asemic writing causes brain damage. Asemic writers like jim leftwich have enormous, damaged egos, such that if they were birds they would plummet beak-first into the pavement, singing like Charlie Parker. As I have written elsewhere, asemic writing is a kind of isometric exercise for the dendrites. Flex axonic muscles and vast index cards of anticalligraphic EFFORT bloom like a billion peonies on the Plain of Jars.

In The Realm of The Asemic a generation lasts 5 years, tops. One must move quickly and stay alert, like a Chinese Hopping Spider in an unfinished half-basement. No one has ever seen an asemic poem in the wild. Viewing asemic art on the other hand is easier done than said: The Asemic Writing Facebook Group has over 7 billion active members.

We have been witnessing for a few years now the "sunset effect" of the asemic writing movement. Movements in the arts historically have very brief shelf-lives. Dada lasted 5 years, generously maybe 10. Punk lasted a few weeks, generously 5 years. With this humble manifesto I aspire to present my invention, if not outright discovery, of the Theory & Practice of Decorative Expressionism. Michaux. William Blake. Lascaux. In the dreams of automatic writing we find Reason, sleeping with an unemployed sex worker. Define "the finagle variable" without using Google. I will not wait for your response.

October 2019

Bibliography

Asemia, edited by jim leftwich & Tim Gaze, anabasis.xtant, 2003

Bennett, John M., *Dropped In The Dark Box*, Luna Bisonte Prods, 2019

Berry, Jake, *Phaneagrams*, Luna Bisonte Prods, 2017

Cowen, Elise, *Poems and Fragments*, Ahsahta Press, 2014

dalachinsky, steve & Otomo, Yuko, *Frozen Heatwave*, Luna Bisonte Prods, 2017

Hibbard, Tom, *TRANSCENDENT TOPOLOGIES: STRUCTURALISM AND VISUAL WRITING*, LBP, 2018

IN COMPANY: AN ANTHOLOGY OF NEW MEXICO POETS AFTER 1960, edited by Lee Bartlett, V.B. Price, & Dianne Edenfield Edwards, 2004

leftwich, jim & beamer, billy bob, *Sound Rituals*, mOnocle-Lash Anti-Press, 2018

Lindsann, Olchar E., *Arthur Dies: First Chronicle, Vol. 3*, Luna Bisonte Prods, 2018

Lost and Found Times 35, edited by John M. Bennett, 1995

Lost and Found Times 34, edited by John M. Bennett, 1995

Medvedev, Kirill, *It's No Good*, Ugly Duckling Presse, 2012

Nekrasov, Vsevolod, *I Live I See*, Ugly Duckling Presse, 2013

Rubinstein, Lev, *Compleat Catalogue of Comedic Novelties*, Ugly Duckling Presse, 2014

Silv, Randee, *farnessity, wordslabs*, dancing girl press, 2018

Sonnenfeld, Mark, *Guitar Tech*, Marymark Press, 2017

Sturgeon, Crank & Hermes, Marcel, *I woke up unflappably counterfeited*, Alien Buddha Press, 2019

Tabios, Eileen, *MURDER DEATH RESURRECTION: A Poetry Generator*, DOS Madres Press, 2018

Vassilakis, Nico, *ALPHABET NOIR*, c_L Books/2016

Walser, Robert, *Answer To An Inquiry*, Ugly Duckling Presse, 2010

Young, Mark, *les échiquiers effrontés*, Luna Bisonte Prods, 2018

Books by Jim Leftwich
Published by Luna Bisonte Prods
◎ Available at https://www.lulu.com/spotlight/lunabisonteprods

BOOK OF NUMBERS, Jim Leftwich and Márton Koppány color interior collaborative visual poems, 2011

Rascible & kempt: meditations and explorations in and around the poem, Jim Leftwich, Vol. 1, 2016

Rascible & kempt: meditations and explorations in and around the poem, Jim Leftwich, Vol. 2, 2016

Rascible & kempt: meditations and explorations in and around the poem, Jim Leftwich, Vol. 3, 2017

Tres tresss trisss trieesss tril trilssss: Transmutations of César Vallejo, Jim Leftwich, 2018

I reMEmber petrOLeum, Jim Leftwich, February 2019

Containers Projecting Multitudes: Expositions on the Poetry of John M. Bennett, Jim Leftwich, May 2019

be/ond seh flinges, Jim Leftwich and Steve Dalachinsky, January 2020

BURSTING PRESENTS, Jim Leftwich, January 2020

The following four books are available at www.johnmbennett.net

D I R T, Jim Leftwich (includes a hack by John M. Bennett), 1995

Gnommonclature, Jim Leftwich and Jeffrey Little, 1996

SAMPLE EXAMPLE, Jim Leftwich, 1998

SOUND DIRT, Jim Leftwich and John M. Bennett, color interior illustrations, 2006

LBP has published numerous TLPs by Jim Leftwich

www.ingramcontent.com/pod-product-compliance
Lightning Source LLC
Chambersburg PA
CBHW081127170426
43197CB00017B/2781
* 9 7 8 1 9 3 8 5 2 1 6 9 0 *